I0793358

IMAGES
of America

The Dutch in the Calumet Region

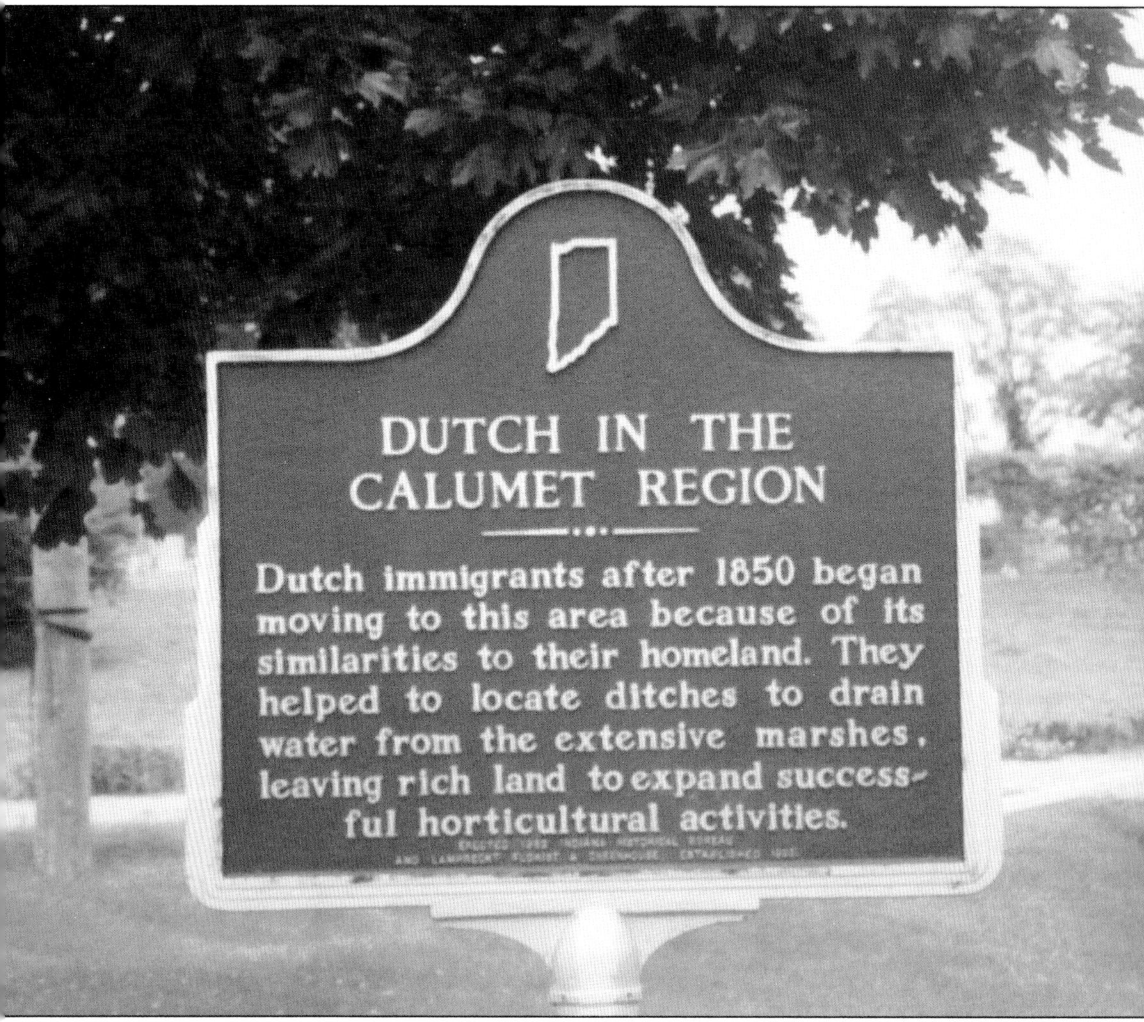

Leaving the Netherlands in search of religious freedom and a better way of life, the Dutch began arriving in the Calumet region in the middle part of the 19th century. By clearing and draining the land and establishing stable communities, they left a permanent impression on the region, which still reflects their heritage today. This sign, erected in 1992 by the Indiana Historical Bureau, stands at 8941 Kleinman Road in Highland, Indiana. (Photograph by the author.)

On the Cover: The light, sandy soils of the Calumet region were well suited for the production of garden crops. (Courtesy of the South Holland Historical Society.)

IMAGES
of America

THE DUTCH IN THE CALUMET REGION

Ken Bult

ARCADIA
PUBLISHING

ISBN 978-1-4671-1378-6

Published by Arcadia Publishing
Charleston, South Carolina

Printed in the United States of America

Library of Congress Control Number: 2014952139

For all general information, please contact Arcadia Publishing:
Telephone 843-853-2070
Fax 843-853-0044
E-mail sales@arcadiapublishing.com
For customer service and orders:
Toll-Free 1-888-313-2665

Visit us on the Internet at www.arcadiapublishing.com

For my family
Nothing is more important

Contents

ACKNOWLEDGMENTS

As much as I tried my hardest to make this book free of errors, I apologize in advance for any that may have slipped in despite my best efforts. In many cases, I have reverted to original Dutch names and spellings. I know there is a lot more that could have been included here, but there was not a secret agenda with any omissions—just factors of time and space. That being said, I would like to offer my thanks to the following people, without whose help this project would have been impossible. Thank-yous go to Robin Sheldberg and Ed Smith at the South Holland Historical Society, Susan Douthett at the Highland Historical Society, Shirley Schmueser at the Munster Historical Society, Richard H. Harms at the Calvin College Archives, Julia Simpson at Arcadia Publishing, my friend Marie Eenigenburg Min, my wife and research assistant, Carol, and my daughter Kaylee, for helping me do research on a particularly rainy night in Highland.

INTRODUCTION

Every year on Labor Day in South Holland, Illinois, not many miles from Chicago's southern border, the descendents of the town's early settlers gather to celebrate their heritage at the Paarlberg Farm and Park. While South Holland may not be the solidly Dutch community it once was, the descendents of the Dutch immigrants still populate this region. The area settled by their ancestors in the 19th century is a part of the Calumet region. Geographically, the region includes the northern parts of Lake and Porter Counties in Indiana and southeastern Cook County in Illinois that are drained by the Grand Calumet River and the Little Calumet River This region happens to run along the south shore of Lake Michigan. For the purposes of this book, the region's loose boundary runs from what today is part of Chicago's South Side to the western border of Griffith, Indiana, forming a Dutch crescent that includes the communities of Roseland, South Holland, Lansing, Munster, and Highland. Even before the towns existed, then into the 20th century, the Dutch were a community that transcended the borders of the towns they established. Once in the region, the Dutch carved communities out of the wilderness by clearing and draining the land and raising large families. Throughout the region, there is evidence of the early Dutch settlers in the churches they built, the businesses they started, and the loved ones they buried. But what was it that brought the Dutch to this region? What drove them to leave the comfort and security of the land to which they were born and brave a long and dangerous sea journey into the unknown?

In order to understand what kept the Dutch communities unique when everything around them was changing, one needs to understand that many of the people who immigrated to the Calumet region from the Netherlands were not typical 19th-century Dutchmen and -women. Religious zeal and the desire for religious freedom brought many of the region's founding families here. The Dutch immigration to the United States that took place in the second half of the 19th century began as a result of conditions that these people considered intolerable. While the reasons that other ethnic groups immigrated were more often than not based on economics, the Dutch immigration was largely religious in nature.

Beginning in 1815, with the defeat of Napoleon and the accession of Willem I of the House of Orange to the throne of the Netherlands, the religious problems arose. King Willem became the guiding force that put into place a number changes designed to modernize the Dutch church when he placed the Reformed Church of Holland under state control. The change put forward by Willem included all church property; salaries and education of the clergy were placed under state control; and a new wording allowed pastors who denied the Trinity and other church doctrines to continue preaching. With these changes, the movement for religious freedom through immigration was taking root. The Secession of 1834 began in Ulrum, a town in the north of the Dutch province of Groningen, when pastor Hendrik de Cock was forbidden by the government to preach or baptize children whose parents believed their own ministers were not true to the faith.

On December 14, 1834, a large majority of the congregation of the Dutch Reformed Church in Ulrum signed the Act of Secession and Return, breaking with the state church. The members of the new church were not only harassed by the state when meeting to worship, but they were also not allowed to establish their own schools As a result, by 1845, some congregations led by their pastors felt they could no longer live with the restrictions being forced upon them by the government. As a result, two prominent leaders of the secession movement decided that immigrating to America could be a solution to many of their problems. One of the leaders in the search for religious freedom was Albertus Van Raalte. He and members of his congregations left the Netherlands for America on September 24, 1846. They began their new life in Holland, Michigan, on February 9, 1847. The other leader was Hendrik Pieter Scholte. On August 26, 1847, his followers arrived at what was to become Pella, Iowa. Meanwhile, the Dutch were slowly settling in the Calumet region as well. With the homestead of Hendrick De Jong, a Dutch foothold was established in the region. Others, like the Widow Paarlberg and Klaas Pool, arrived, followed by Rev. Willem Wust and 30 followers from his former congregation in 1848. In the summer of 1849, the founders of Roseland, Illinois, started their new lives at de Hooge Prairie (High Prairie).

When George Pullman needed land for his railroad-car factory and company town, many of the early Roseland settlers made a nice profit and some, in turn, bought land in Lage Prairie (South Holland). Because large farms of 160 acres or more were hard to work, they were broken down into more manageable sizes, to be divided among the many Dutch sons. The resulting lots, 20 to 40 acres in size, were perfect for truck farming. When there were no more parcels to be handed out, many Dutch sons moved east to Lansing and Munster. While the rest of the country was moving west, the Dutch were expanding to the east. During the period immediately following the Civil War, the farmers of South Holland began to seriously sell their produce at the Chicago South Water Street Market. The Calumet region, with its light, sandy soil, was well suited for the production of garden crops, especially onions. In South Holland, the eventual change to onions led to the onion-set farmers and co-ops that kept agriculture a major factor in South Holland until after World War II. Eventually, the Dutch made their way south as well, to Wichert, Illinois, and DeMotte, Indiana, where they still reside in significant numbers. This is, in part, the untold story of the Dutch in the Calumet region.

One

Churches, Schools, and Cemeteries

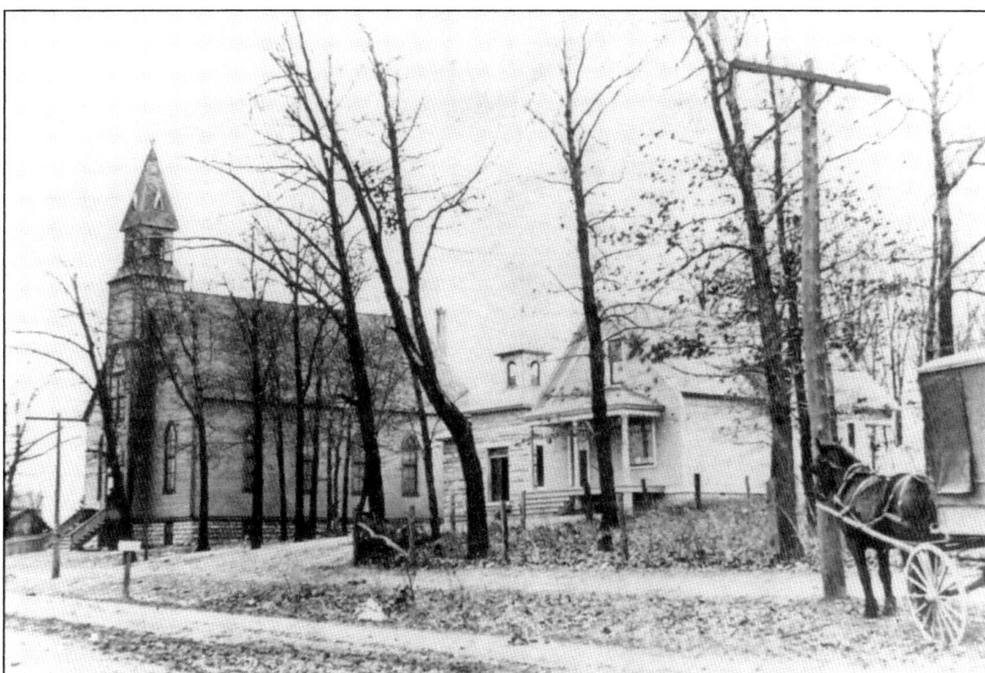

John Swart's grocery wagon stops near the Munster Reformed Church and the Munster Christian School on Ridge Road. Born in the Netherlands, Swart (1871–1954) came to America in 1891 and married Anna H. Eriks (1886–1976) in 1909. He is at rest in Hope Cemetery in Highland, Indiana. (Courtesy of the Munster Historical Society.)

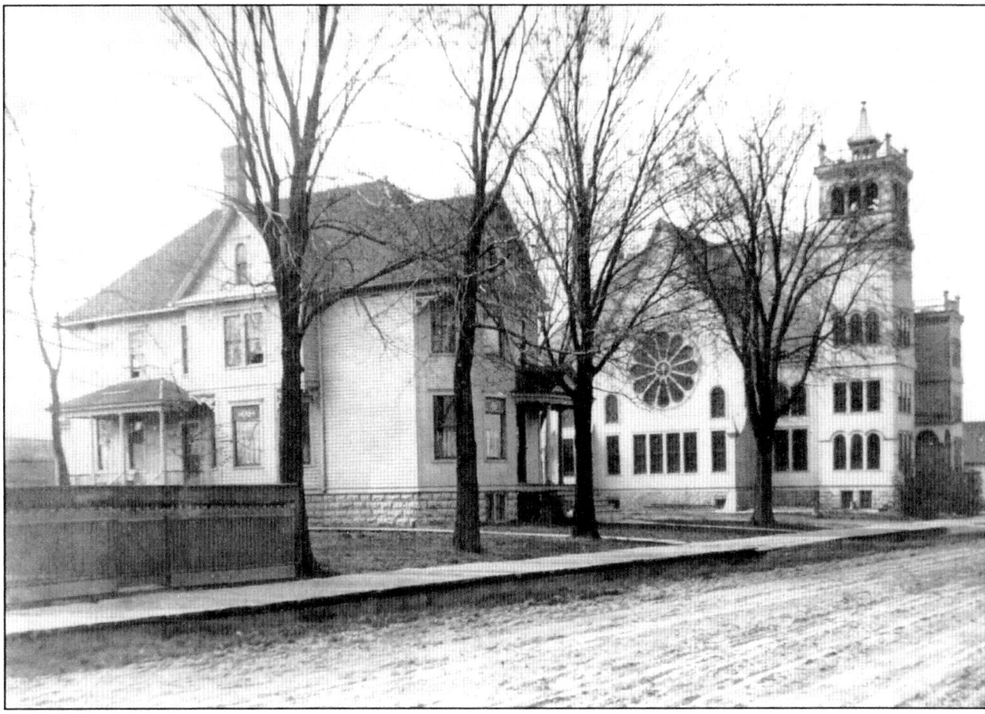

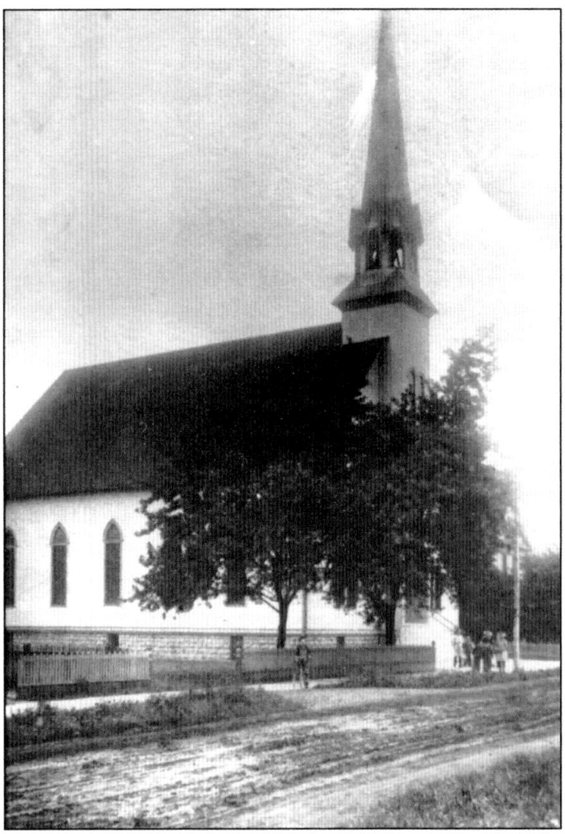

The First Reformed Church of South Holland, Illinois, and the parsonage are seen here in 1906. The Low Prairie Church, formed in 1848, was later known as Reformed Protestant Church, then First Dutch Reformed Church, and, finally, First Reformed Church of South Holland. (Courtesy of the South Holland Historical Society.)

The First Christian Reformed Church of South Holland, Illinois, is located at 163rd Street and South Park Avenue. The church got its start when some members of the First Reformed Church of South Holland left that church and began True Dutch Reformed Church. The building shown here was constructed in 1896. (Courtesy of the South Holland Historical Society.)

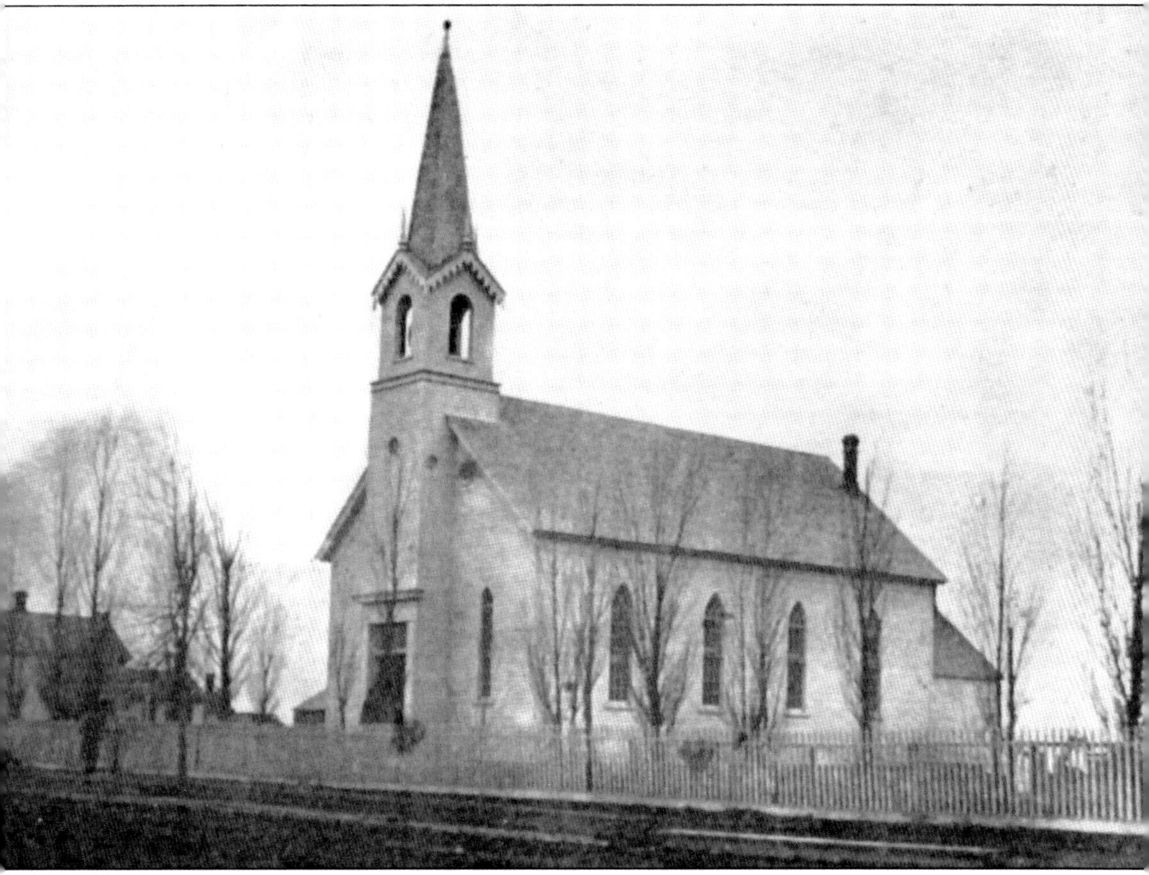

In 1867, the First Reformed Church of Roseland moved into this building. It was soon decided that a board of trustees was needed to supervise the church properties. To that end, the first board, consisting of Harm Van der Belt, Klaas Madderom, Pieter De Jong, and Dirk De Jong, was appointed on May 20, 1869. (Courtesy of Marie Eenigenburg Min.)

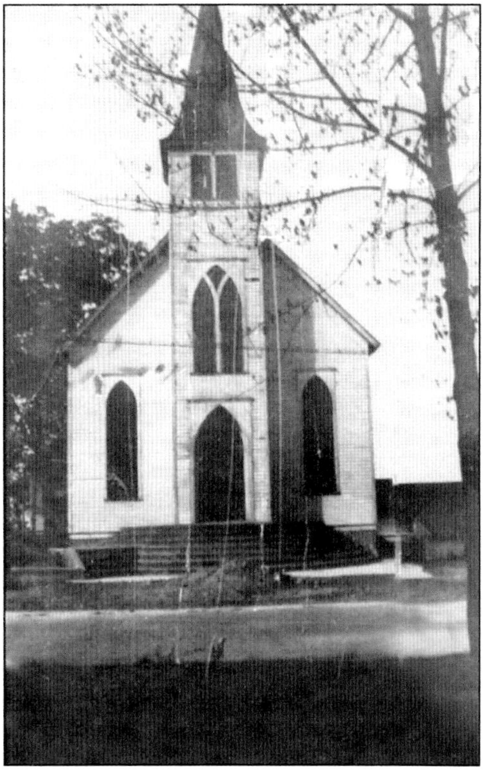

The First Reformed Church of Lansing, located at 3134 Ridge Road, was organized on August 21, 1861, as the Dutch Reformed Church of Lansing. In 1870, most of the congregation seceded to form the True Holland Reformed Church, which later became Munster Christian Reformed Church. In 1874, nine families came together to reorganize the Lansing church. The use of the Dutch language for services was discontinued in 1942. In 1945, a fire destroyed the church building (pictured), which was constructed in 1897. The new church was completed in 1947. (Courtesy of the Lansing Historical Society.)

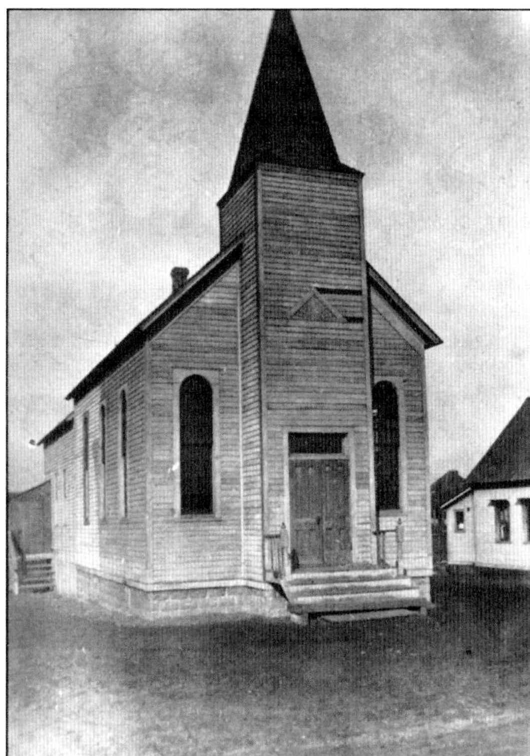

Jacob Schoon (1825–1904) married Henderika Ronk on May 17, 1862, following the death of his first wife, Elizabeth, on May 21, 1861. They arrived from the Netherlands on June 19, 1865. Schoon's Church (pictured) was built for Jacob by Gerbrand Kooy in 1891, after a dispute with the Lansing church. (Courtesy of the Highland Historical Society.)

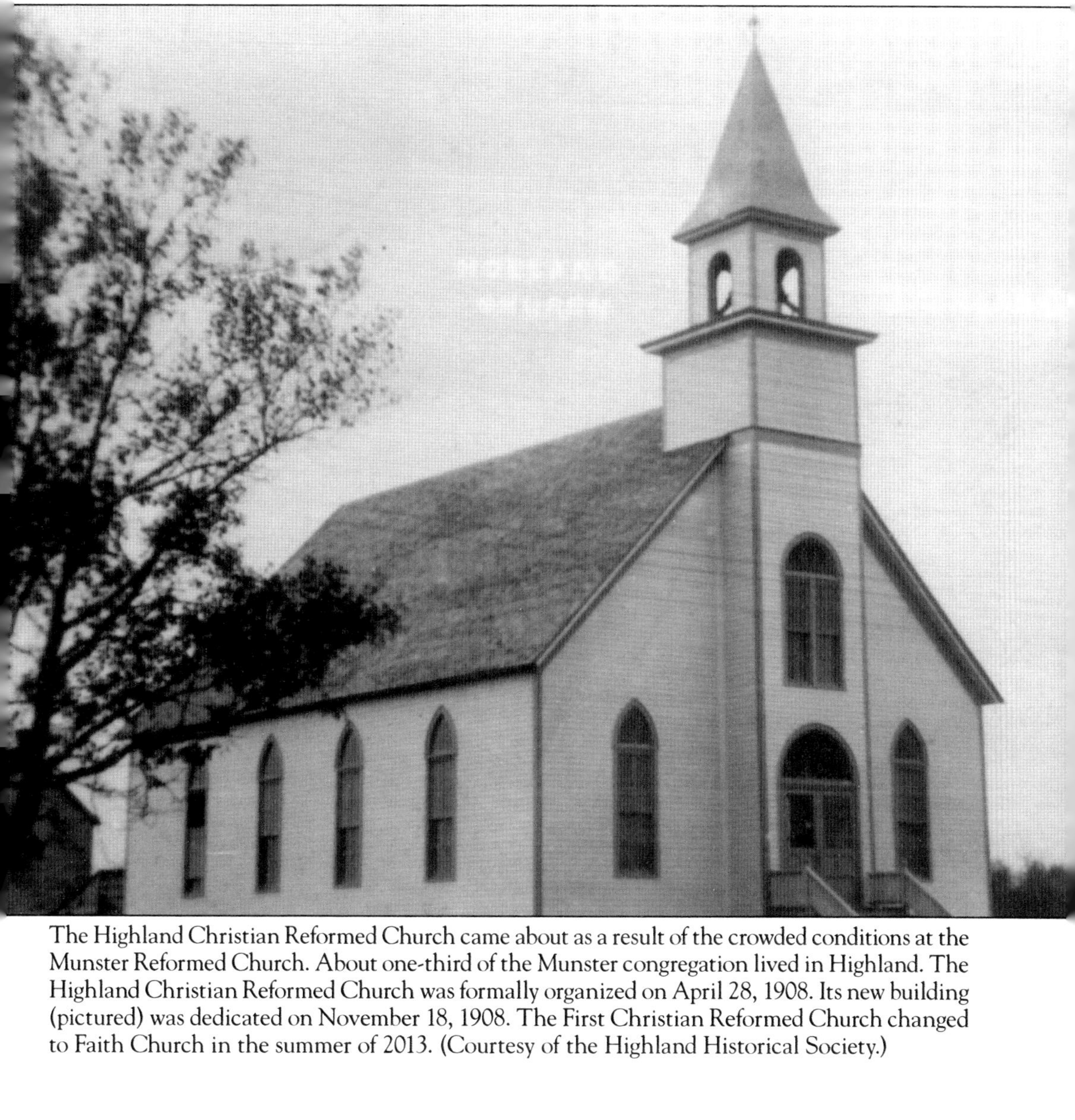

The Highland Christian Reformed Church came about as a result of the crowded conditions at the Munster Reformed Church. About one-third of the Munster congregation lived in Highland. The Highland Christian Reformed Church was formally organized on April 28, 1908. Its new building (pictured) was dedicated on November 18, 1908. The First Christian Reformed Church changed to Faith Church in the summer of 2013. (Courtesy of the Highland Historical Society.)

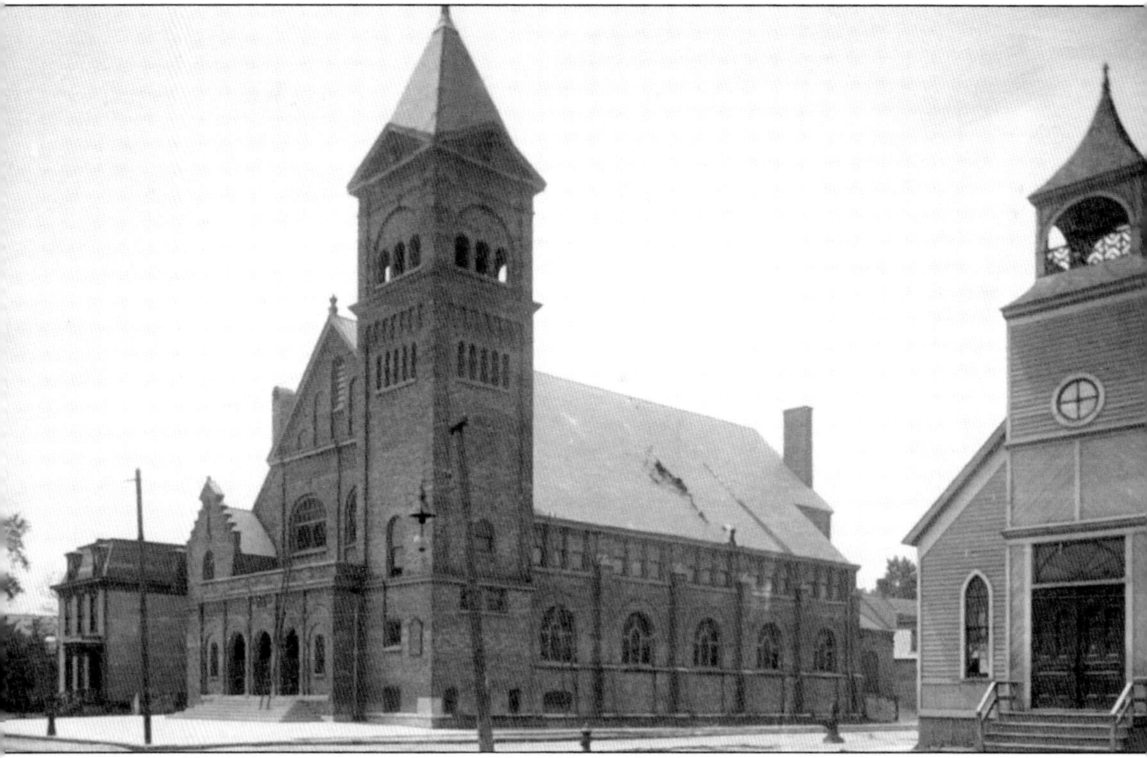

The First Reformed Church of Roseland had humble beginnings in 1849 in Klass Dalenberg's barn. In 1850, Peter De Jong donated land for a church to be built at what today is the corner of 107th Street and Michigan Avenue in Chicago. Shown here are the third church building (right), erected in 1867, and the fourth, built in 1888. (Courtesy of the Calvin College Archives.)

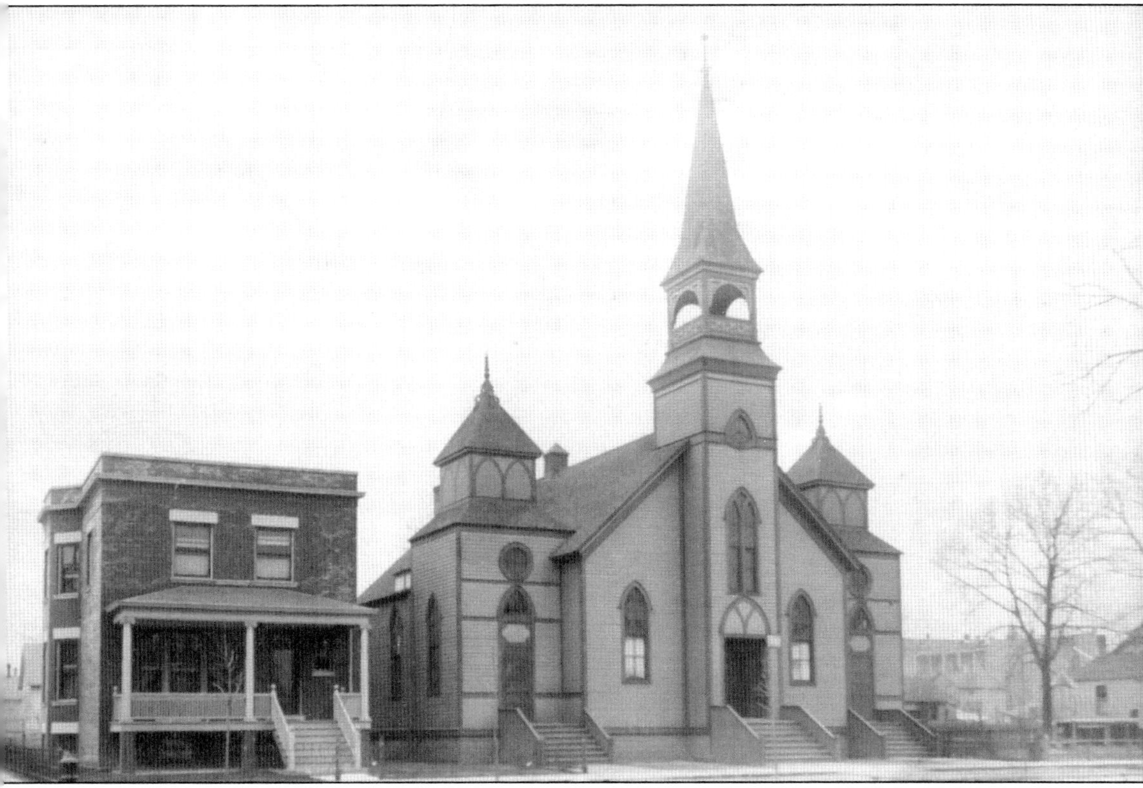

The First Christian Reformed Church of Roseland was organized on December 28, 1877, and the first building (pictured) was dedicated on May 19, 1878, at 111th and State Streets. The final church service was held in Roseland on December 26, 1971, after the decision was made to move to Lynwood, Illinois. On July 13, 1972, the name was changed to the Lynwood Christian Reformed Church, and services began in the new building on November 22, 1973. (Courtesy of the Calvin College Archives.)

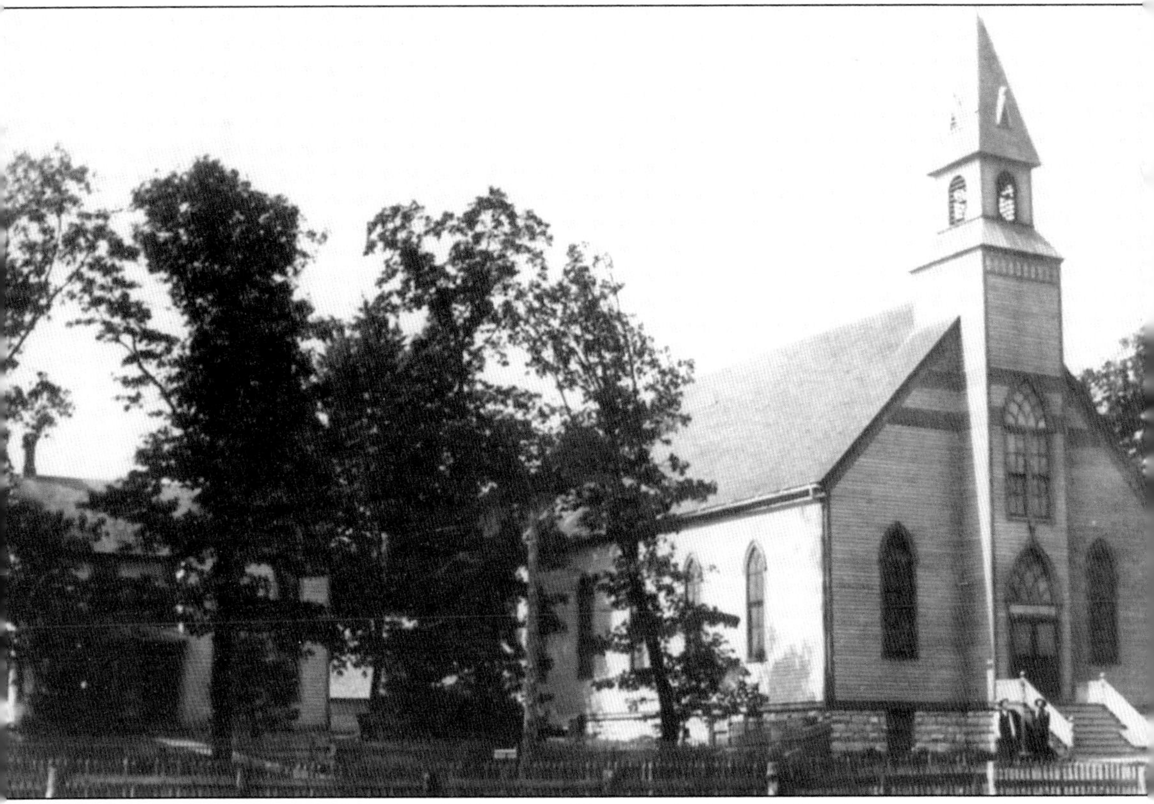

It was on August 25, 1870, that the Munster Christian Reformed Church came into being as the True Holland Reformed Church. It was not until 1874, after years of meeting in private homes, that land was acquired on Ridge Road in Munster to build a church. This version was built in 1900. (Courtesy of the Munster Historical Society.)

This bulletin from the centennial year of the First Reformed Church of Roseland was handed out to worshipers on September 11, 1949. Among the congregational news inside was the announcement of the marriage of Wilma Dyksta and Clarence De Haan, which had taken place on Thursday, September 1, 1949. (Courtesy of Marie Eenigenburg Min.)

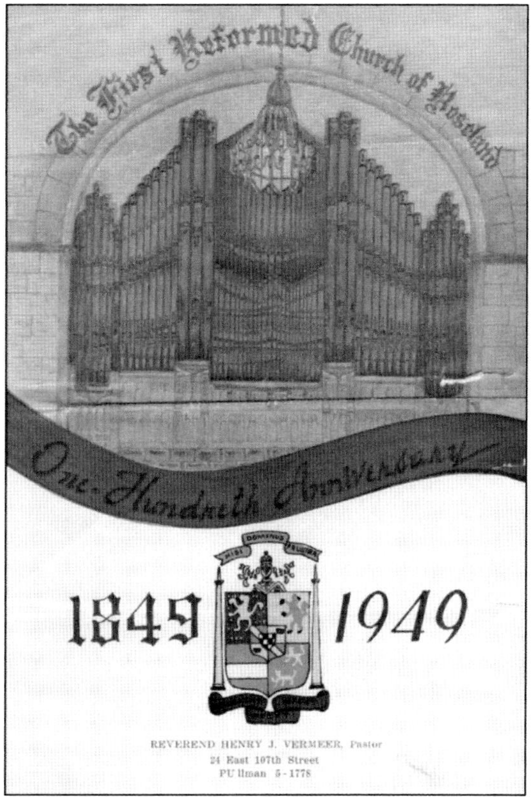

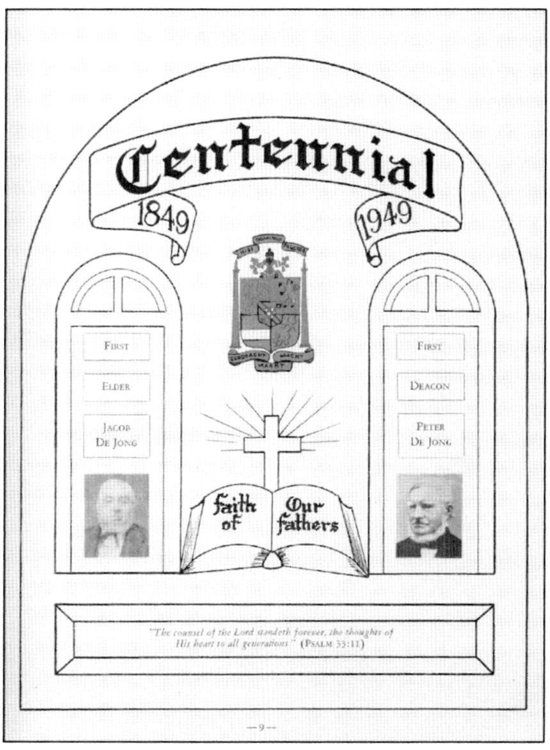

Pictured on page nine of the First Reformed Church of Roseland's A *Century for Christ* centennial book are Jacob De Jong (1808–1875) and his brother Peter (1811–1893). They were two of the founding fathers of Roseland, Illinois, and were instrumental in the founding of the church, as well. (Courtesy of Marie Eenigenburg Min.)

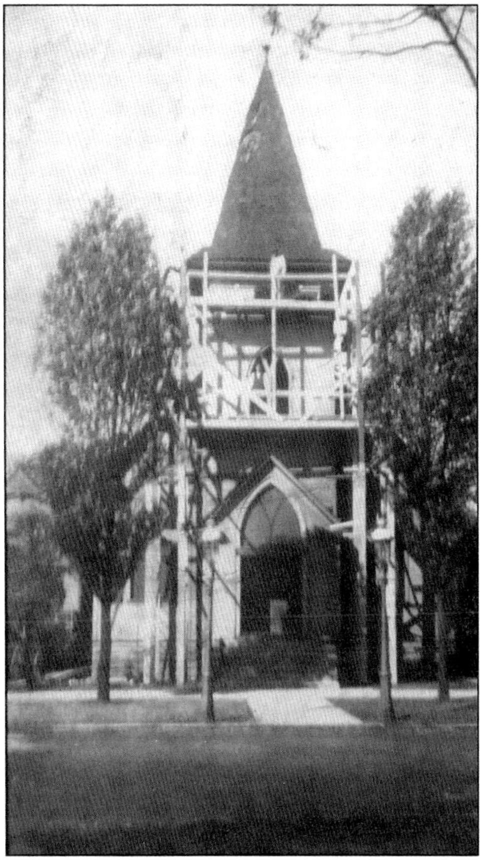

Established as the Second Reformed Church of Roseland on November 19, 1890, the church name was changed to Bethany Reformed in 1891. Erected by Harry Eenigenburg, the building was started in June 1891 and dedicated on November 23, 1891. The first minister was Gerrit Hekhuis, and the first couple to be married in the new church was Katie Kuyper and Albert Van Keimpema, on October 4, 1893. (Courtesy of Marie Eenigenburg Min.)

One of the hallmarks of Dutch Calvinism is the keeping of the Sabbath. Farming was hard, physical labor. After 10-hour days all week long, a farmer needed a day of rest in order to look after both his physical and spiritual well-being. (Courtesy of the South Holland Historical Society.)

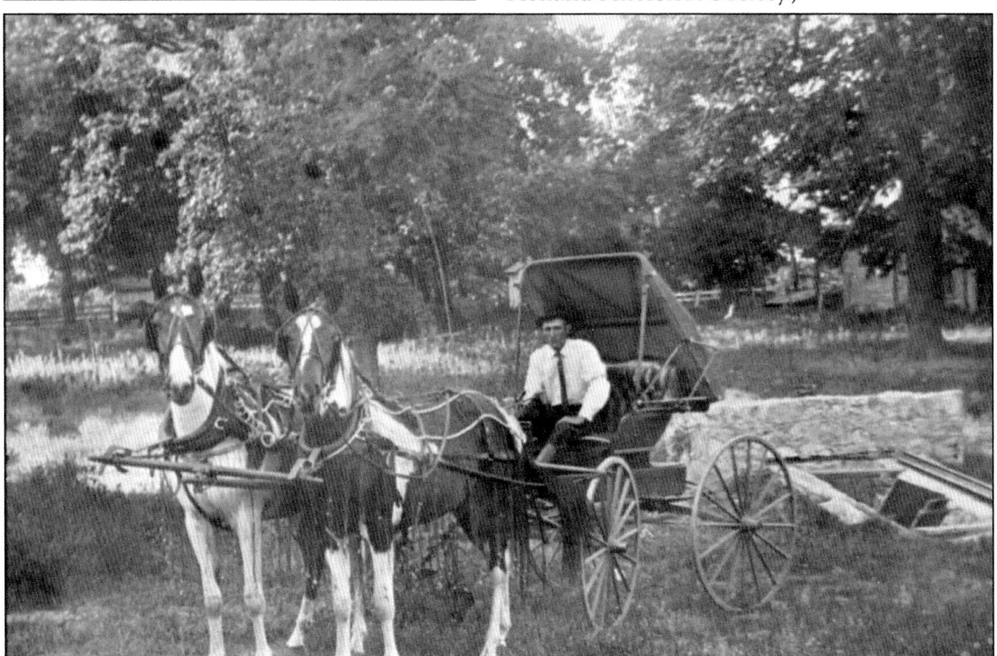

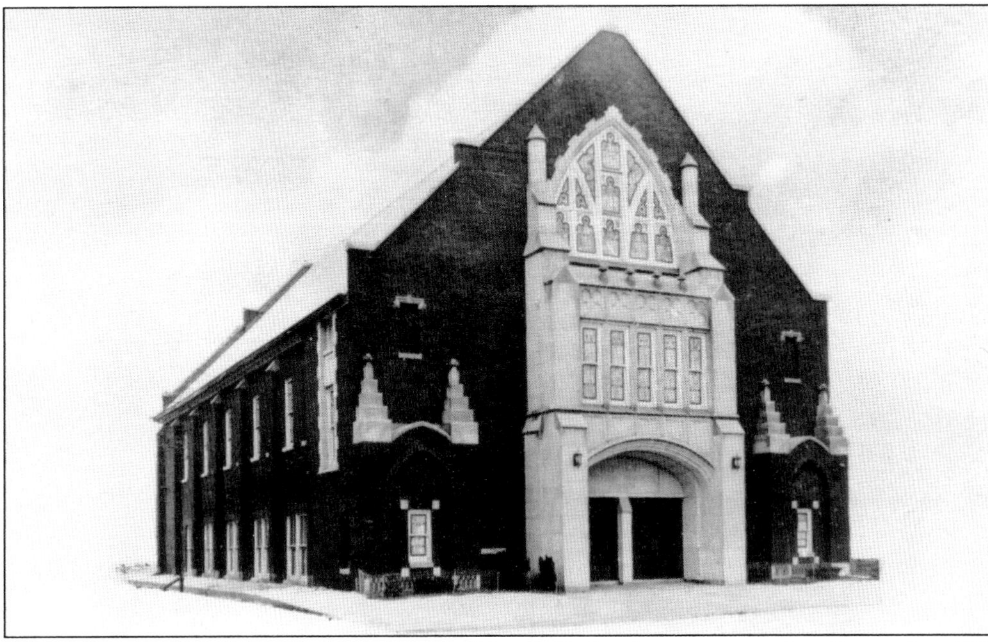

The Bethany Christian Reformed Church of South Holland was organized in September 1925 for the purpose of conducting services in the English language. It was the first church in South Holland to hold all of its services in English. The first pastor was Rev. E. Kooistra. (Courtesy of the South Holland Historical Society.)

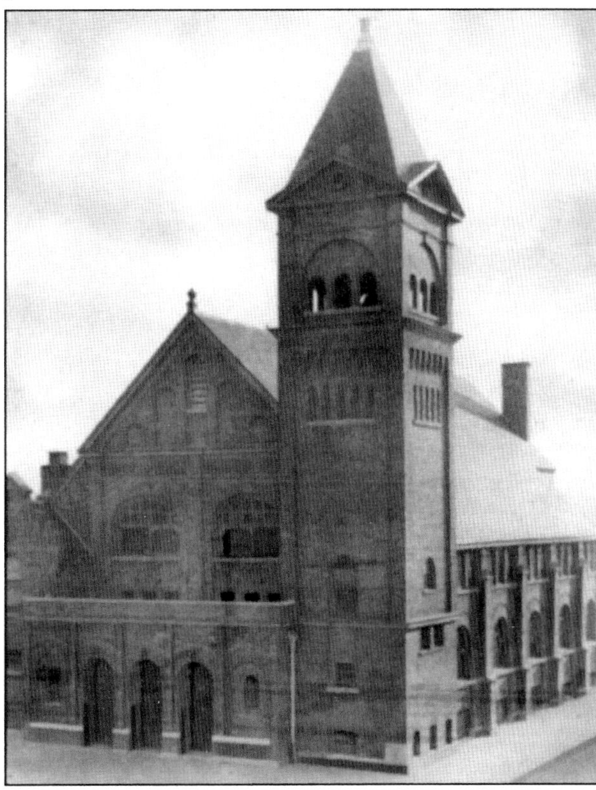

The First Reformed Church of Roseland (pictured) had several "daughter" congregations establish new churches, including Bethany Reformed Church in 1890, the First Reformed Church of Gano in 1891, the First Reformed Church of Mount Greenwood in 1913, and Emmanuel Reformed in 1914. John W. Warnshuis arrived in September 1891 to serve as Gano's first dominie. (Courtesy of Marie Eenigenburg Min.)

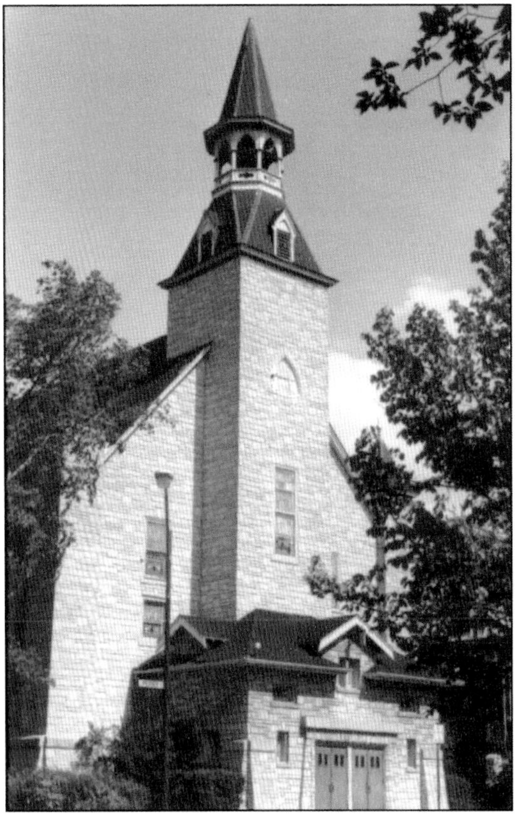

With 109th Street as the dividing line, the overcrowded congregation of the First Reformed Church of Roseland split to form the Second Reformed Church of Roseland. The officers elected at the first congregational meeting of the new church, held on July 20, 1893, included elders Peter De Boer, Simon Dekker, Abraham Moll, and John Zylstra. The first pastor, Hendrik Van Hoogen, was installed on May 11, 1894. (Courtesy of the Calvin College Archives.)

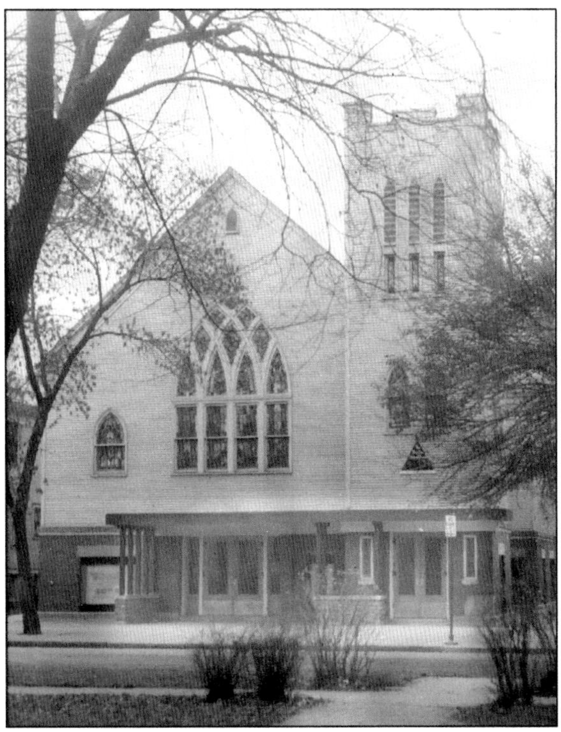

The Third Reformed Church of Roseland was organized in August 1907. The Reverend William Stuat became dominie in 1908 and was the first of three short-serving pastors before being called to Grand Rapids, Michigan, in 1915. Gerrit Hoeksema arrived in 1926 and stayed on until he retired 32 years later. The Reverend John Potts became pastor in 1959. (Courtesy of the Calvin College Archives.)

On June 12, 1945, a congregational meeting of the First Reformed Church of Roseland was held to discuss finding a replacement for Rev. John A. Klaaren, who had delivered his final sermon on October 31, 1944. The call went out to Rev. Henry J. Vermeer (pictured), who accepted and was installed on March 1, 1946. (Courtesy of Marie Eenigenburg Min.)

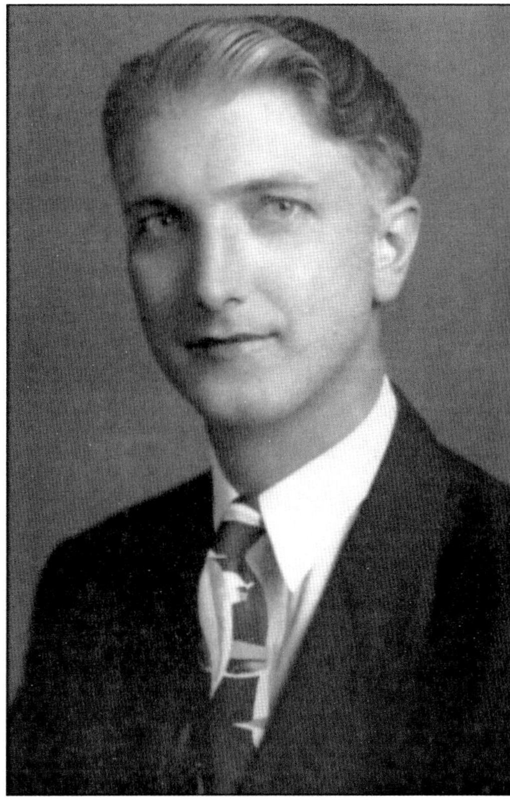

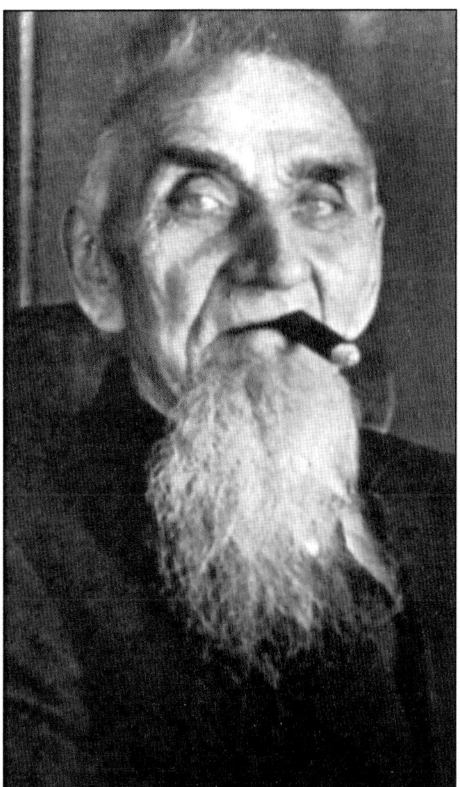

In 1879, the Reverend Dirk Mollema arrived from Steam Boat, Iowa, to become Munster's first dominie. In the United States, the word *dominie* is used to describe a pastor in the Christian Reformed Church. Reverend Mollema left in 1882 to accept a call to the Reformed Church in Lafayette, Indiana. (Courtesy of the Munster Historical Society.)

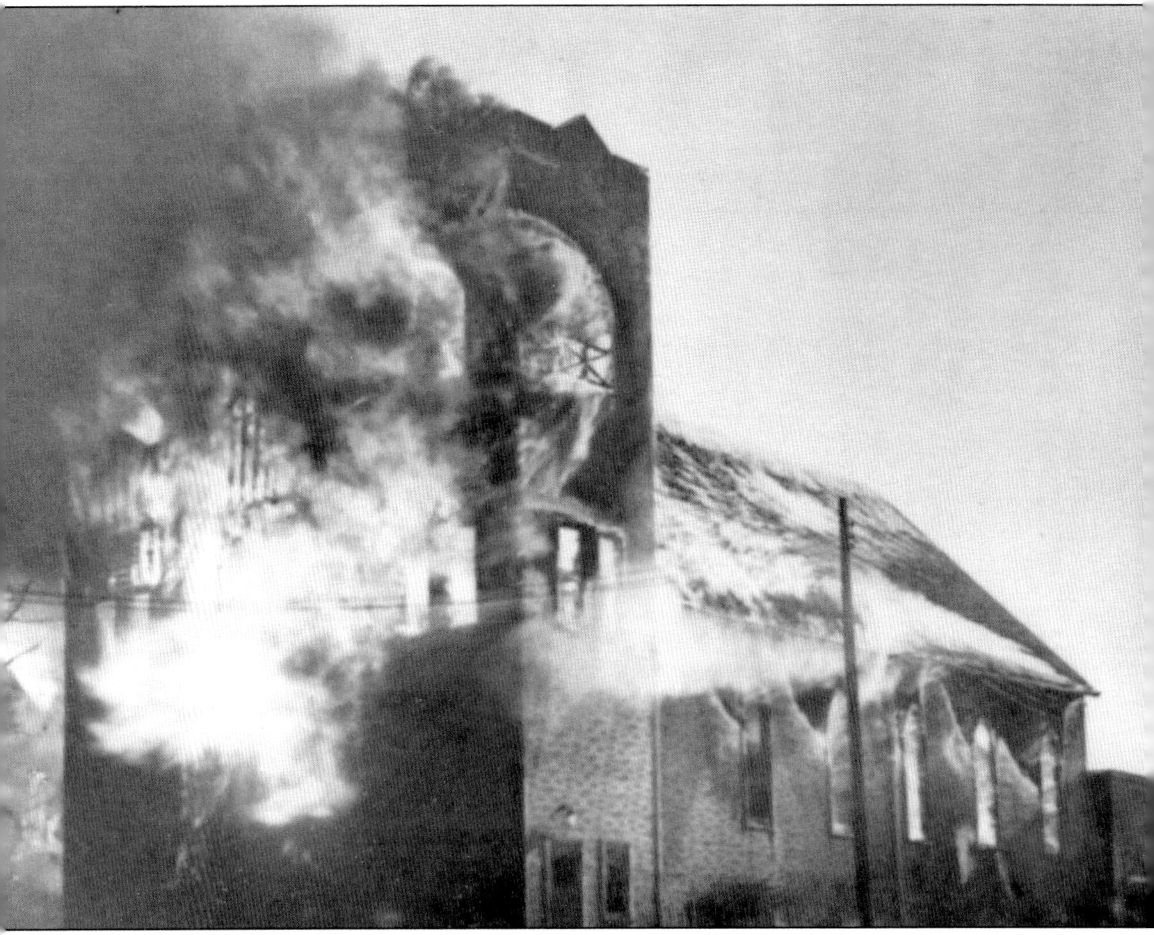

On January 3, 1952, the First Christian Reformed Church of Munster, Indiana, caught fire, and the entire building was destroyed. Before the fire had even been put out, representatives from both the First Reformed Church of Lansing, Illinois, and the Lansing Christian Reformed Church had offered the use of their buildings for services. By the end of the day, St. John's Lutheran Church of Lansing also offered the use of its facilities. (Courtesy of the Munster Historical Society.)

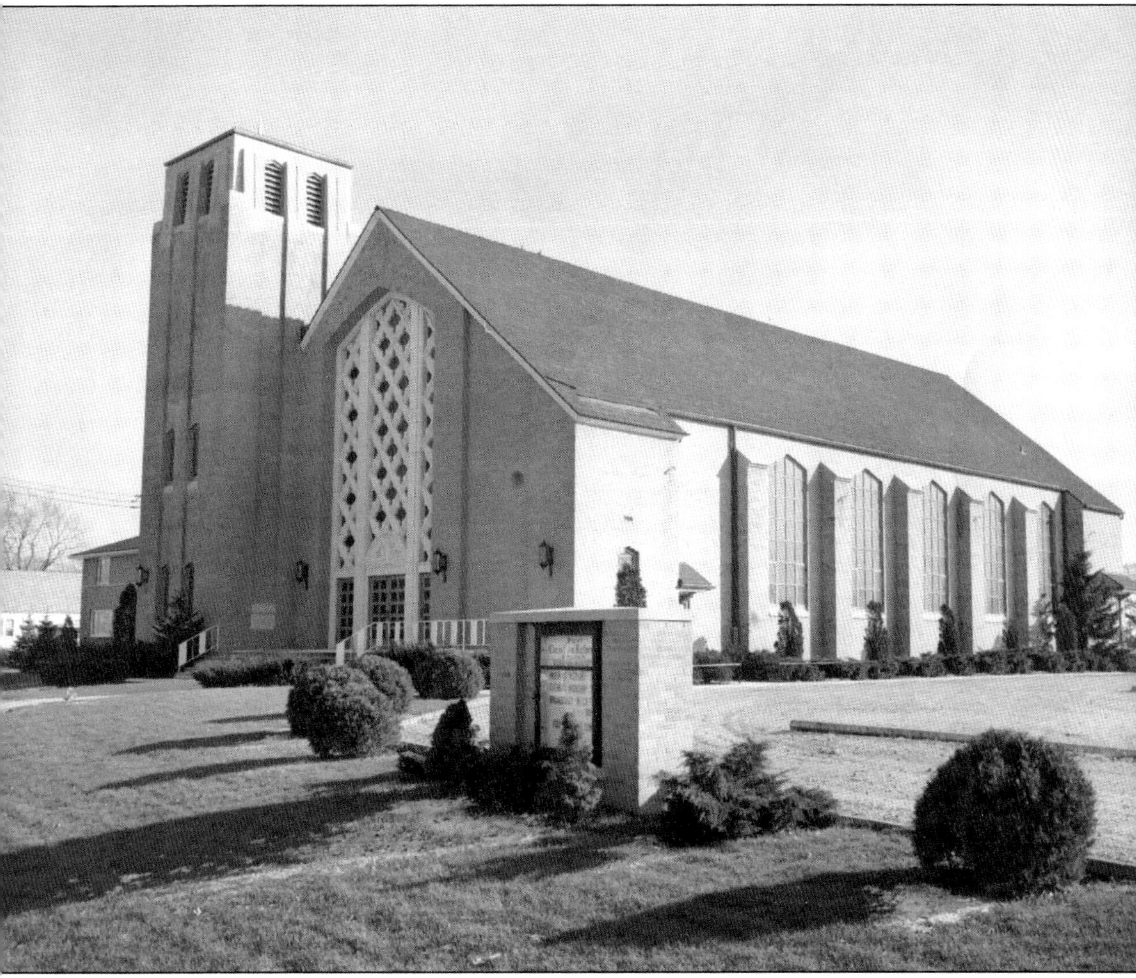

The structure shown here was built after the fire on the same site, and it is presently home to the Munster Christian Reformed Church. It is located at 214 Ridge Road, on the corner of Ridge Road and Homan Avenue. (Courtesy of the Munster Historical Society.)

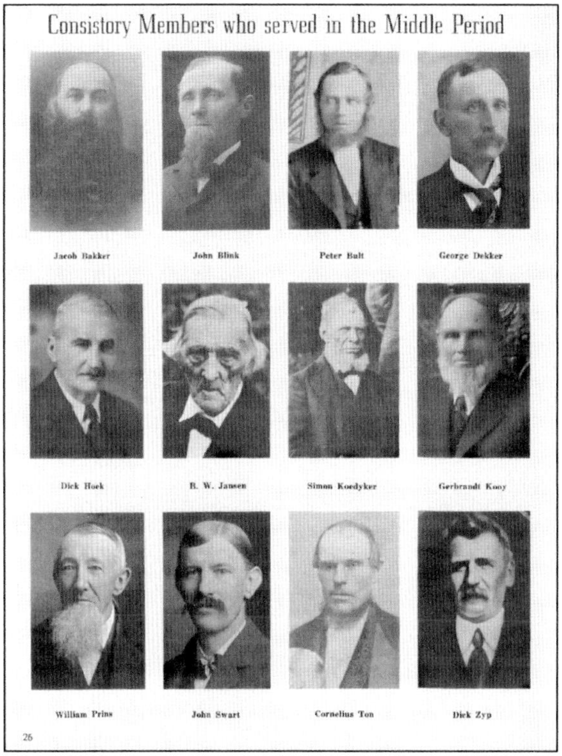

In 1861, Gerrit Eengenburg bought two and one-quarter acres of land at Ridge Road and Burnham Avenue from John Lansing. It is here that Eengenburg built Lansing's first church. He called it the North Creek of Thornton Holland Reformed Church. The church was closed from 1868 to 1873, when parishioners founded a new church in Munster. In 1875, twenty families reorganized under the name of the Reformed (Dutch) Church of Lansing, later known as the First Reformed Church of Lansing. Shown here are consistory members from the middle period. (Courtesy of the Lansing Historical Society.)

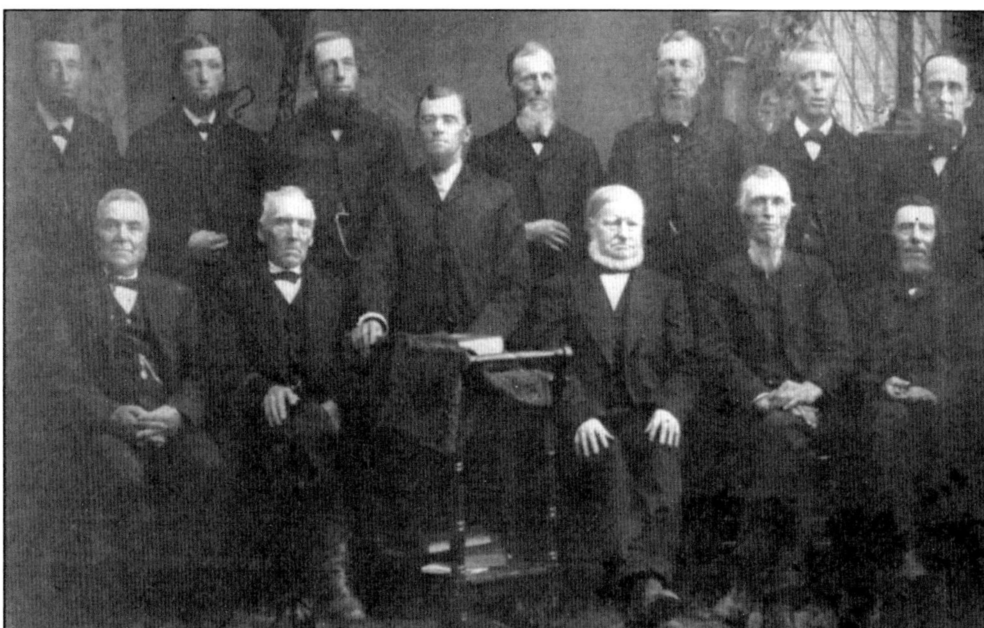

Some of Roseland's first settlers were among the First Reformed Church of Roseland's consistory of 1886. Shown here are, from left to right, (first row) Klass Madderom, Barend Van Mynen, Rev. Balster Van Ess, Peter De Jong, Jan Ton, and Arie Vander Myde; (second row) William Swart, Peter Prince, Dirk De Jong, Heert Tysen, John De Jong, Dirk Van Vuren, and Johannes Vanderbilt. (Courtesy of Marie Eenigenburg Min.)

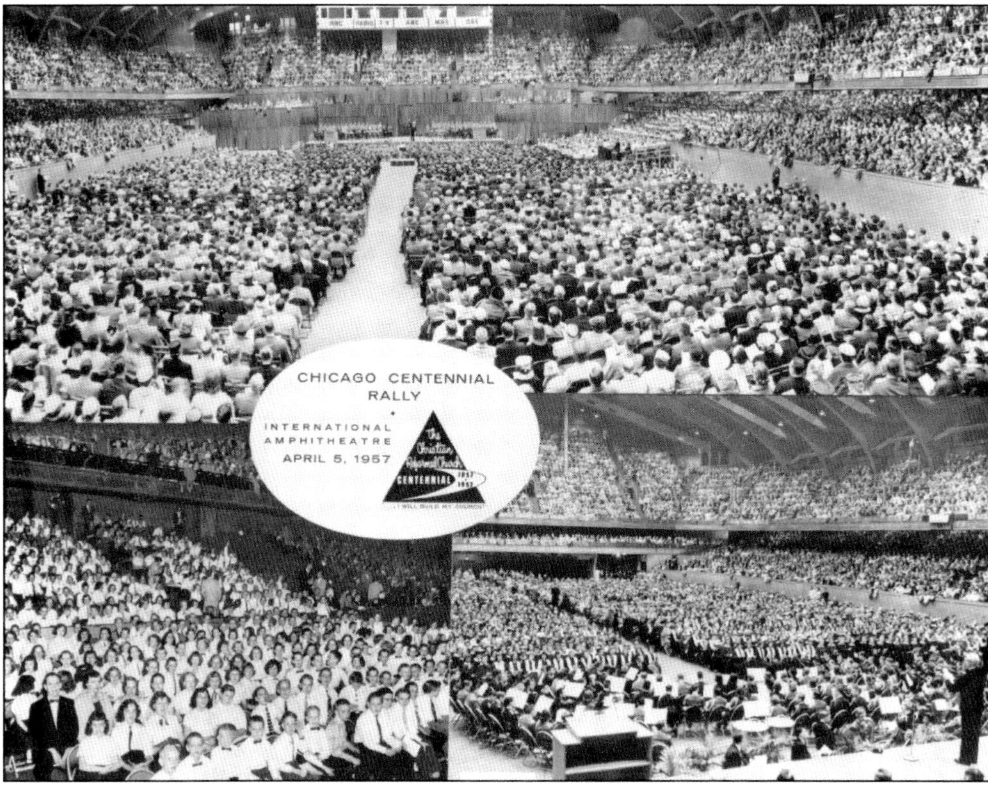

Lead by Gijsbert Haan (1801–1874), a meeting was held on April 5, 1857, to form a classis (governing body) of a new denomination that was to one day become the Christian Reformed Church. In 1957, a centennial celebration was held at Chicago's International Amphitheater, attended by an estimated 12,000 people. (Courtesy of the Calvin College Archives.)

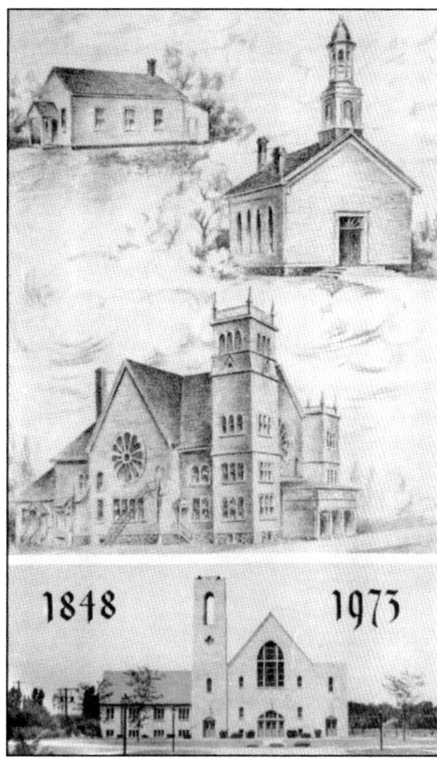

The first organized church in South Holland, Illinois, got it start shortly after the arrival of Rev. Willem Coenran Wust and 30 followers from his former congregation. The church was originally named the Grerformeerde Kerk onder het Kruis, or the Reformed Church under the Cross, in English. (Courtesy of the South Holland Historical Society.)

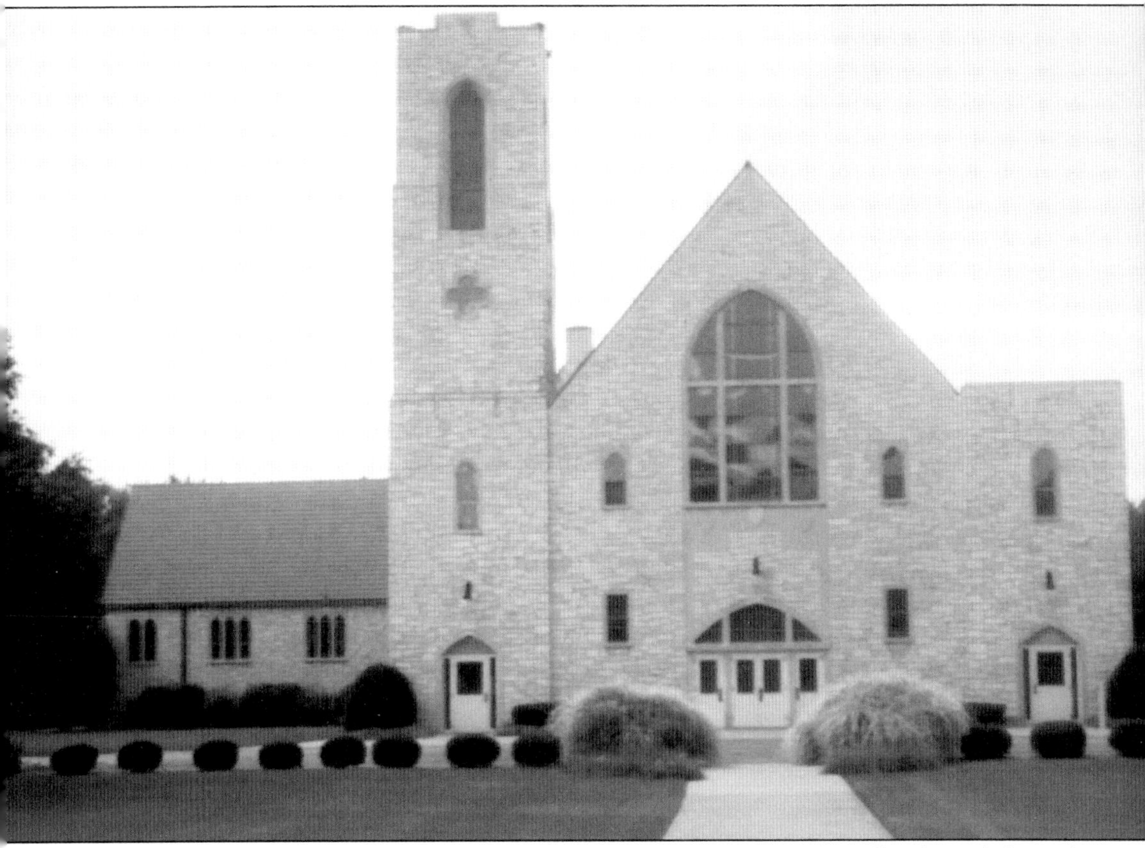

The present-day building housing the First Reformed Church of South Holland was dedicated in 1951. The Reverend Theodore F. Zandstra was the minister at the time. In 1967, an annex was added to accommodate meeting rooms, a kitchen, and a youth room. (Photograph by the author.)

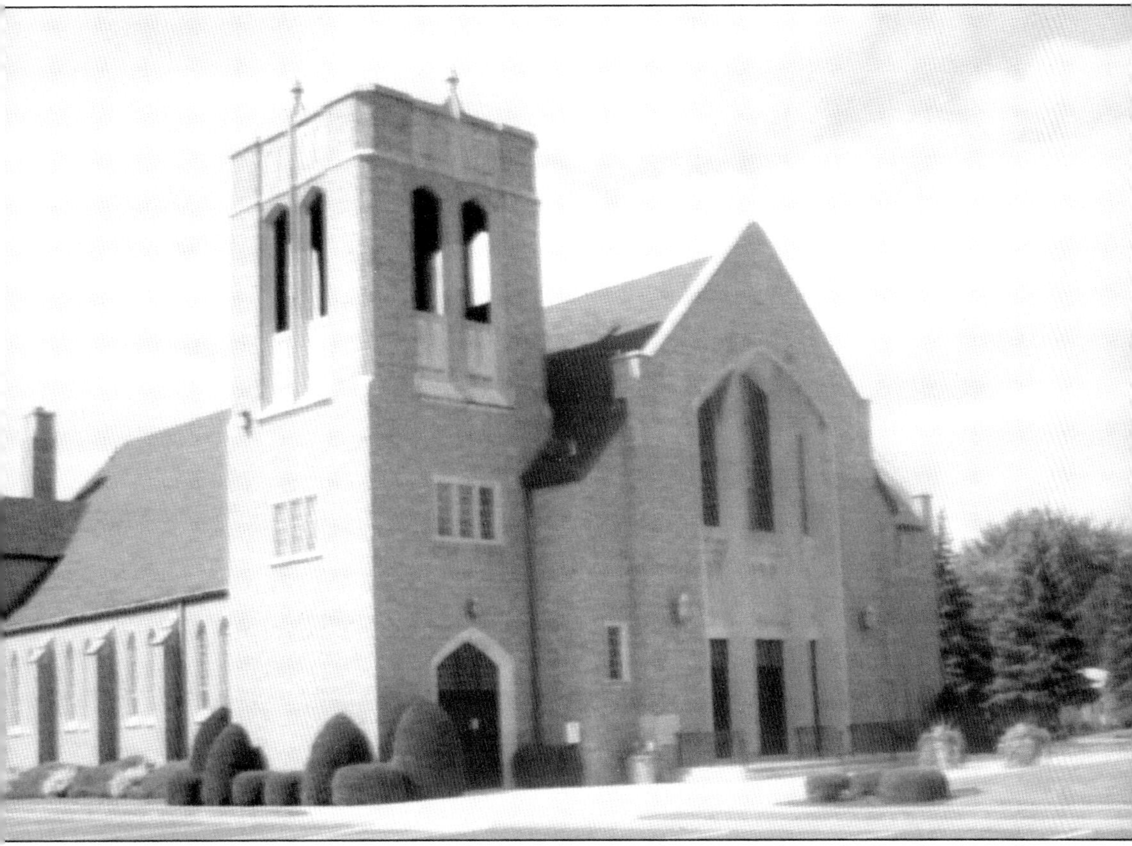

On April 30, 1955, the cornerstone was laid for the First Christian Reformed Church of South Holland's new building. A year later, the new structure was dedicated. The old building, with its hand-rung bell and tall steeple, was torn down to make room for more parking. (Photograph by the author.)

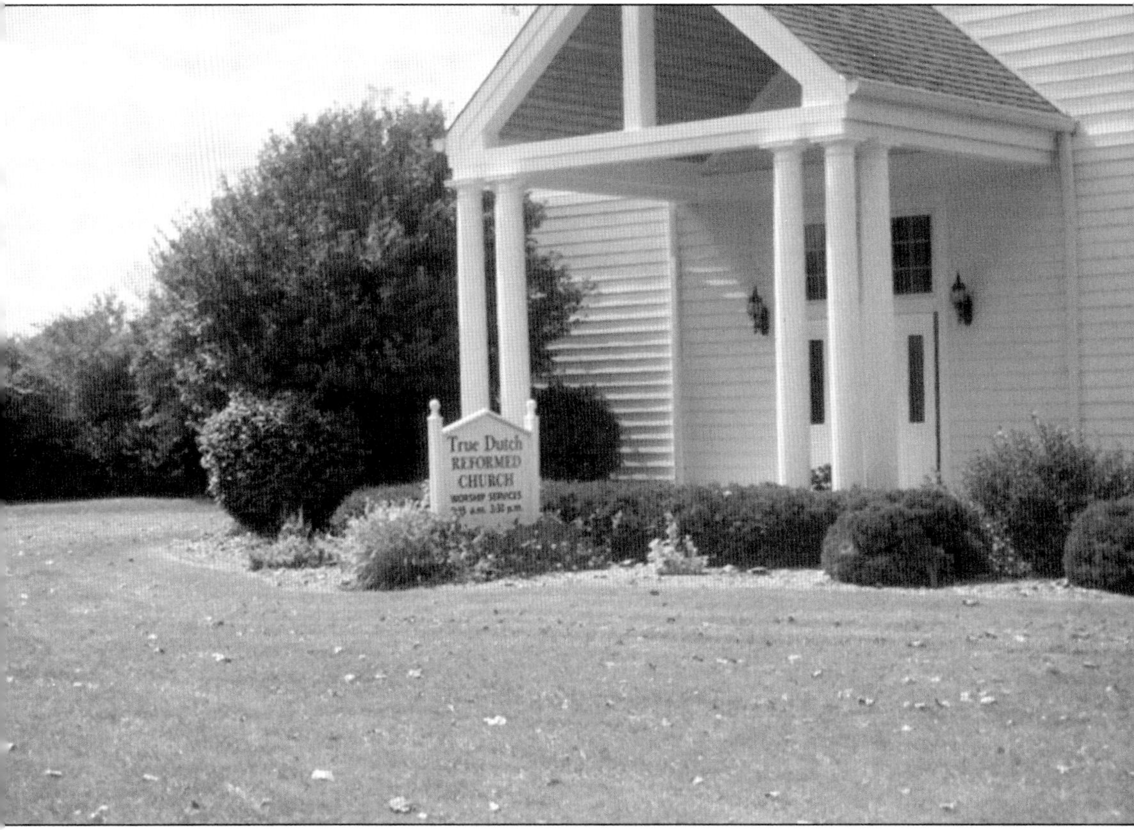

The True Dutch Reformed Church of South Holland had its beginnings when several members of the original South Holland Reformed congregation left the church in part due to the perceived moderate preaching of Rev. Seine Bolks. On January 27, 1865, this group became officially known as the True Dutch Reformed Church of South Holland. The church is presently located at 18340 Dante Avenue in Lansing, Illinois. Reverend Bolks went on to accept a call from Orange City, Iowa, where he was dominie from 1872 to 1878. (Photograph by the author.)

In 1908, after many meetings, the first consistory of the First Christian Reformed Church of Highland called on the Reverend J.M. Blyeveld, and he became the first pastor of the new church. The members of that first consistory are shown here, from page 4 of the 50th-anniversary booklet. (Courtesy of the Highland Historical Society.)

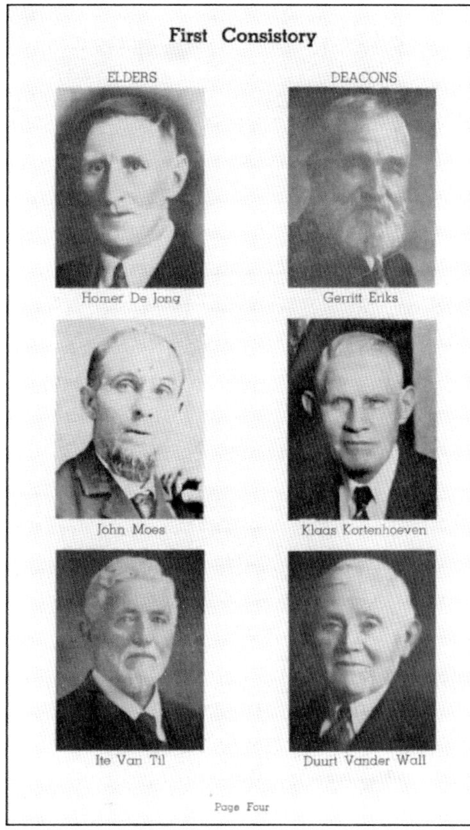

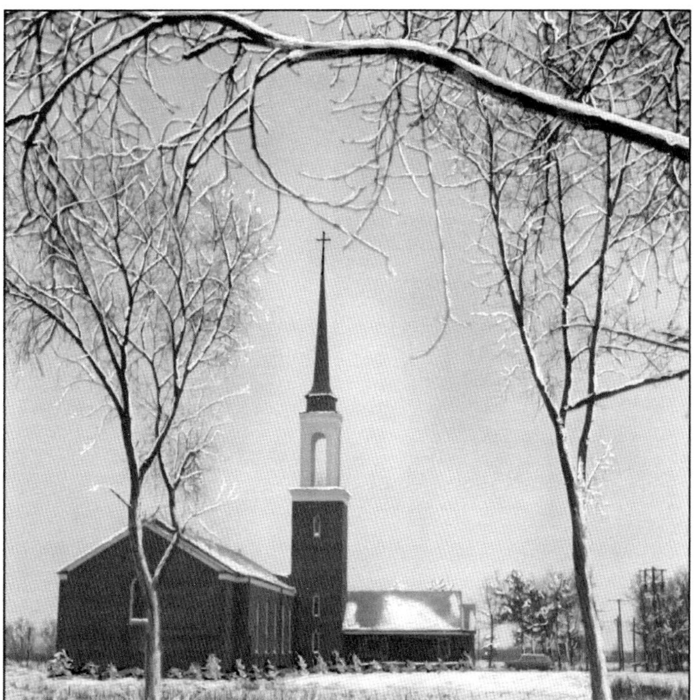

The Second Christian Reformed Church of Highland came into being in 1953, due to the crowded conditions at the First Christian Reformed Church of Highland. Now known as the New Life Christian Reformed Church, it is located at 3010 Ridge Road in Highland, Indiana. (Courtesy of the Calvin College Archives.)

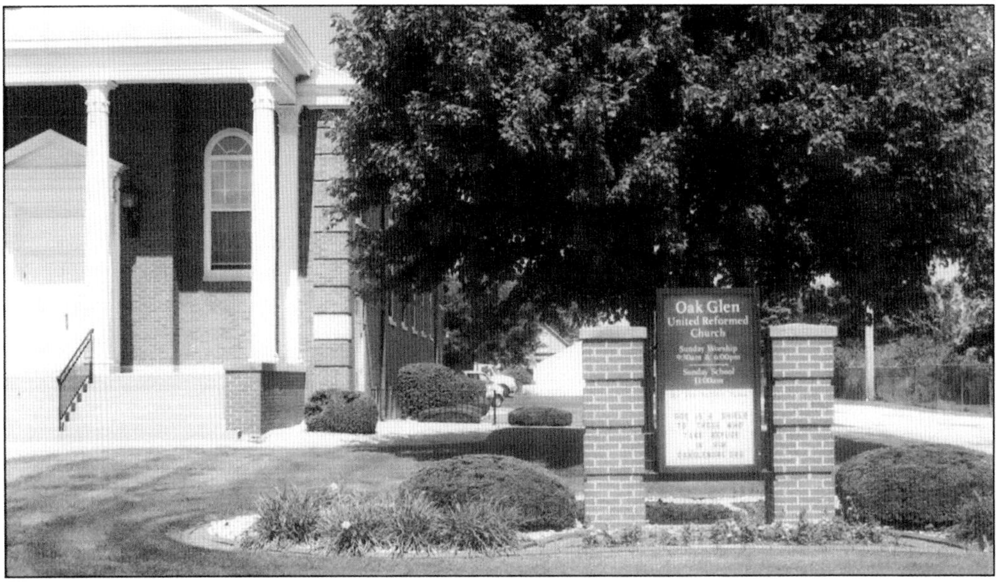

The Oak Glen United Reformed Church, located at 2244 Indiana Avenue in Lansing, Illinois, was originally known as Oak Glen Christian Reformed Church. The congregation was formed due to the overflow crowds attending both the Munster Christian Reformed Church and the Lansing Christian Reformed Church. Starting on January 4, 1948, with 52 families, the Oak Glen Christian Reformed Church met for six years in the auditorium of Illiana Christian High School. The congregation broke ground on its own building in June 1953. By 1954, when the structure was completed, the church had a membership of 445 individuals from 96 families. (Photograph by the author.)

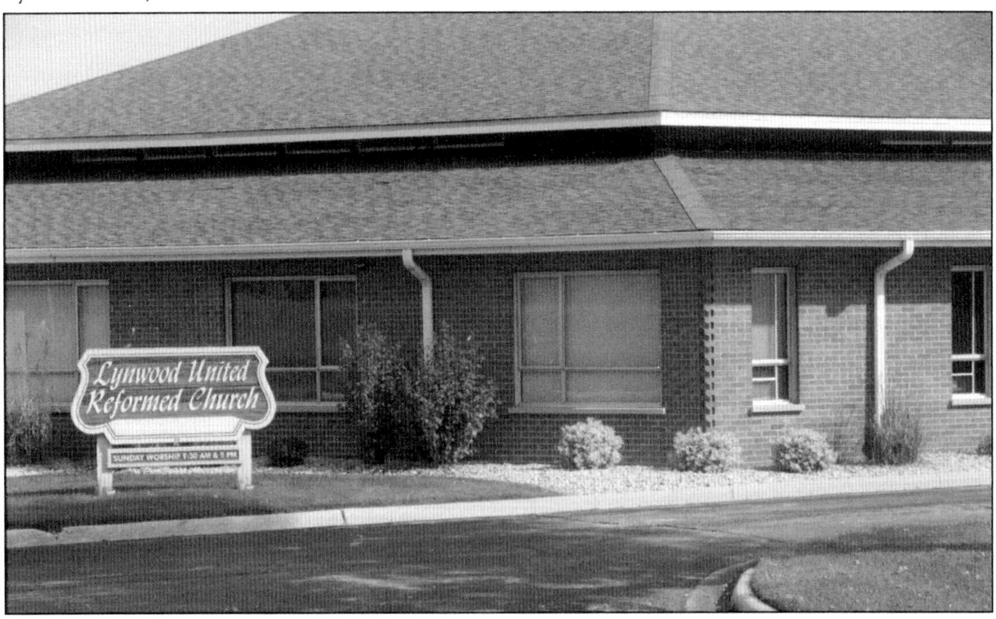

In 1972, the First Reformed Church of Roseland became the Lynwood Christian Reformed Church. In November of that same year, ground was broken on seven acres of land on Glenwood-Dyer Road in Lynwood, Illinois, for a new church building (pictured). In 1990, the Lynwood Christian Reformed Church joined the new United Reformed denomination. (Photograph by the author.)

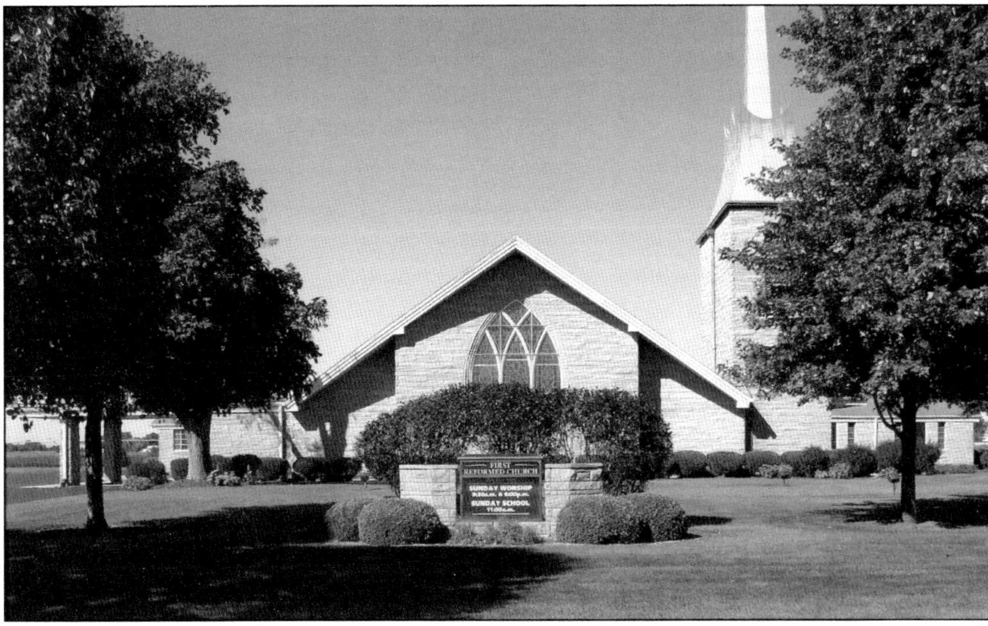

The First Reformed Church of Wichert was incorporated under the name First Reformed Church of Koster in 1895. At the time, worship services were held in a barnlike structure. In 1898, a new church was built on two acres of donated land, and the first services were conducted in Dutch by Rev. J.W. Poot, and in English by Rev. G. J. Hekhuis. Some of the furniture was donated by the First Reformed Church at Roseland, Illinois. (Photograph by the author.)

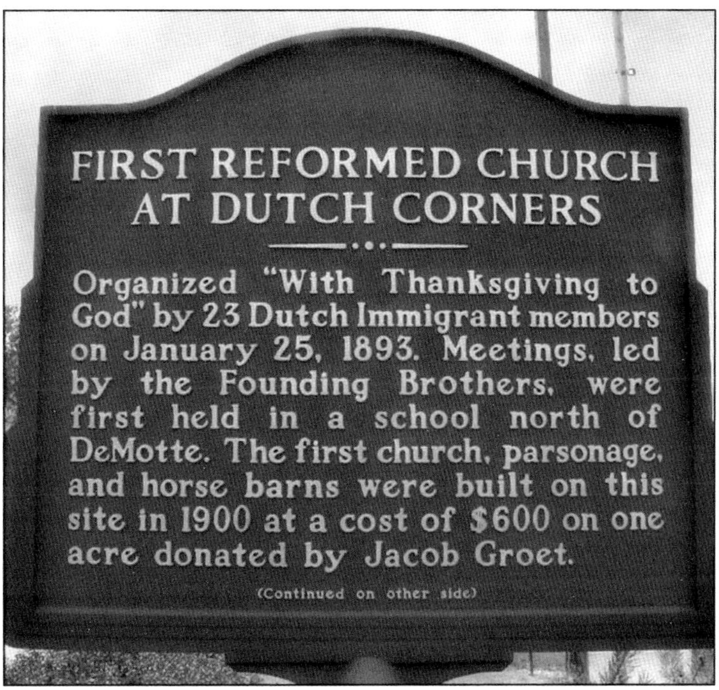

The First Reformed Church of DeMotte is located about three miles west of town, at what is referred to as "Dutch Corners." The congregation was organized in 1893. During the early years, all services were held in the Dutch language. Disagreement concerning English replacing Dutch led to a split in the congregation. Those who wanted English services became the congregation of the American Reformed Church in DeMotte. (Photograph by the author.)

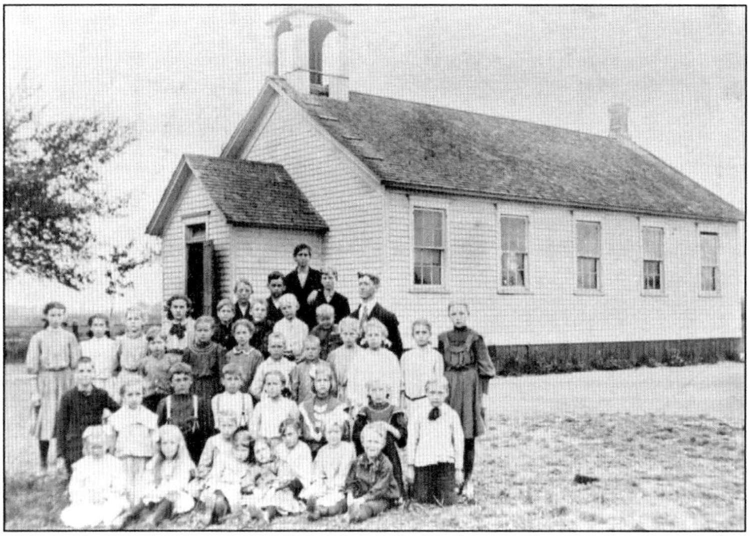

South Holland's first school, a one-room building with living quarters for the teachers, was erected in 1854. It was replaced with a two-room building in 1884 and was called the Gouwens School, in honor of J.C. Gouwens, who served as president of the school board for many years. (Courtesy of the South Holland Historical Society.)

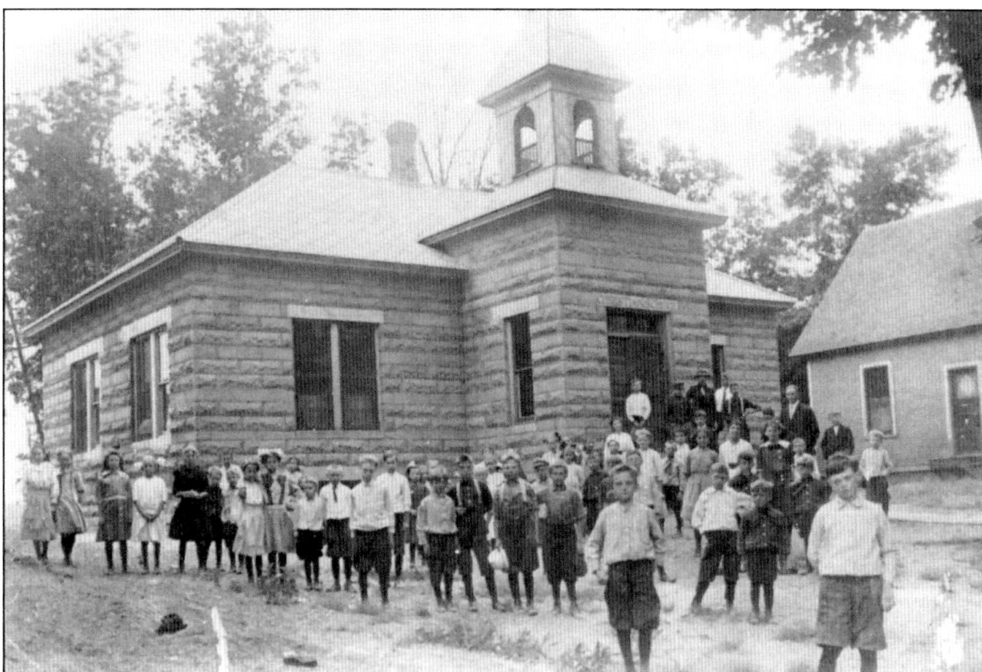

The Munster Christian School, built on the corner of Ridge Road and Hohman Avenue, first held classes on September 16, 1907, when 56 children began attending the two-room school. In 1942, a new, larger building opened in Lansing, Illinois, and the name was changed to Lansing Christian School. (Courtesy of the Munster Historical Society.)

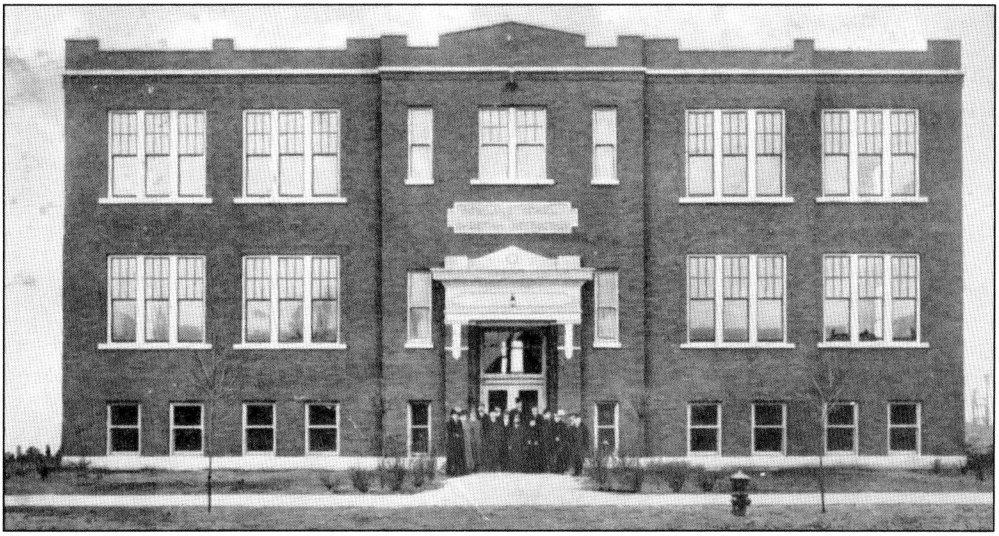

The Roseland School for Christian Instruction, founded in 1884, was originally known as De Hollandsche Christelijke. The first location was at the back of the First Christian Reformed Church of Roseland on 111th and State Streets. Classes at the 104th Street and Princeton Avenue location (pictured) began on October 5, 1891. Students there were taught in Dutch until 1911. (Courtesy of the Calvin College Archives.)

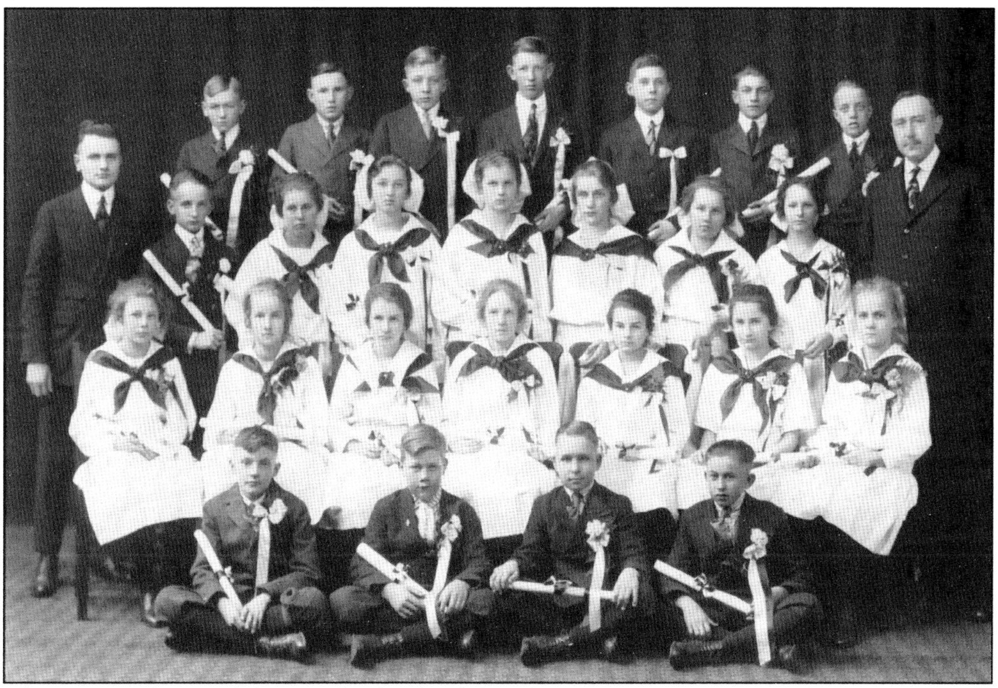

The 1922 graduates of the Roseland School for Christian Instruction include, in alphabetical order, John Boersma, Cornelia Bulthuis, Gerrit De Heer, Katie Dekker, Grace De Roos, Richard De Vries, Rudolph De Vries, Martin De Jong Cicilia Dykstra, Amelia Hoekstra, Oscar Hofstra, Andrew Knipper, Dora Kuiken, Martin Kuiken, William Maatman, Charles Miedema, Angeline Nydam, Grace Posthuma, Theodore Radius, Edith Schaap, Helen Vander Poel, Katie Vander Woude, Grace Voorn, Fred Worman, and Mary Yff. (Courtesy of the Calvin College Archives.)

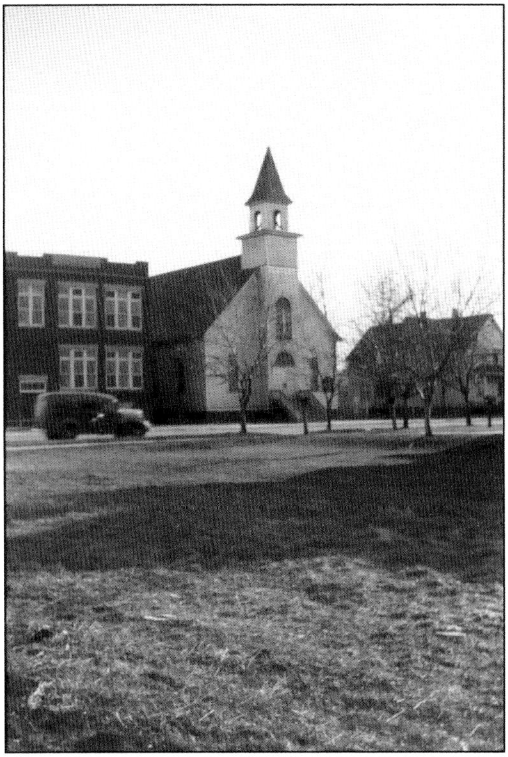

The Highland Christian School (left) is shown in 1939. The school, founded in 1909, was formally incorporated on January 10, 1910, as the Association for Christian Instruction at Highland. The two-story brick building was located on Highway Avenue. (Courtesy of the Calvin College Archives.)

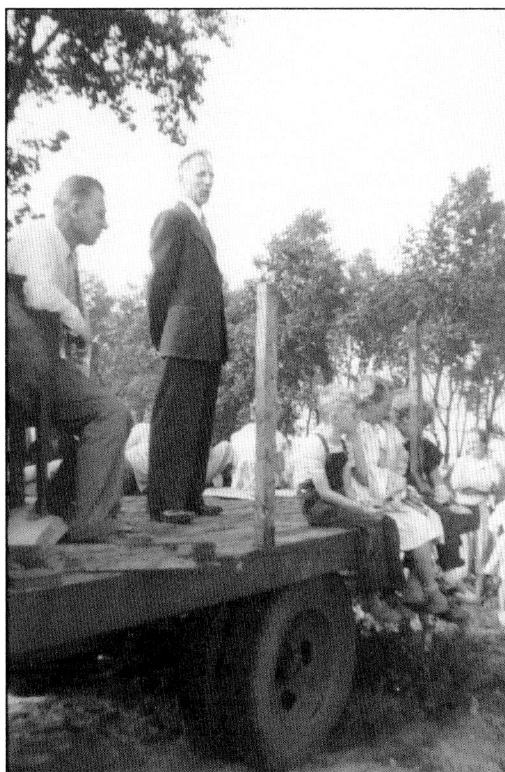

John Van der Zee (left), principal at the Highland Christian School, listens as Dr. Martin Van Dyke, pastor of the Highland Reformed Church, speaks at the ground breaking for a new school building in 1950. As of 2014, the school was located at 3040 Ridge Road in Highland, Indiana. (Courtesy of the Calvin College Archives.)

Illiana Christian High School met for a time in two barracks at the former Civilian Conservation Corps (CCC) camp in the Thornton Forest Preserve. The faculty was allowed to make improvements in order to convert the barracks into classrooms. In the fall of 1946, a student body of 135 filled the six classrooms in one barracks. The additional barracks was used for recreational purposes. (Photograph by the author.)

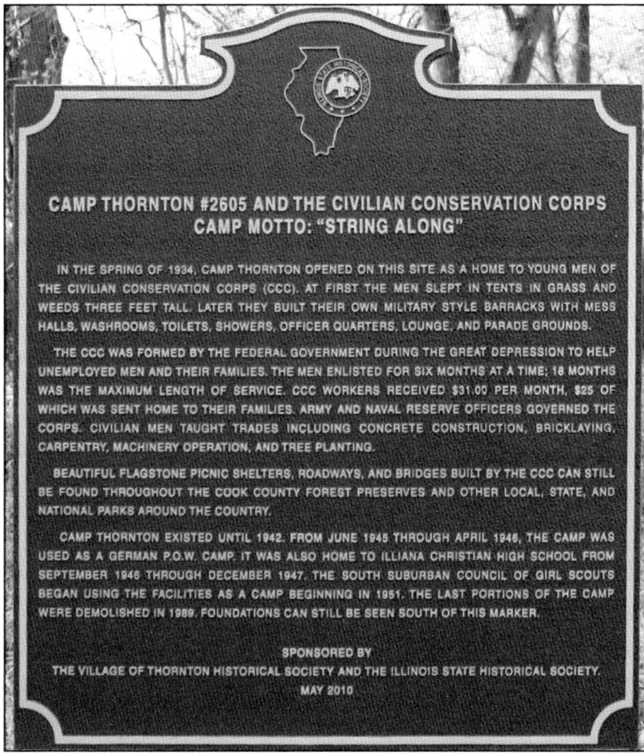

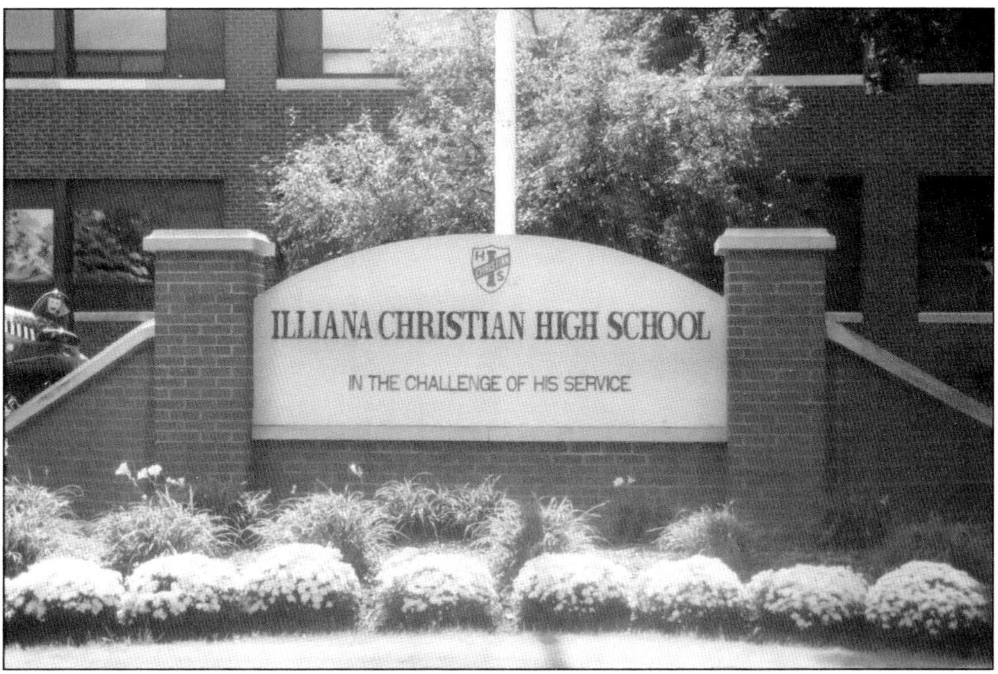

As of summer 2014, plans were under way to move Illiana Christian High School from Lansing, Illinois, to a 40-acre site at the southwest corner of 109th Street and Calumet Avenue in Hanover Township, Indiana. The school has been at its present location since January 1948. (Photograph by the author.)

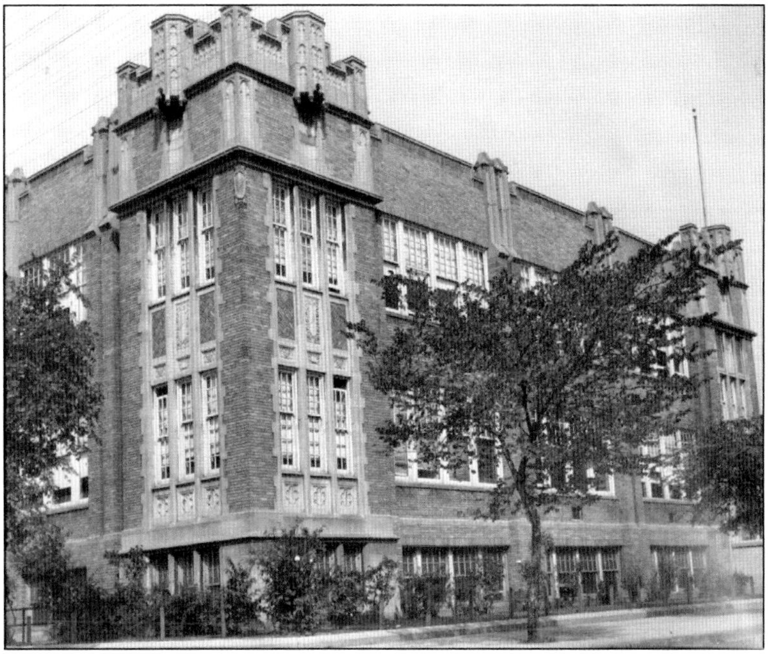

Chicago Christian High School first held classes in 1918. The student population of 13 met in a building located at Seventy-second Place and Loomis Street in Englewood. Mark Fakkema was the principal from 1918 to 1926. (Courtesy of the Calvin College Archives.)

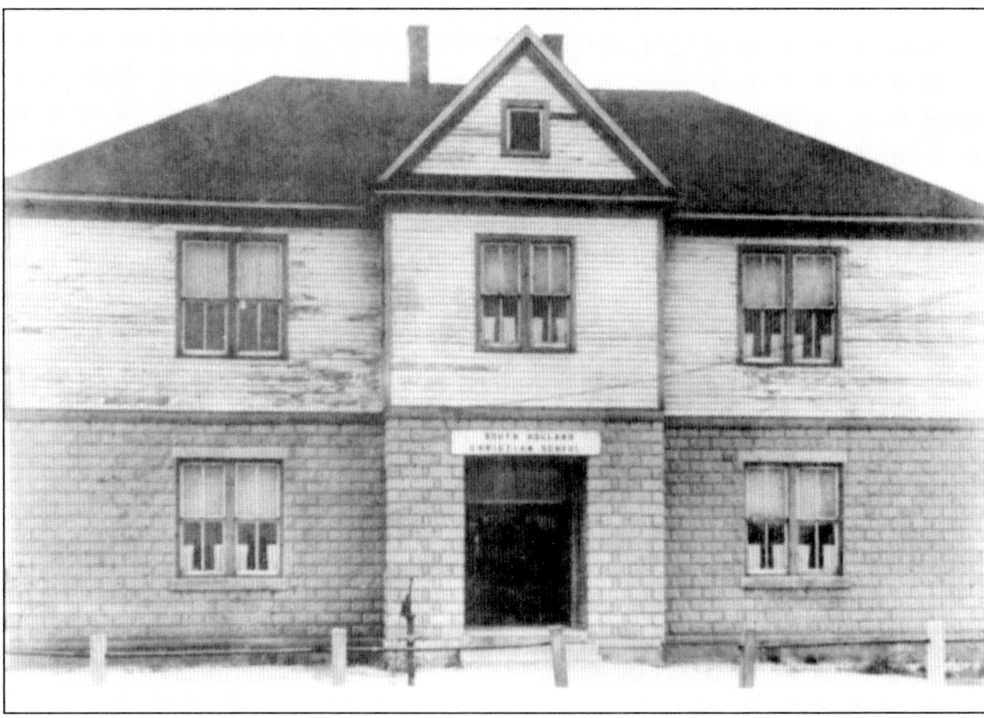

Calvin Christian School opened its doors to students in 1913. The first school building consisted of two rooms, in which 20 students and their teacher met. In 1914, the original building was raised, and a brick-and-concrete new first floor was built underneath it. (Courtesy of the South Holland Historical Society.)

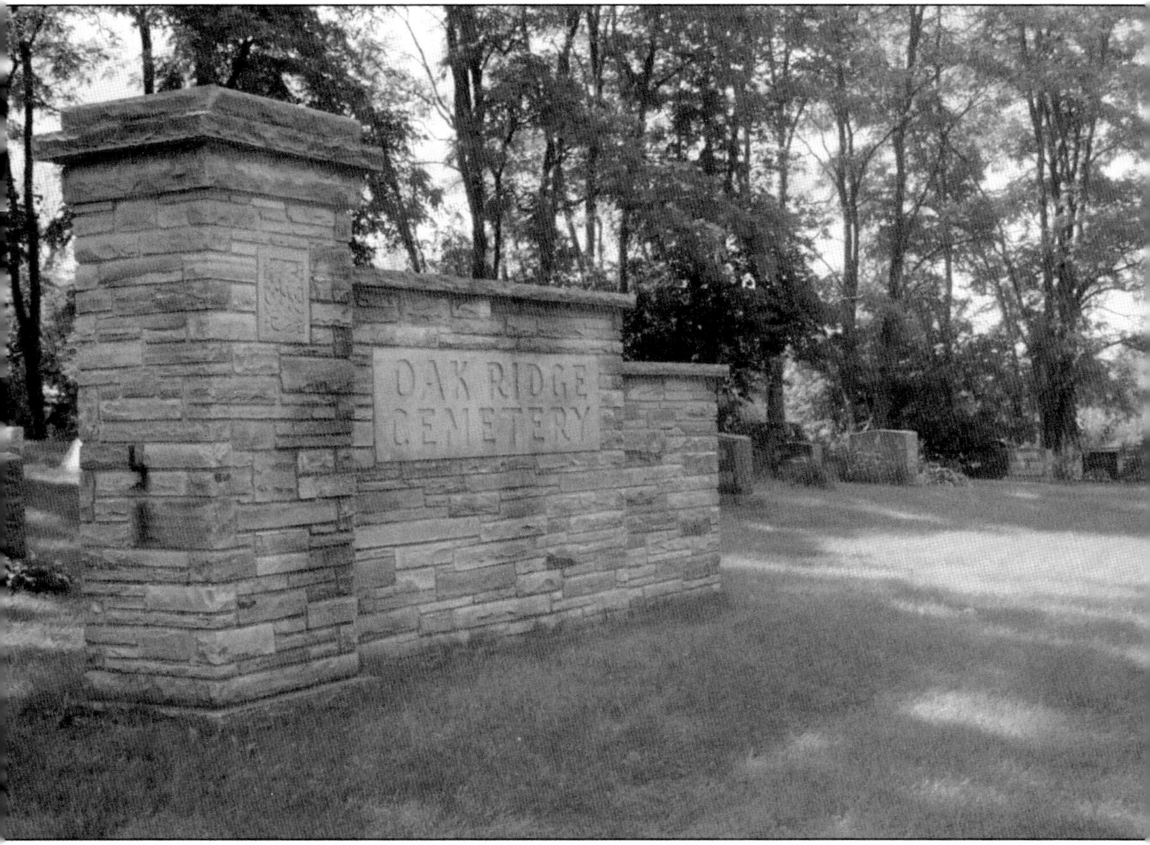

Owned and operated by the First Reformed Church of South Holland, Illinois, Oak Ridge Cemetery had its beginnings on November 28, 1912, when the idea was put forward to purchase seven acres near Oak Glen for a cemetery. Located on Thornton-Lansing Road, the land was purchased in 1913 for $3,300. (Photograph by the author.)

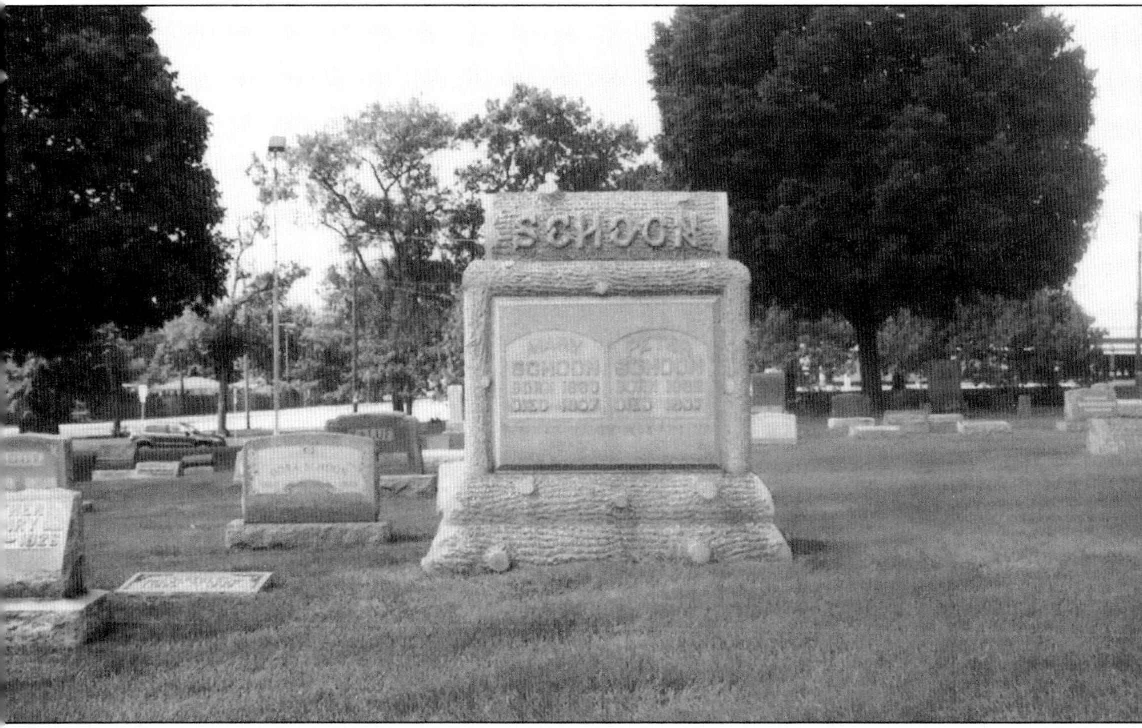

The Schoon Cemetery, also known as Munster Christian Cemetery, is located on the grounds of Munster Christian Reformed Church, at Ridge Road and Hohman Avenue in Munster, Indiana. In the 1890s, brothers Jacob and Pieter Schoon each bought an eighth of an acre of land from Pieter's son Dirk next to the Munster Christian Reformed Church. This land became the Schoon family cemetery. (Photograph by the author.)

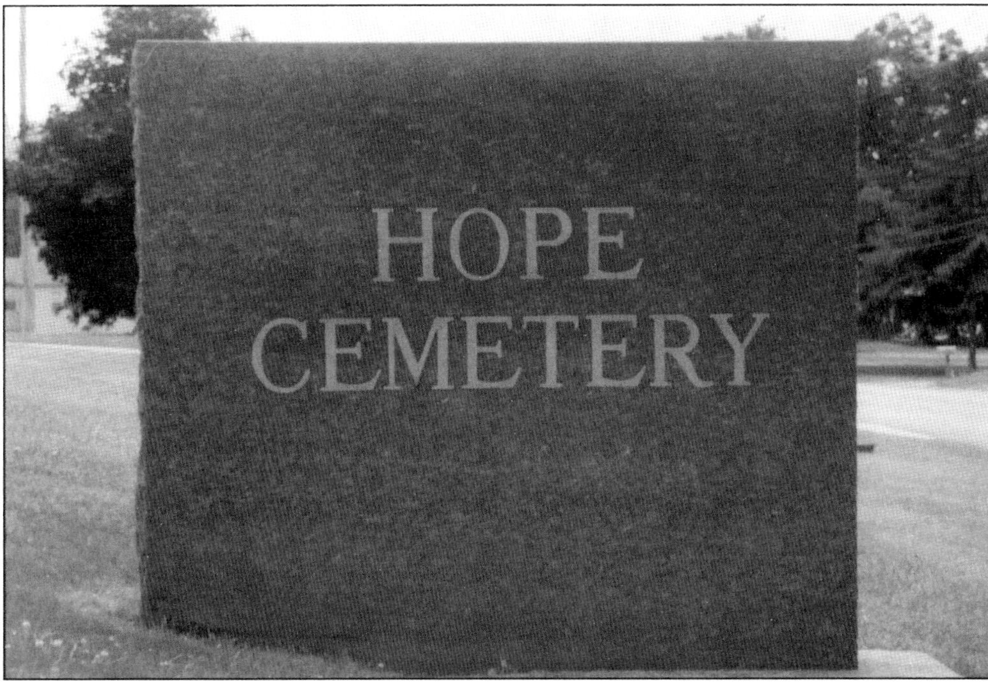

Hope Cemetery is located at 8917 Kleinman Road in Highland, Indiana. The one-and-a-half-acre property sits on a former sand dune and was bought by the Highland Christian Reformed Church in 1909 from Peter Zyp for $300. It is now owned and operated by both of the Christian Reformed churches in Highland. (Photograph by the author.)

On May 20, 1857, the congregation of the First Reformed Church of South Holland purchased land to be used for final resting. It was known at the time as Mount Holland Cemetery. Among the early settlers buried here is Hendrick De Jong. The cemetery is now known as Homewood Memorial Gardens. (Photograph by the author.)

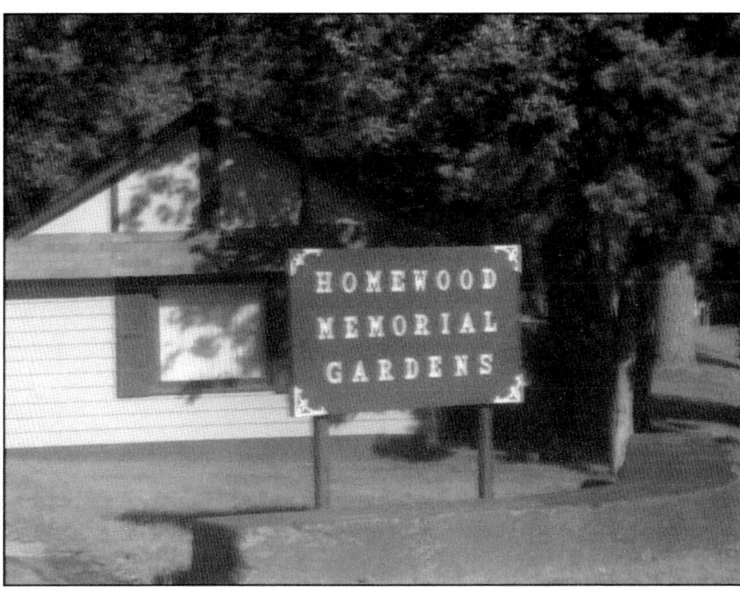

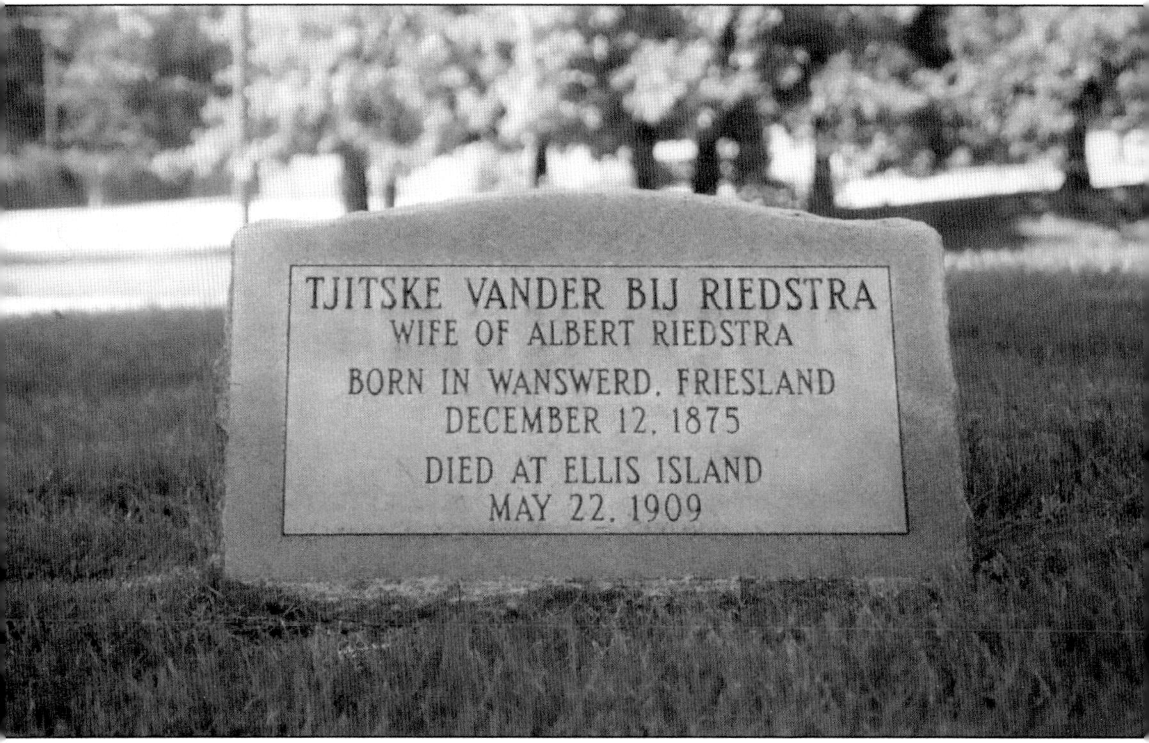

Tjitske Vander Bij was born in Wanswerd, Ferwerderadiel, Friesland, Netherlands, on December 12, 1875. She married Albert Riemerts Riedstra on October 10, 1896, in Dantumadeel, Friesland. They arrived, with their six children, at Ellis Island on April 12, 1909. Tjitske died 40 days later, still at Ellis Island. She is at rest in the Schoon Cemetery in Munster. (Photograph by the author.)

Two

People

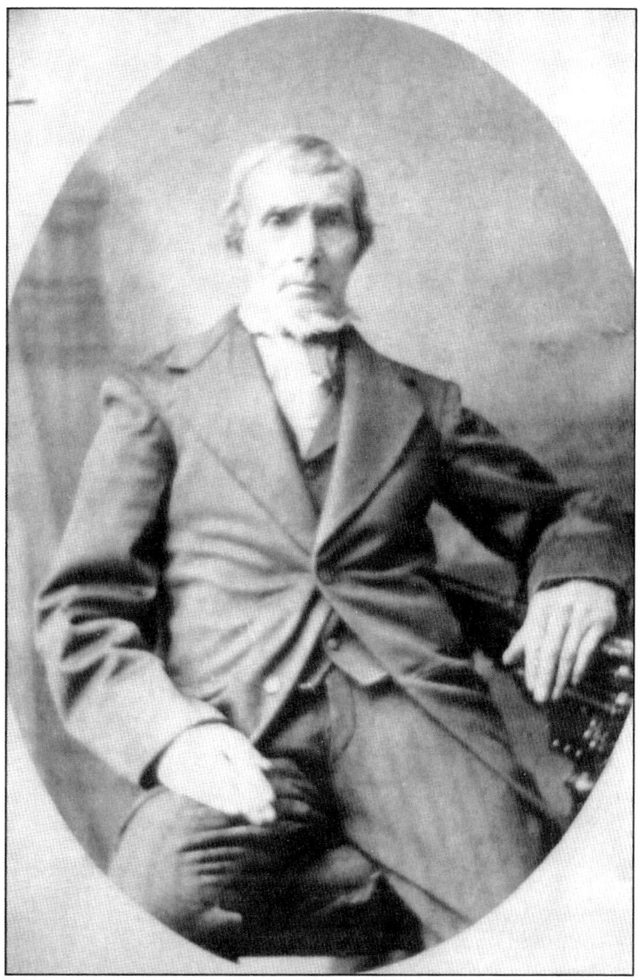

The first Dutch settlers in the Calumet region were Hendrik De Jong, his wife, Geertje, and their 12 children. They had lived in Holland, Michigan, for about a year before moving on to Illinois. In 1847, Hendrik purchased 300 acres along the Little Calumet River in what is now South Holland. (Courtesy of the South Holland Historical Society.)

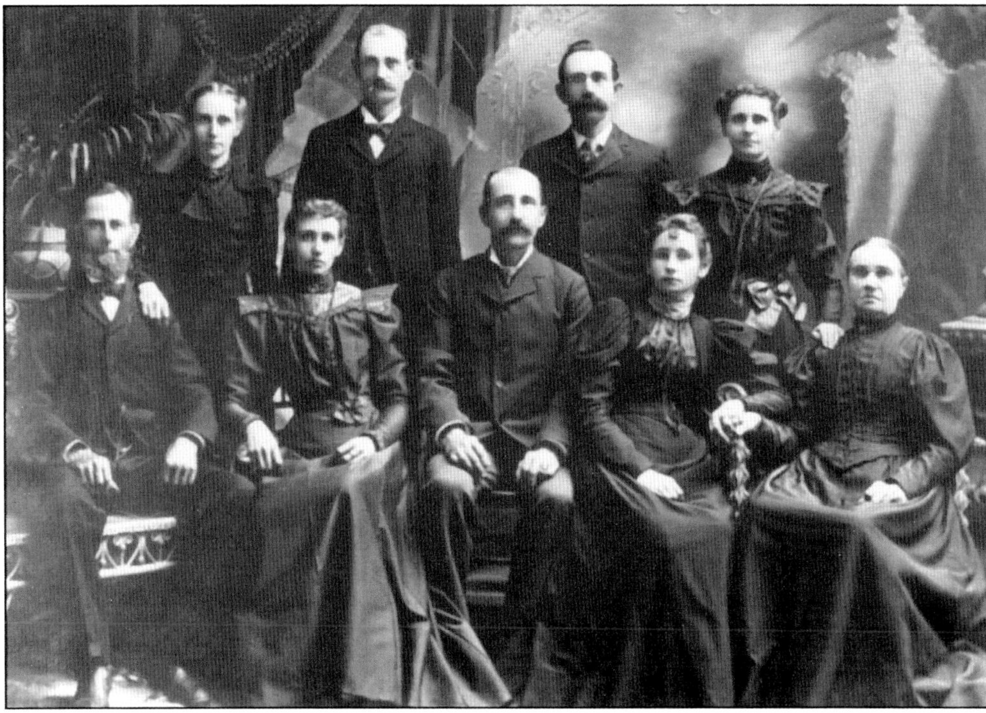

Members of the Pieter Schoon family are, from left to right, (first row) Pieter, Lizzie, Simon, Katie, and Mary; (second row) Alice, Dirk, Cornelius, and Mary. Pieter came to the United States from Broek op Langedijk, Noord-Holland, the Netherlands, in 1867. After arriving in the United States, the family first settled in Roseland before moving to Riverdale and, eventually, to Munster. (Courtesy of the Munster Historical Society.)

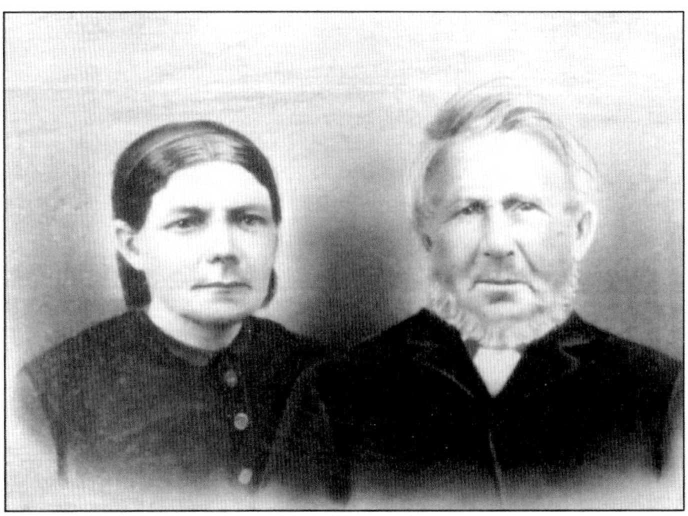

The Dutch settlement of the area that would one day become Munster began in 1855 with the arrival from the Netherlands of Peter and Aartje Jabaay (pictured). Other early settlers included the families of Dingeman and Gurtje Jabaay, Arie and Sarah Jabaay, Cornelius and Lena Klootwyk, Peter and Gertrude Kooy, and Giel Swets. (Courtesy of the Munster Historical Society.)

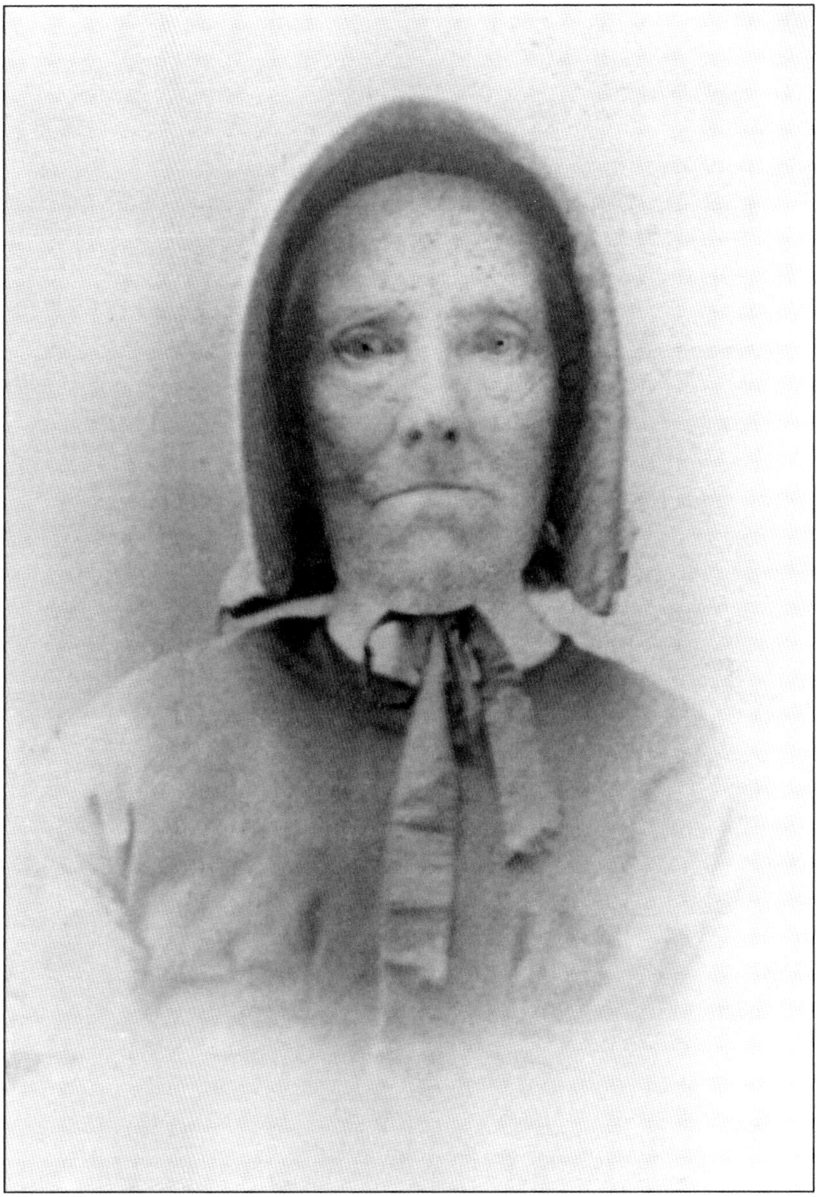

In the spring of 1847, in the North Holland town of Spanbroek, Klass Paarlberg and his wife, Antje, were busy making plans to leave their home and start a new life together in America. Like many who emigrated from Holland to the United States at this time, the Paarlbergs were not leaving because of any economic situation. They owned a dairy farm and lived a reasonably comfortable life for the times. Like many in the Netherlands, it was their desire for religious freedom that brought them to this decision. The voyage, which had begun with such high hopes, soon turned tragic, when Klass died en route and was buried at sea. The ship's captain offered free passage back to the Netherlands for Antje and her children, but she declined. After making the canal journey from New York to the Great Lakes, the ship that the Widow Paarlberg was on was blown off course on its way to Holland, Michigan. She instead ended up in Chicago and went on to become one of the earliest settlers of South Holland, Illinois. (Courtesy of the South Holland Historical Society.)

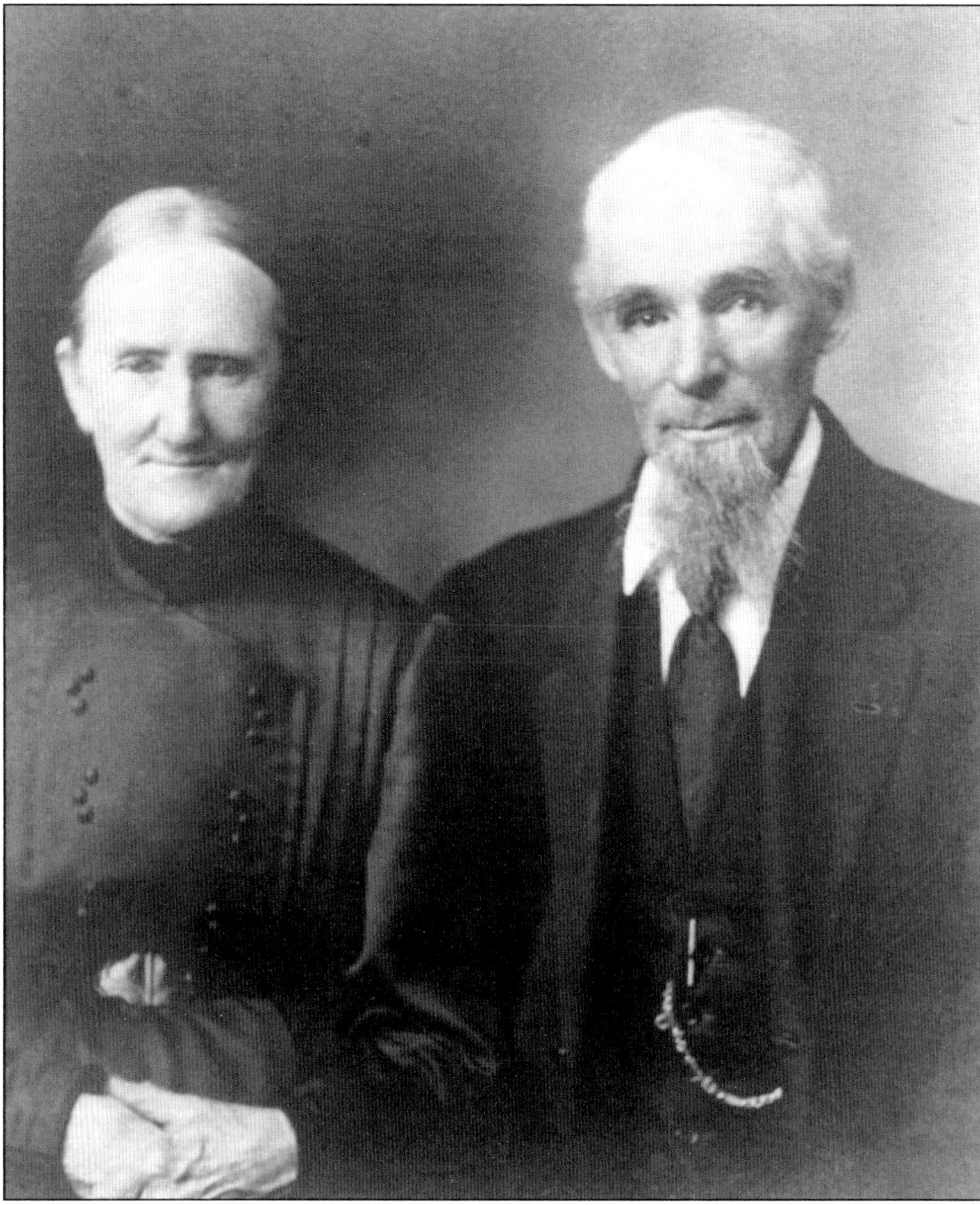

Matthijs Van der Wolf (1849–1921) married Trijntje Paarlberg (1843–1933) on November 26, 1876, in South Holland, Illinois. Trijntje's father, Klass Paarlberg (1804–1847), died during the dangerous sea journey she made with her mother, Antje, in 1847. Antje also buried her three-month-old son near what today is Lincoln Park. Antje would thereafter be known as the Widow Paarlberg. (Courtesy of the South Holland Historical Society.)

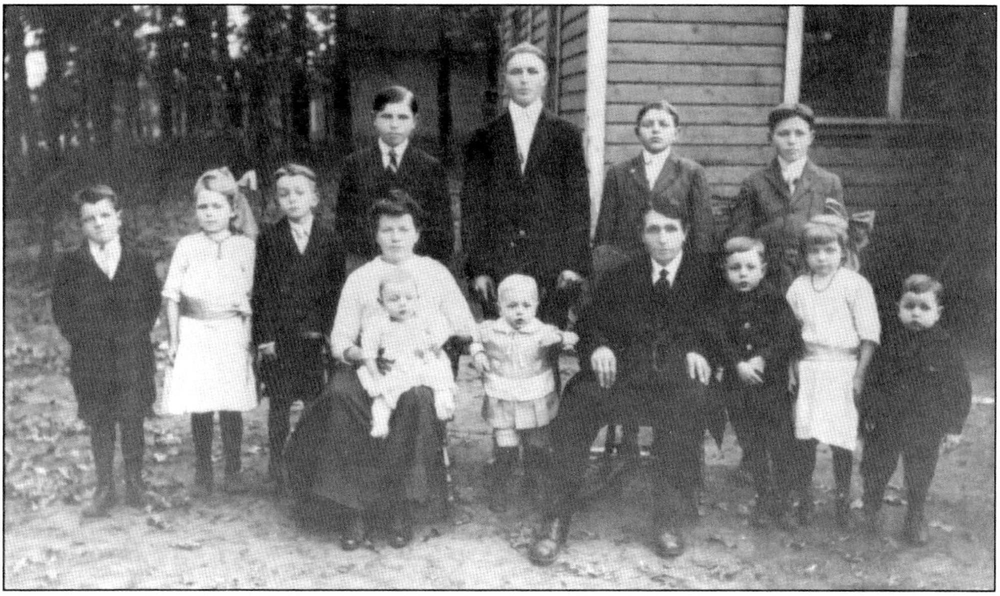

The Dutch who settled the Calumet region, like the Kuiper family (pictured), raised large families and established their own homesteads as early in life as possible. The church encouraged the establishment and maintenance of large families. This was the way it had been in the Netherlands for generation after generation, and it did not change because they happened to be living in America. (Courtesy of the Highland Historical Society.)

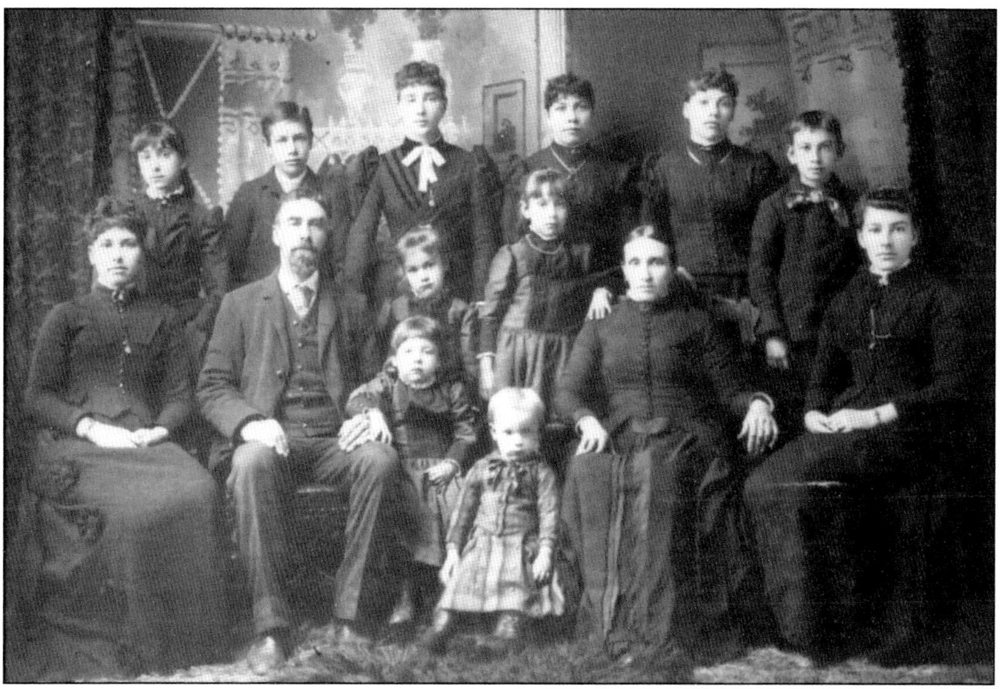

Sometime around 1870, after serving under Gen. William Sherman during his March to the Sea in the Civil War, Jacob Munster, shown here with his wife, Hendrike (Henrietta), and their children, opened the Munster General Store on Ridge Road. It also served as the area's first post office. (Courtesy of the Munster Historical Society.)

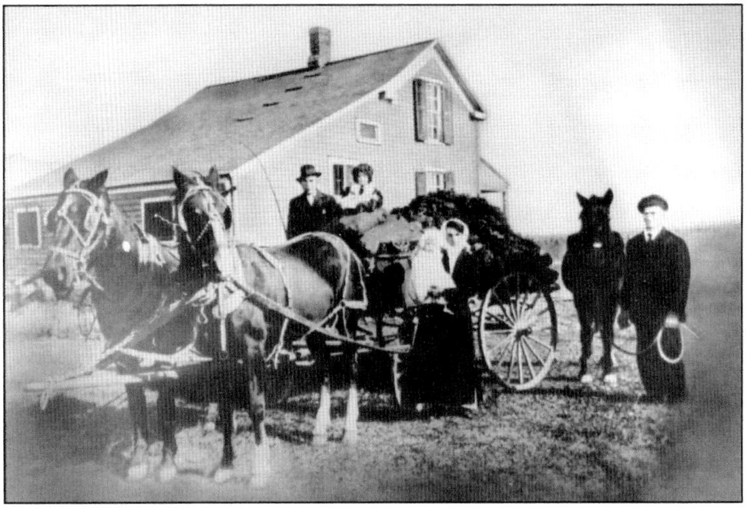

At their home on Indiana Avenue in South Holland are, from left to right, Peter, Johanna, Maude (holding Nellie) Van der Griend, with their hired hand Gerrit Kramer. This wagon of kale is ready to be peddled on the streets of Chicago Heights. (Courtesy of the South Holland Historical Society.)

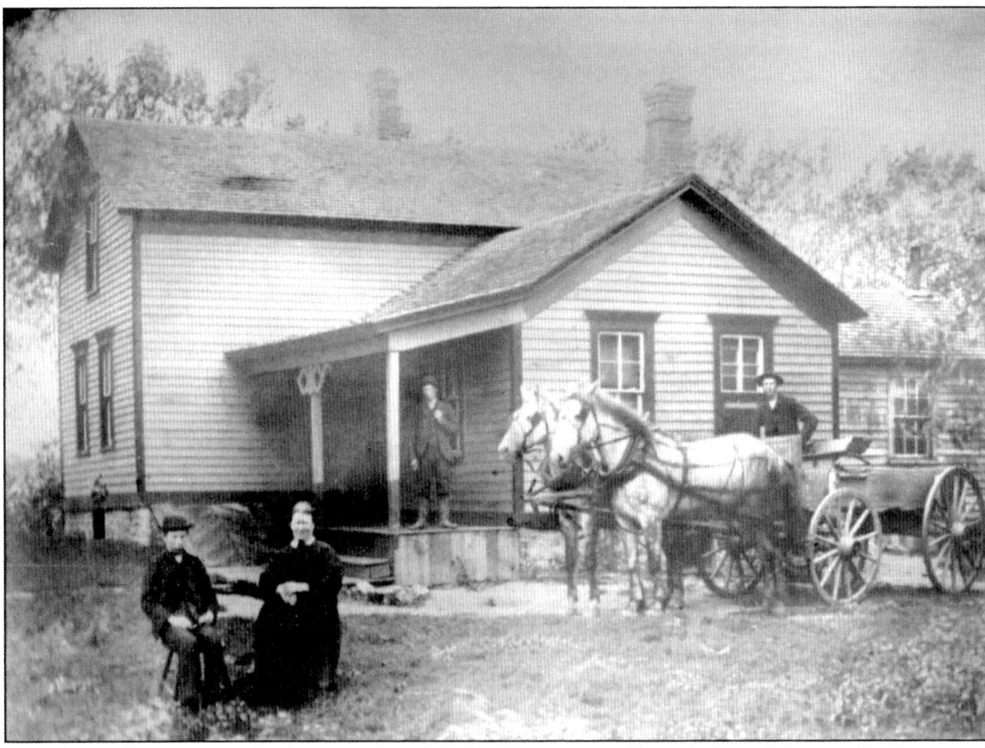

Seen here about 1890, the home of Jacob P. De Jong, son of Hendrik and Geetje De Jong, was located at the northwest corner of Route 6 and Indiana Avenue, in South Holland. It is the present-day site of South Suburban Community College. Seen here are, from left to right, Harry J. De Jong, Grietje (Wiersma) De Jong, Henry J. De Jong, and Jacob P. De Jong. (Courtesy of the South Holland Historical Society.)

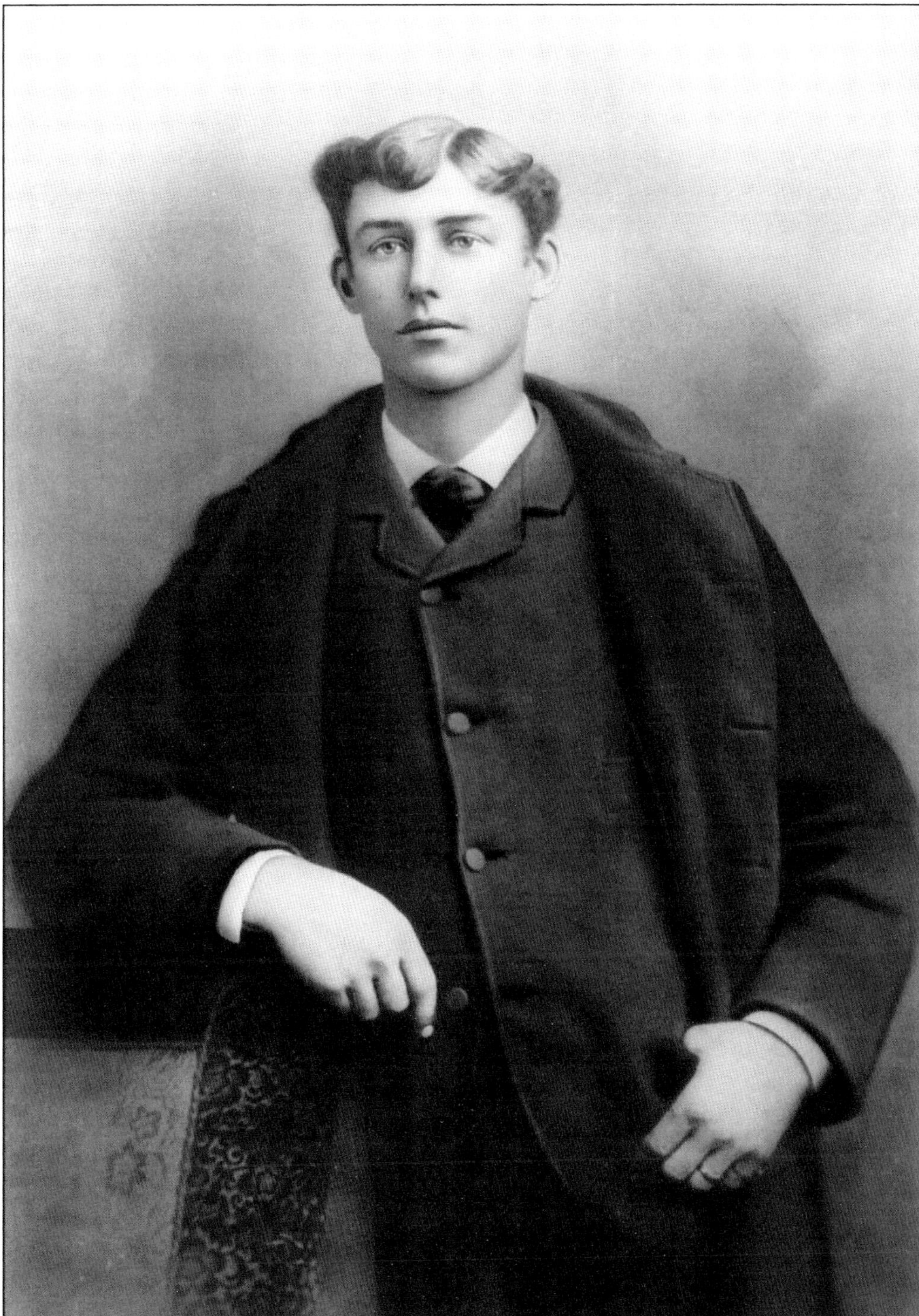

Harry Eenigenburg (1859–1943) was the son of Gerrit and Jannetje (Ton) Eenigenburg, who were two of the original Roseland settlers. In 1853, the family moved to Oak Glen, which would one day become part of Lansing, Illinois. Harry (pictured) published an early history of the region in 1935. (Courtesy of Marie Eenigenburg Min.)

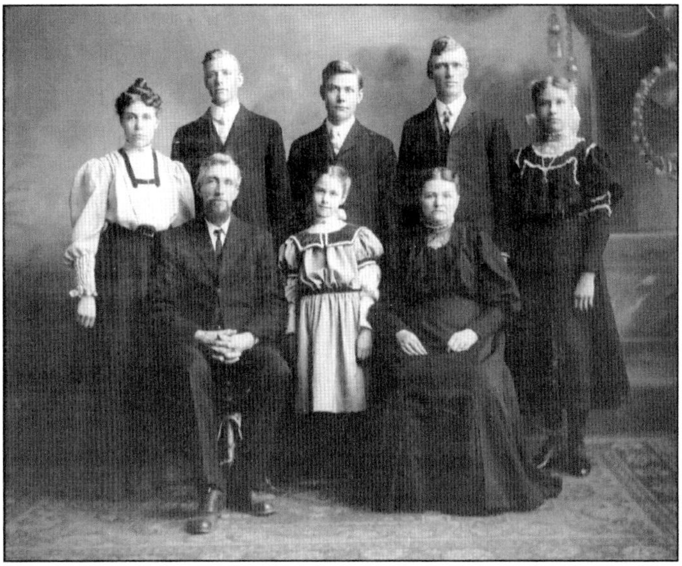

Seated are George Eenigenburg (1854–1935) and Nellie (Bult) Eenigenburg (1857–1944). Their children are, from left to right, Petronella Keesen (1882–1981), Peter (1886–1946), John (1888–1950), Gerrit (1878–1974), Jeanette Jabaay (1892–1961), and, standing between her parents, Dorothy (1898–1984). Gerrit married Pietertje Dekker (1881–1974) in 1902. Dorothy married Dirk Schoon (1896–1974). (Courtesy of Marie Eenigenburg Min.)

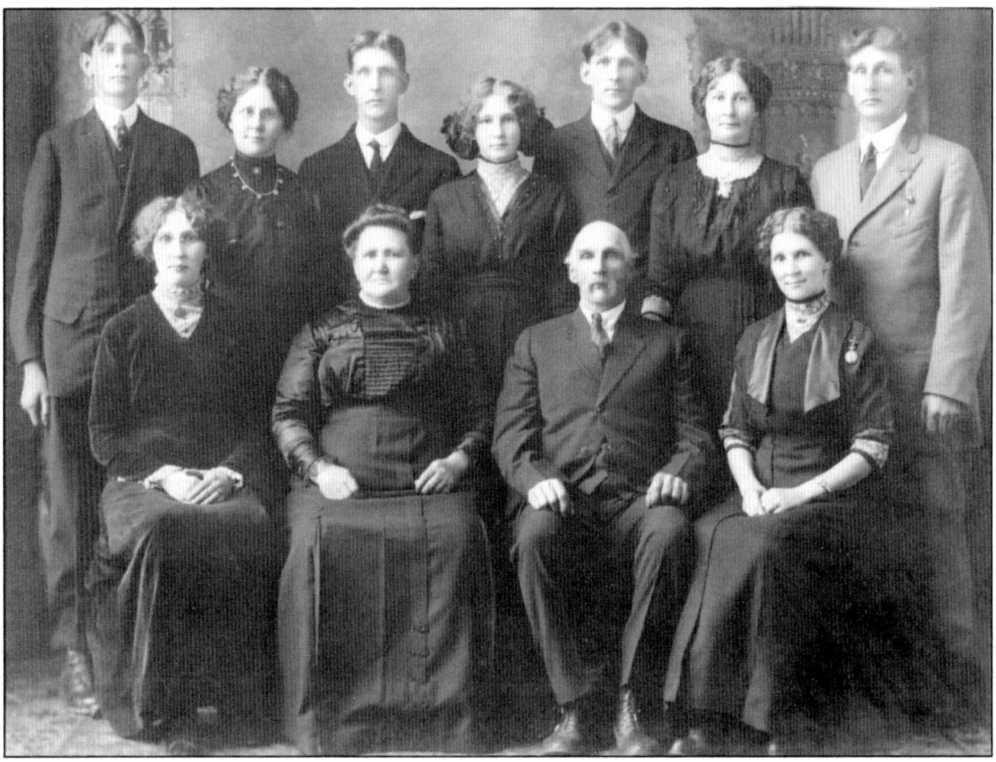

Members of the Jansen family are, from left to right, (first row) Ada, Mary, Garrett, and Peachie; (second row) John, Sarah, Harry, Maggie, Peter, Minnie, and William. Not only did Garrett served as Munster's first treasurer, but, as the Monon Depot station agent, he sold train tickets right out of the Jansen home, which was located near the tracks. (Courtesy of the Highland Historical Society.)

Cornelius and Aaltje Tanis sit in front of their home at the corner of 160th Place and South Park Avenue in South Holland. Cornelius (1835–1917) and Aaltje (1837–1920) were married on February 18, 1865, in Zijpe, Noord-Holland, Netherlands. They came to the United States in 1876. (Courtesy of the South Holland Historical Society.)

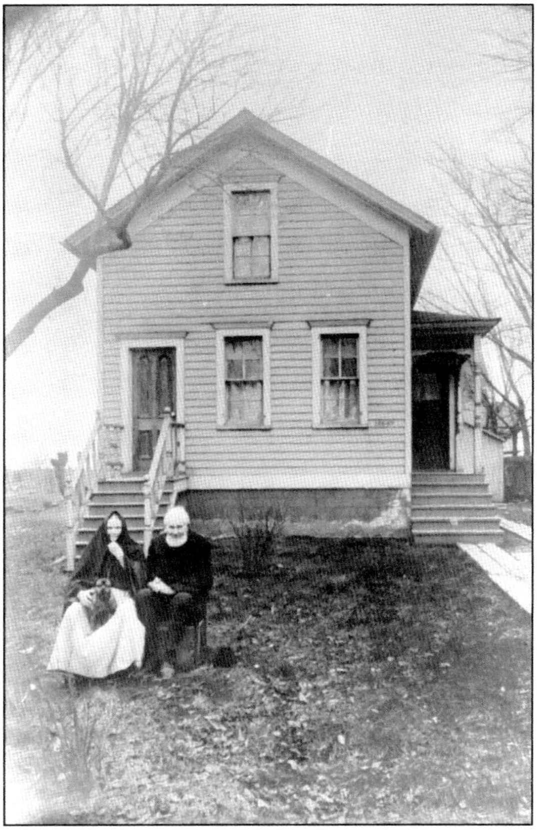

Jan Paarlberg's farm was located between Cottage Grove Avenue and Van Dam Road at about 163rd Street. Shown here are, from left to right, Pearl, Jannigje (Anker), Minnie, Jan, and Cora. Seated in the buggy is Audie Van Dam. (Courtesy of the South Holland Historical Society.)

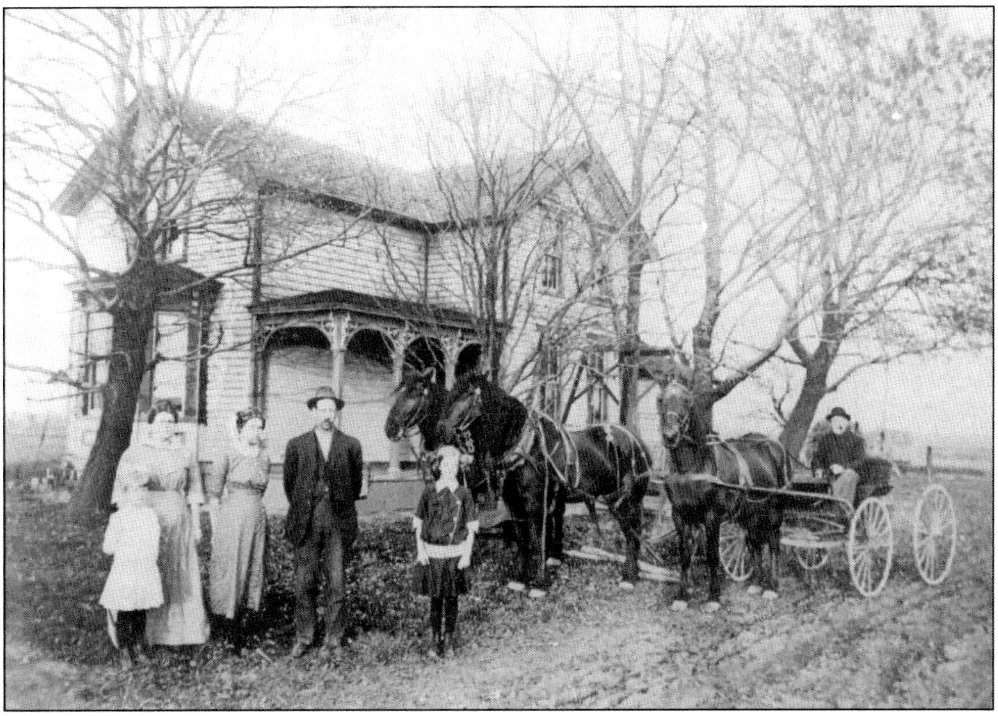

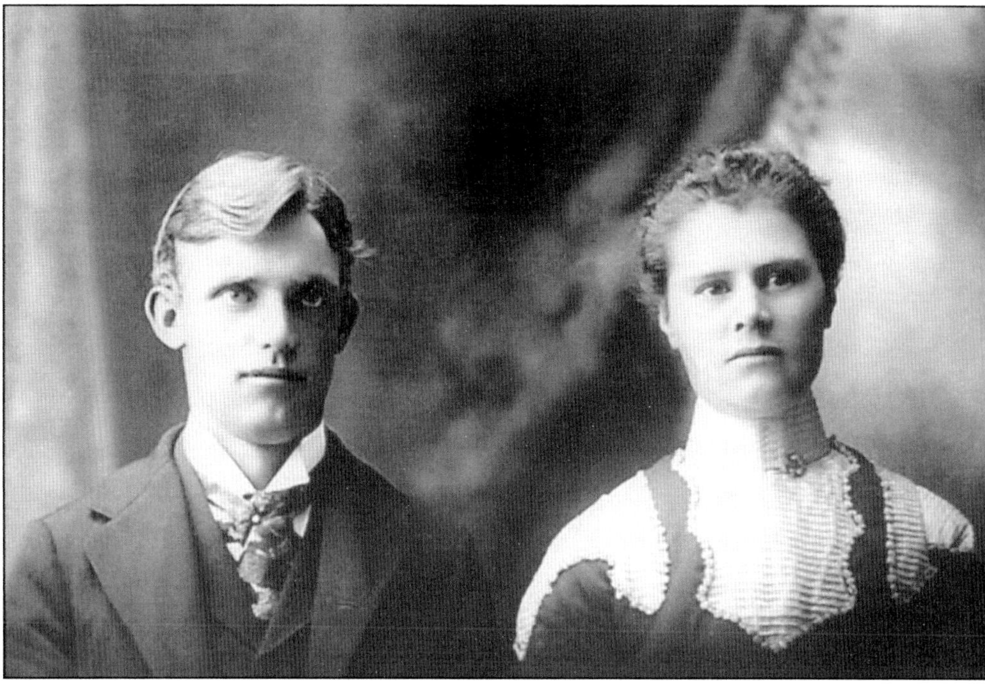

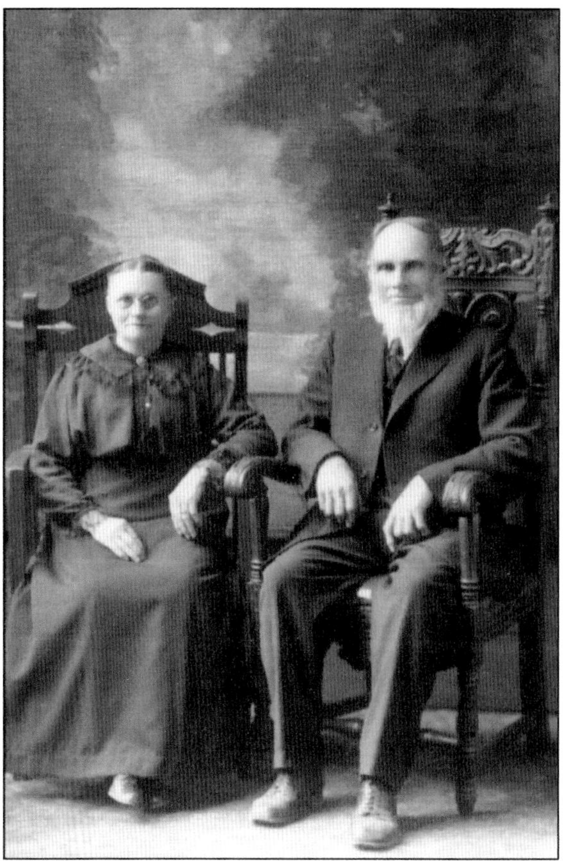

Peter J. Kooy (1874–1929), son of John and Johanna Kooy, and Grace Koedyker (1879–1968), daughter of Simon and Jane Koedyker, pose on their wedding day, April 11, 1900. Peter was appointed postmaster for Highland on May 15, 1905. In 1910, he was elected one of Highland's first town trustees. (Courtesy of the Highland Historical Society.)

Gerbrand Kooy was born in Pieter De Jong's barn in Roseland on September 5, 1855. He married Mary Schoon (1860–1938) on December 5, 1871. Gerbrand served as a Munster town trustee from 1914 until 1917. This photograph of the couple was taken in 1906. Gerbrand passed in 1933. Both are at rest in the Schoon Cemetery in Munster, Indiana. (Courtesy of the Munster Historical Society.)

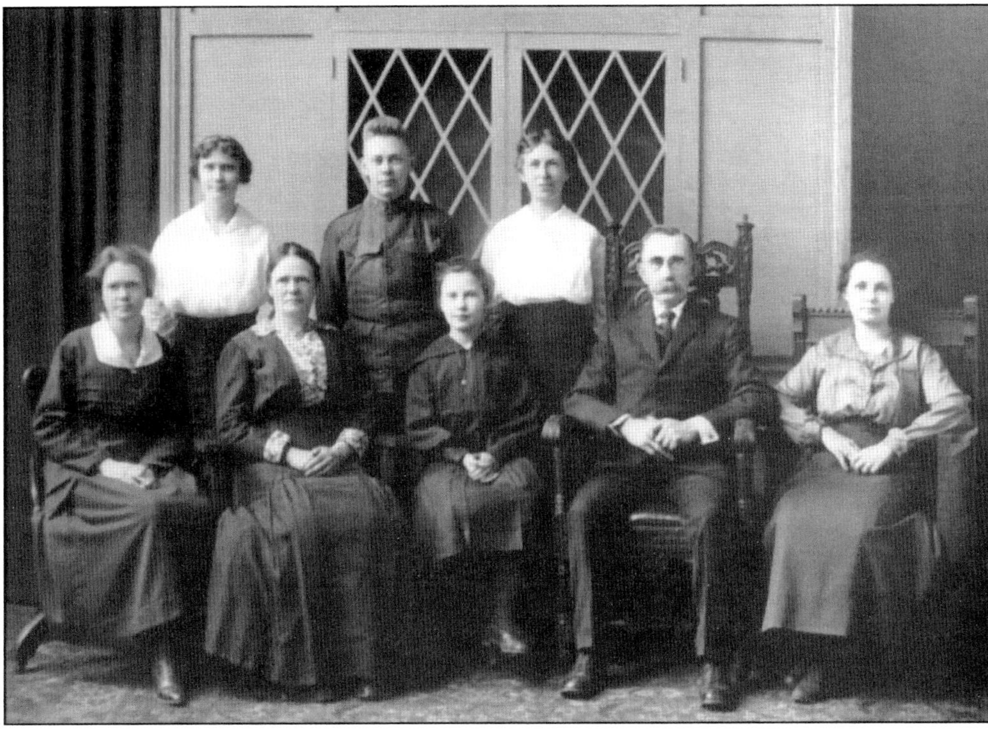

Cornelius Pieter "C.P." Schoon poses with his family. Shown here are, from left to right, (first row) Rose, Susan, Katharine, C.P., and Hilda; (second row) Winnie, Peter, and Mary. C.P.'s farm was located south of Ridge Road and west of Calumet Avenue. (Courtesy of the Munster Historical Society.)

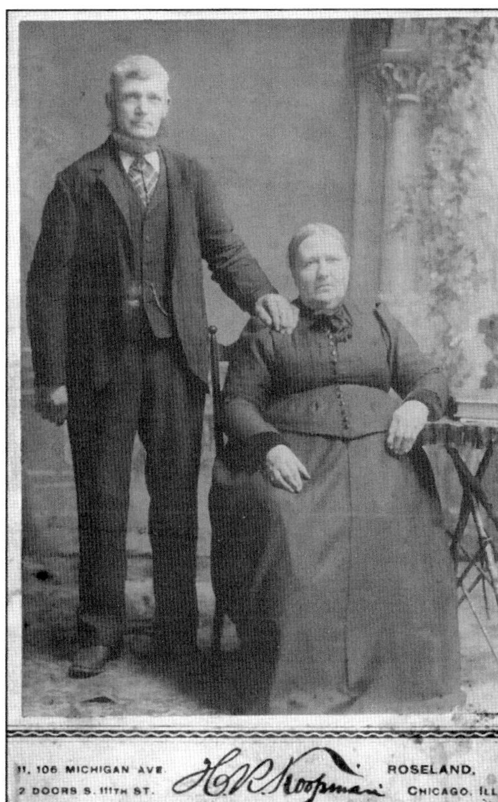

Nicholas De Young (1866–1963) and Sijtje "Sadie" Bult (1874–1963) were married on December 28, 1893. This later photograph of them was taken by H.R. Koopman, who is known for capturing the people and places of Roseland on film. His studio was located at 11106 Michigan Avenue. Klaas Nicholas Madderom (1819–1902) was grandfather to both Nicholas and H.R.'s wife, Katie. (Courtesy of Marie Eenigenburg Min.)

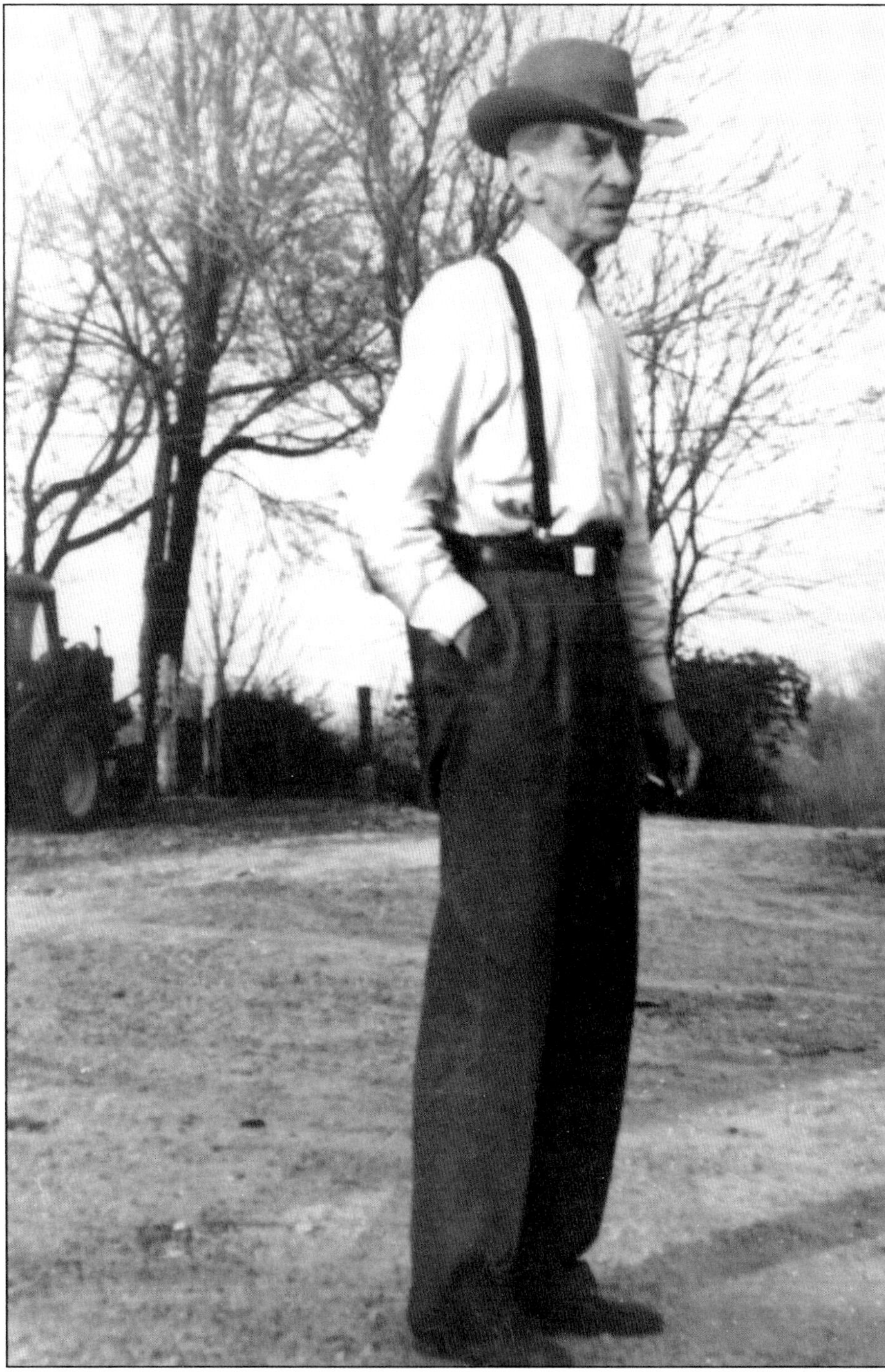

Jan "John" Witvoet (1878–1961) was 13 years old when, on August 9, 1893, his family began their long journey from the Netherlands to America. He was the seventh of Gerrit and Geertje (Aardema) Witvoet's 10 children. Jan's parents, originally from the Friesland province, moved to Grootegast, Gronigan, soon after they were married. It was there that all of their children were born. (Courtesy of the Bult family collection.)

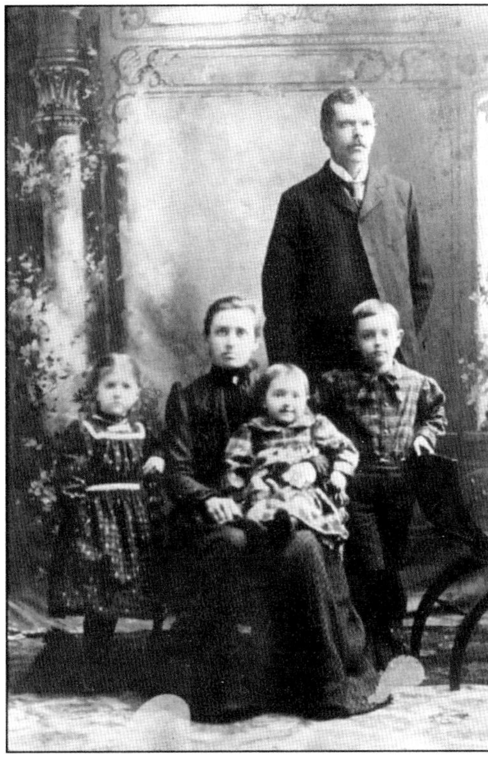

Herman De Mik (1873–1924) stands behind his wife and children, from left to right, Helen, Carrie (Van Kley), Katherine "Katie," and Jake. Herman and Carrie were married on December 17, 1896, and went on to have a total of nine children. Katherine married John Swets on January 8, 1920. (Courtesy of the Munster Historical Society.)

Teunis Arie Benschop was born on September 16, 1840, in Ouderkerk, Zuid-Holland, Netherlands. He died on March 21, 1918, in Lansing, Illinois. His family arrived in the United States in 1848 and settled in South Holland, Illinois. Teunis married Neeltje "Nellie" Klootwijk (1846–1911), and they raised eight children. From oldest to youngest, they are Helena, Simon, Tunis, Catherine (Kate), Arie, Nellie, Cornelia, and John. (Courtesy of Patricia Samsel O'Neill.)

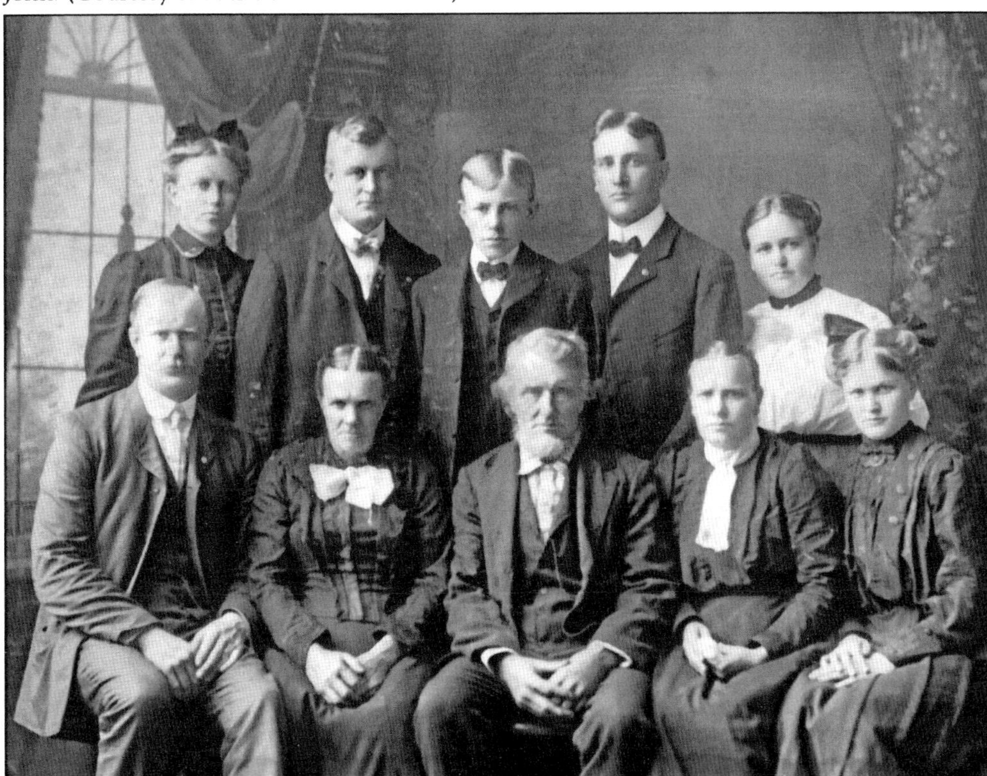

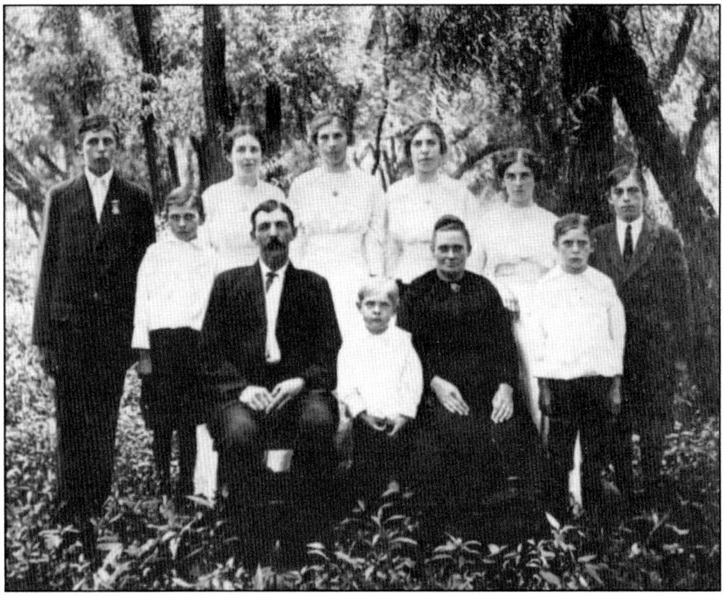

Dirkje "Dickie" Bos (1870–1940) married John DeVries (1866–1921) on March 4, 1891. Shown with them here are nine of their ten children. The children are, from oldest to youngest, Tina, Fannie, Cornelia, Johanna, Teunis, Adrian, Gilbert, Jacob, and Walter. This photograph was taken in Munster, Indiana, sometime shortly before Ruth was born in 1915. (Courtesy of Marie Eenigenburg Min.)

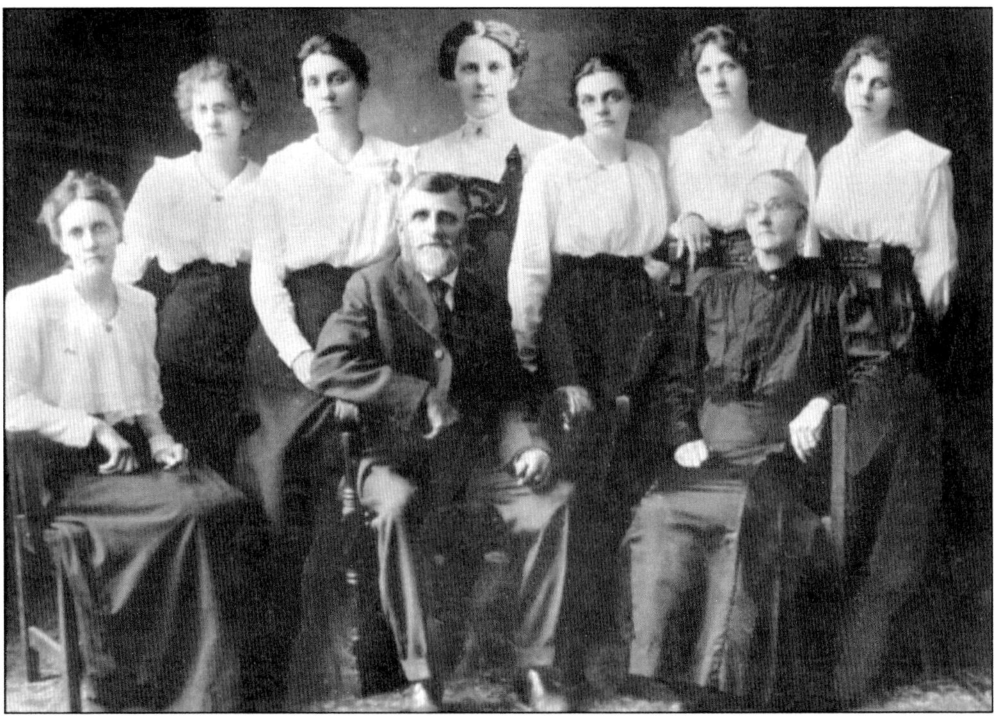

Peter and Mina Zyp pose with their seven daughters sometime before May 16, 1915, when Maggie passed. Shown here are, from left to right, (first row) Gertrude Van Kley, Peter, and Mina; (second row) Myrtle Groot, Mary Blink, Maggie Huizenga, Nellie Moes, Johanna Porter, and Kathryn Groot. Peter was born in the Netherlands and came to the United States with his family in 1869. The daughters are listed here by their married names. (Courtesy of the Highland Historical Society.)

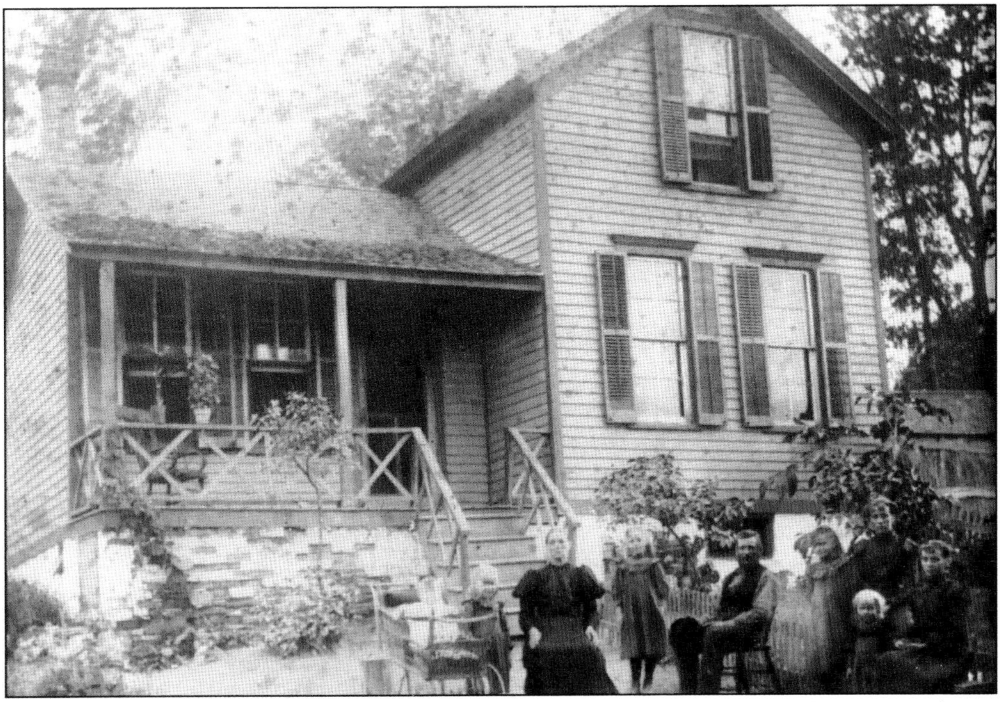

Peter Zyp (1858–1921) married Maaike Maggeltje "Mina" Jansen (1860–1922) on November 2, 1882. This photograph was taken in 1898 in front of their home at the southeast corner of Ridge Road and Kleinman Road, in Highland. The house was later relocated to 8913 Kleinman Road. Also shown in the photograph are Peter and Mina's seven daughters. (Courtesy of the Highland Historical Society.)

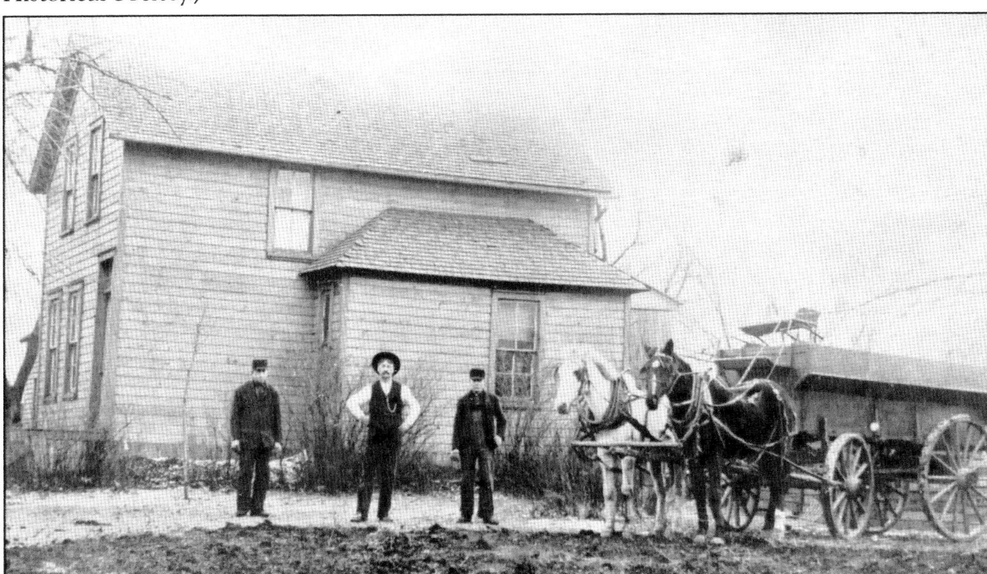

Shown here second from left, Tunis Van der Aa (1857–1942) married Esther De Graaff (1858–1897) on May 15, 1883, in Chicago. Their daughter Jennie (1878–1968) married James Klaas De Jong (1881–1957) on April 8, 1908, in South Holland, Illinois. (Courtesy of the South Holland Historical Society.)

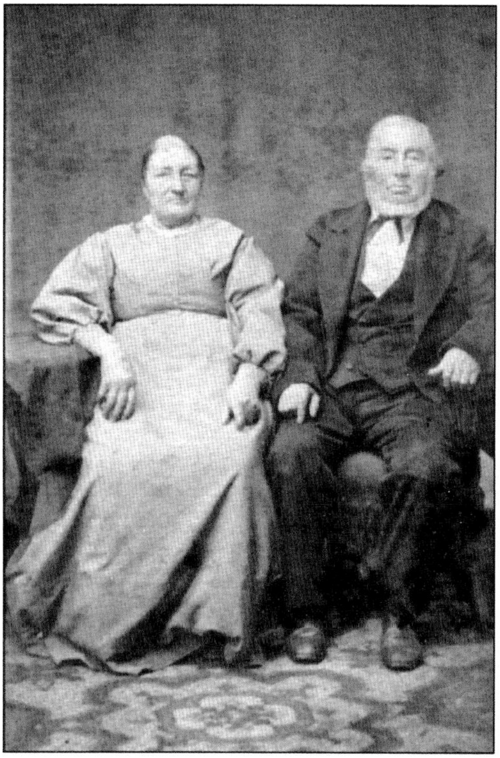

Jacob De Jong was born in Schrool, Netherlands, and married Geertje Eenigenburg (1810–1896) in Akersloot, Noord-Holland, on October 19, 1834. In 1849, Jacob and Geertje were among the first settlers of de Hooge Prairie (High Prairie), as Roseland, Illinois, was first known. Jacob later became the first elder of the First Reformed Church of Roseland. (Courtesy of the South Holland Historical Society.)

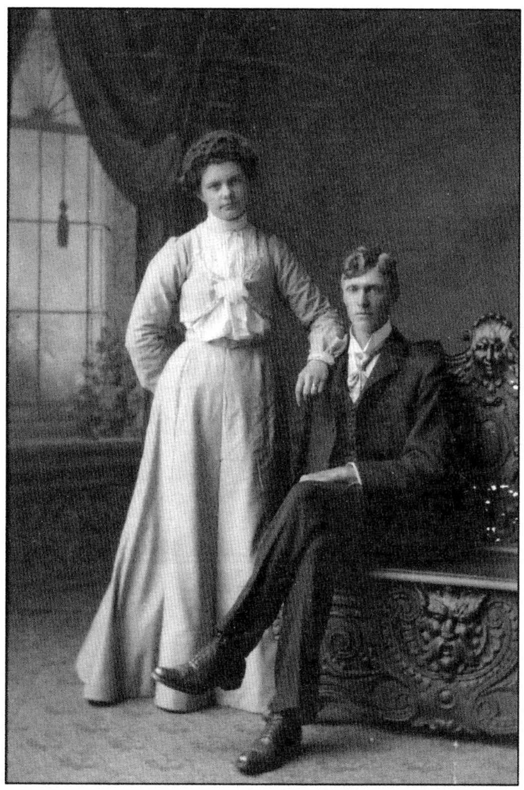

Gerrit Eenigenburg, whose grandparents Gerrit and Jannetje Eenigenburg had made the dangerous trip to America on the schooner *Boston of Massachusetts*, married Pietertje Dekker in Highland, Indiana, on March 7, 1902. They are buried side by side in Maple Grove Cemetery in Fremont, Michigan. (Courtesy of Marie Eenigenburg Min.)

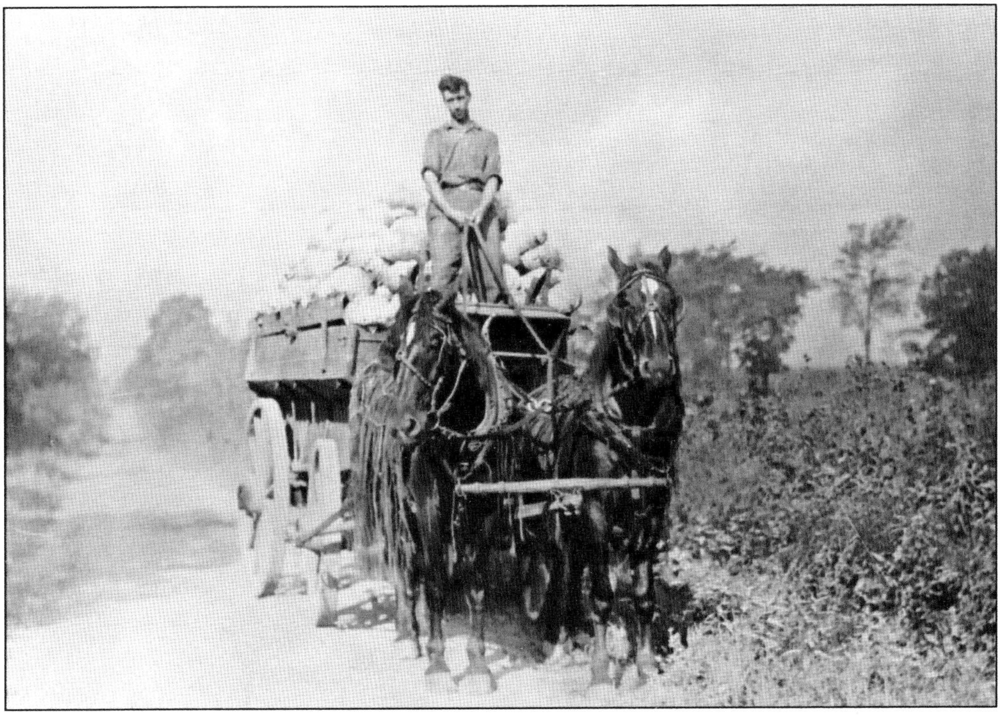

Shown here hard at work, John Peter Santefort (1883–1968), the son of Pieter and Cornelia (VanDerBok) Santefort, married Elska Medema (1887–1979) on April 3, 1908, in South Holland, Illinois. Soon after the wedding, John and Elska move to Snohomish, Washington, where they raised six children. (Courtesy of the South Holland Historical Society.)

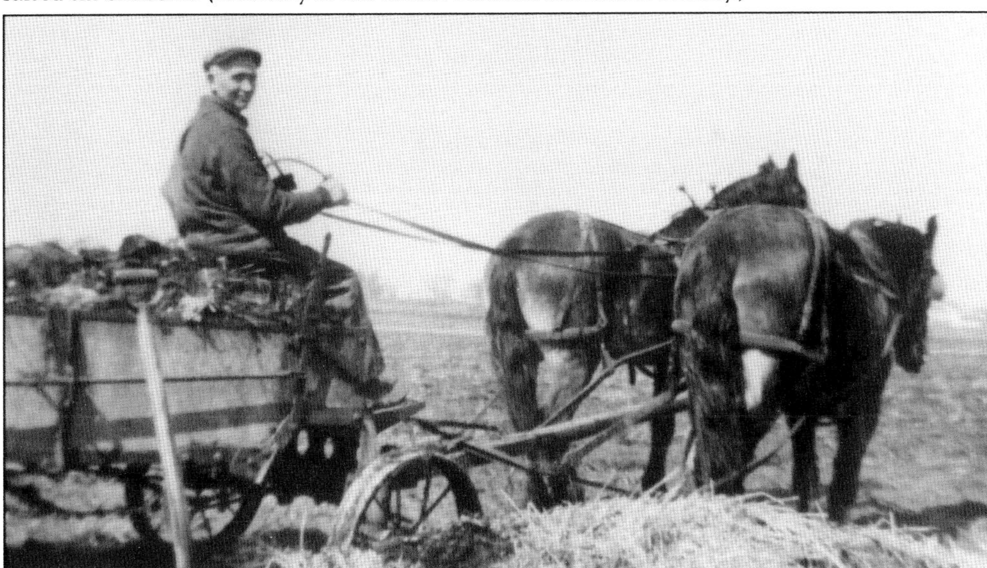

Harm Scheeringa (1893–1982), shown here at work in the fields, arrived from the Netherlands with his parents, Jacob and Grietje (Heuker), in 1912. Jacob and Grietje came here with their seven youngest children. Their three oldest boys had made the journey earlier. Harm married Tena Schoon (1897–1963) on April 9, 1919. (Courtesy of the Highland Historical Society.)

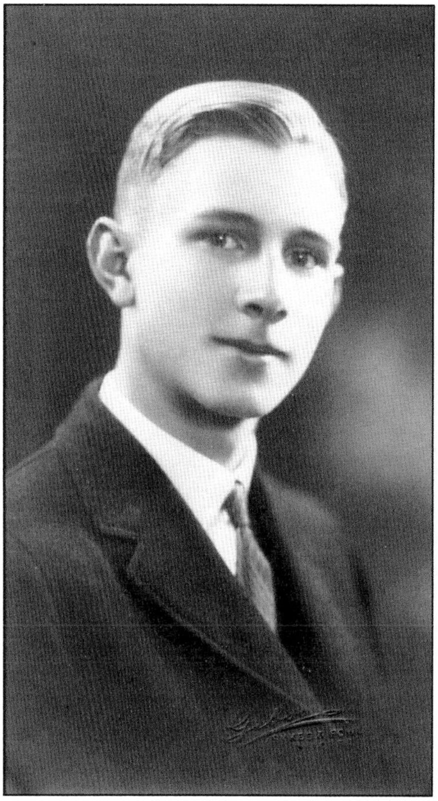

Teunis James De Young (1906–1997) married his first wife, Grace Louise Jaynes, on January 4, 1930. He became a widower on October 23, 1930. On March 14, 1942, he enlisted in the Army. He married Genevieve Lockrem (1915–1978) in Lawton, Oklahoma, on June 27, 1943. (Courtesy of the South Holland Historical Society.)

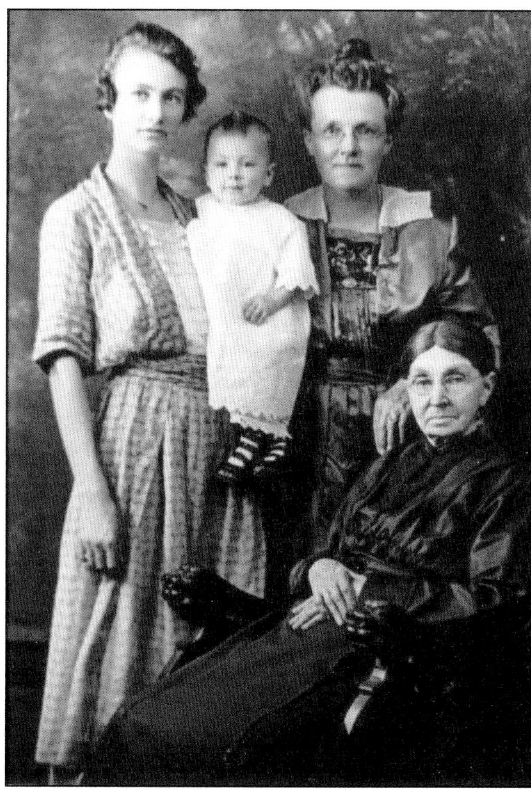

Shown here are four generations of Schoon women. They are, from left to right, Mary D. (Schoon) Jabaay, Henrietta Jabaay, Dora (Talsma) Schoon, and Dora's mother. Mary Schoon married Peter C. Jabaay (1896–1937) on February 26, 1919. Her mother, Dora, married Richard "Dirk" Schoon (1858–1913) in Roseland, Illinois, on March 8, 1883. (Courtesy of the Munster Historical Society.)

Arie Van der Aa (1809–1892) was born in Zijpe, Netherlands. On May 3, 1834, he married Maggettje Baardwijk (1810–1898) in Giessen-Nieuwkerk (now called Giessenburg) in the Netherlands. The family first settled in South Holland, Illinois, in 1854. During the journey, one of their four children died at sea. Another son, Tunnis, was born in 1857. (Courtesy of the South Holland Historical Society.)

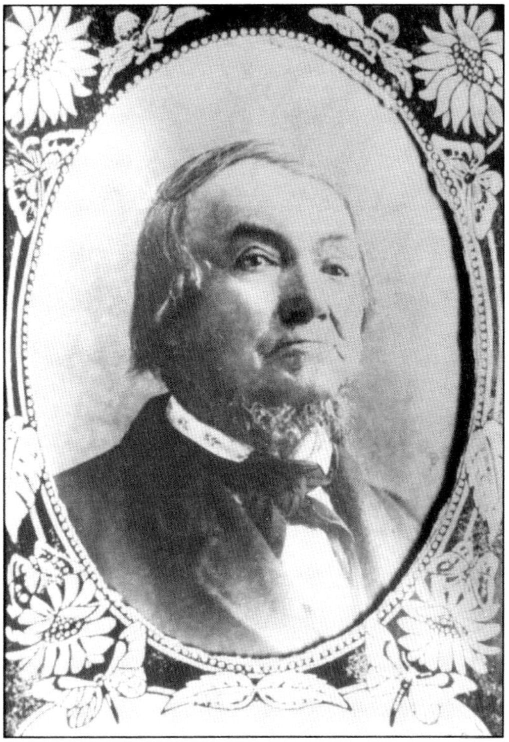

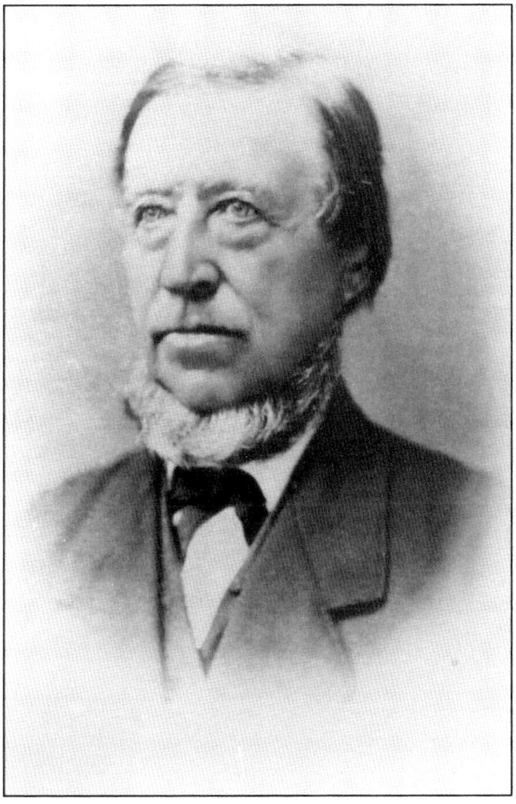

Shown here is Johannes Ravesloot (1813–1900), who married Teunisje Bouwhorst (1811–1891) in Renswoude, Utrecht, Netherlands, on February 2, 1833. They settled in South Holland (Lage Prairie) in 1856. All eight of their children were born before the move to the United States. Their youngest child, Jan, married Pietertje Dalenberg on June 4, 1876. (Courtesy of the South Holland Historical Society.)

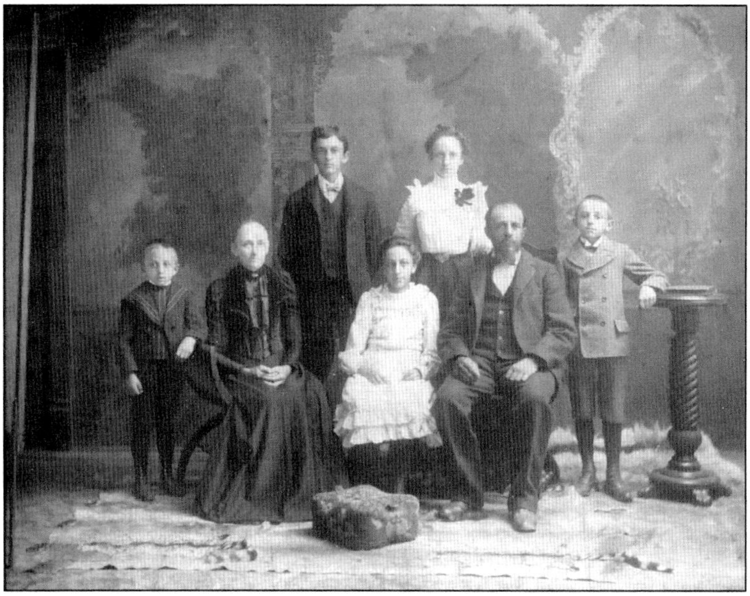

Gerrit Meenwis Van Oostenbrugge (1848–1940) married Antje De Ridder (1854–1933) on February 24, 1878, in South Holland, Illinois. Shown here are, from left to right, (first row) Cour'nelius, Antje, Jennie, Gerrit, and Henry; (second row) John and Evertje. Evertje married Gerrit Tysse on November 29, 1899. (Courtesy of the South Holland Historical Society.)

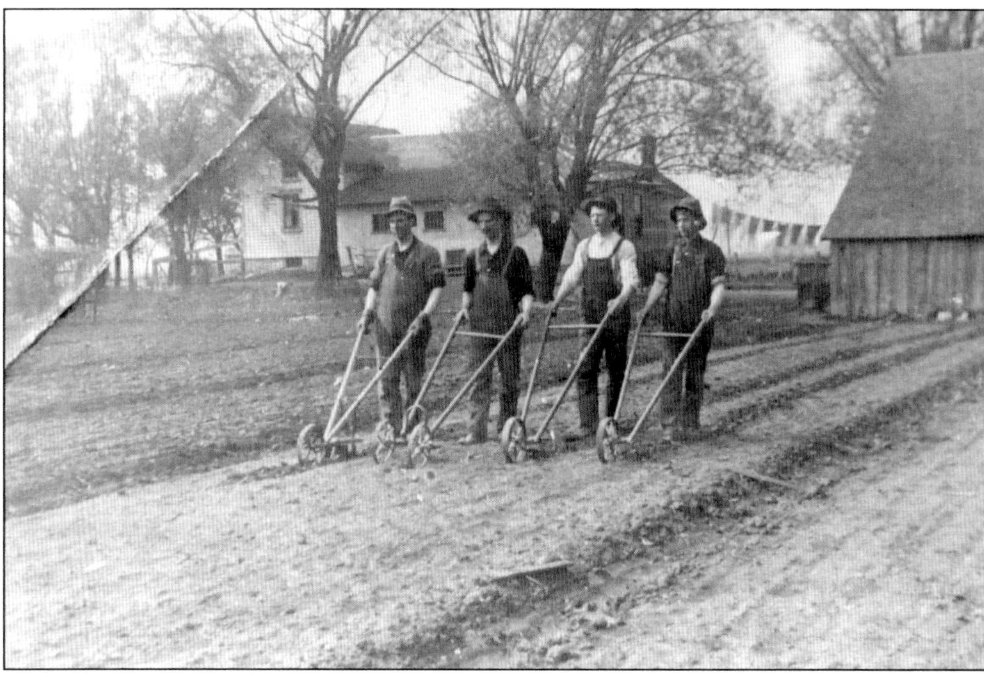

Cultivating onion sets the old-fashion way are, from left to right, brothers John K. and Henry K. De Jong and brothers John J. and Andrew Van der Aa. The parents of the Van der Aa brothers, Jan and Antje Van der Aa, were killed by a train in 1903 in Lansing, Illinois. The sons then lived with Henry K. and Alice De Jong. Alice was Antje's sister. (Courtesy of the South Holland Historical Society.)

Jennie DeMersseman (1838–1938) married Cornelius Arie Hillegonds (1829–1904) on July 20, 1869, in Milwaukee, Wisconsin. She is shown here with grandchildren Casey (standing) and Ruth Paarlberg about 1906. She passed in South Holland, Illinois, just five months short of her 100th birthday. (Courtesy of the South Holland Historical Society.)

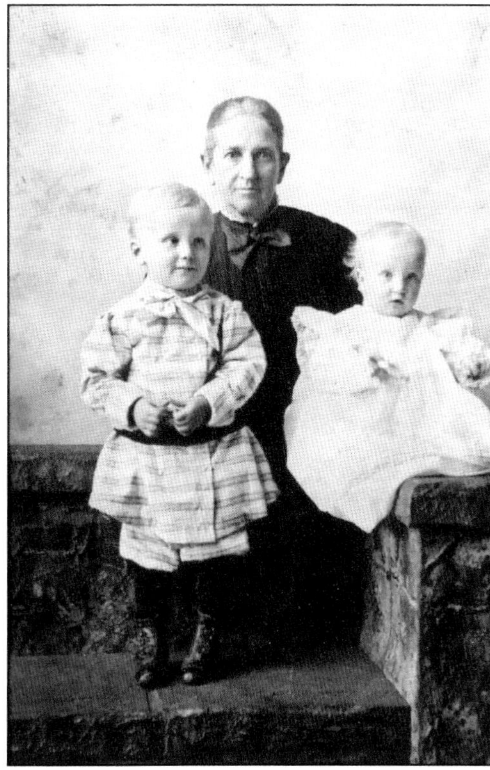

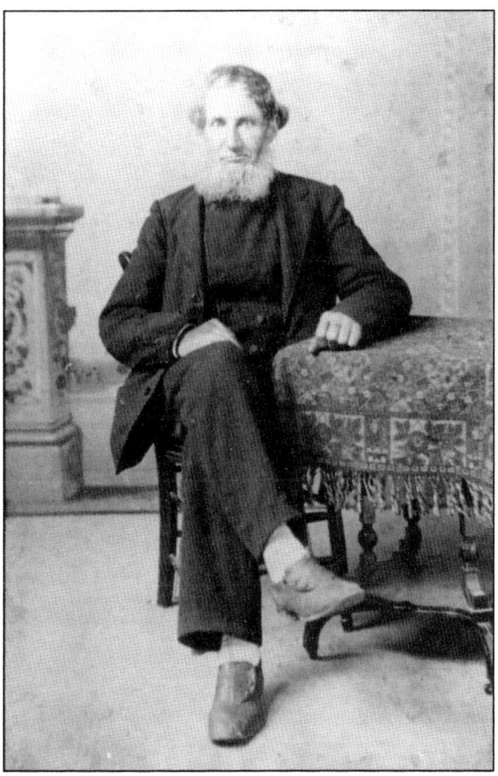

Arie Rietveld (1818–1891) was born in Schellunien, a small village near Gorinchem in the Netherlands. On August 31, 1843, he married Jannigje Gelderblom (1819–1894), and in 1864, they immigrated to the United States and made a new home for their family in South Holland. (Courtesy of the South Holland Historical Society.)

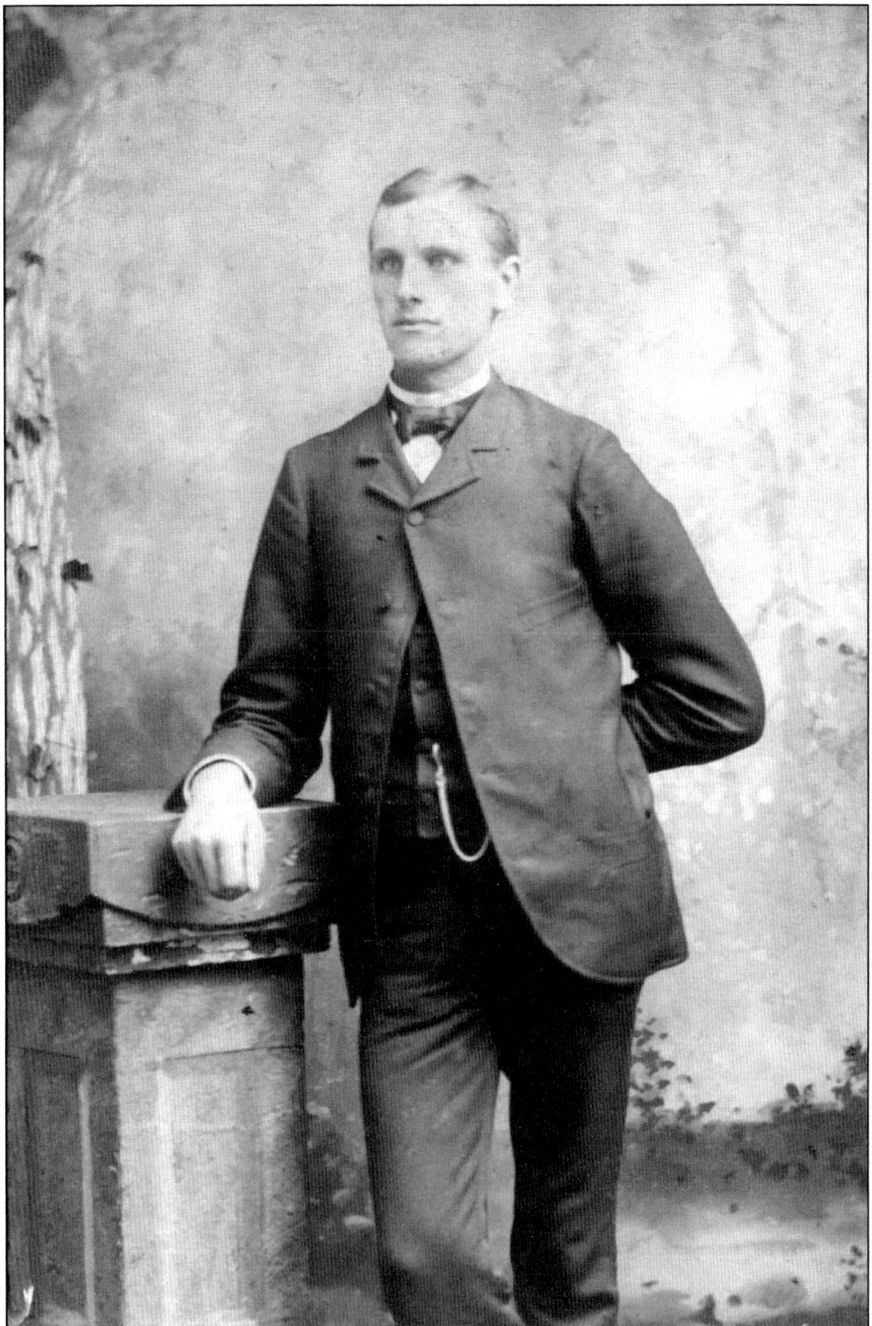

Hendrick Bult (1867–1926) was born in the windmill where his parents were living at the time, in the small village of Wimmenum in the province of Noord-Holland. Wimmenum lies about two miles from the coast of the North Sea and five miles outside the provincial capital of Alkmaar. Shortly after Hendrick's birth, his family immigrated to the United States, where they settled on Chicago's South Side before moving to the Hoxie Farm near Thornton, Illinois, for a while. Hendrick and his wife, Hellagonde, finally settled in Munster. Their farm was on the northeast corner of today's Calumet Avenue and Fisher Street. (Courtesy of Marie Eenigenburg Min.)

Dirk Schaap (1815–1891) married Anneke Van Drunen (1818–1894) on August 29, 1840, in Sleeuwijk, Werkendam, Noord-Brabant, Netherlands. In 1856, the family moved to the United States and settled in South Holland, Illinois. They posed for this photograph about eight years later. Shown here are, from left to right, (first row) Dirk, Dientje, Anerjana, Anneke, and Vyverke; (second row) Maaike, Antonie, Johannes, and Bastiaan. Another daughter, Elizabeth, died in the spring of 1864. (Courtesy of the South Holland Historical Society.)

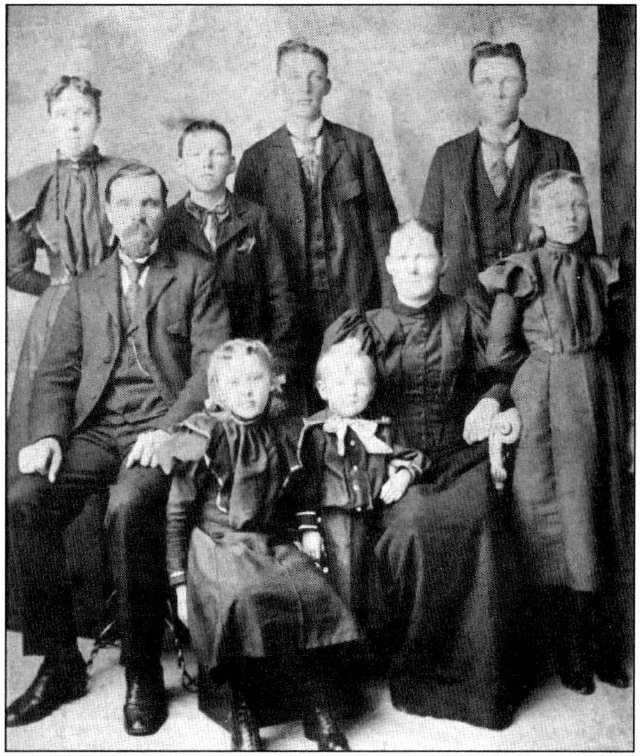

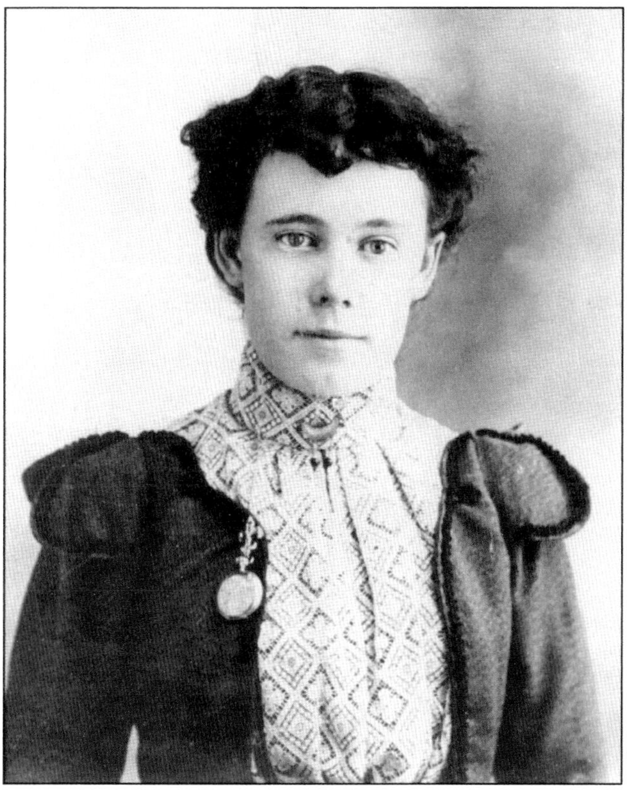

Alice Van Vuren (1878–1958) married Theodore M. Van der Aa (1882–1939) on March 30, 1901. They later ran a store in South Holland. Her grandfather was Dirk Van Vuren (1834–1906), who was born in Uithuistermeede, Netherlands, and became one of South Holland's earliest settlers in 1848. (Courtesy of the South Holland Historical Society.)

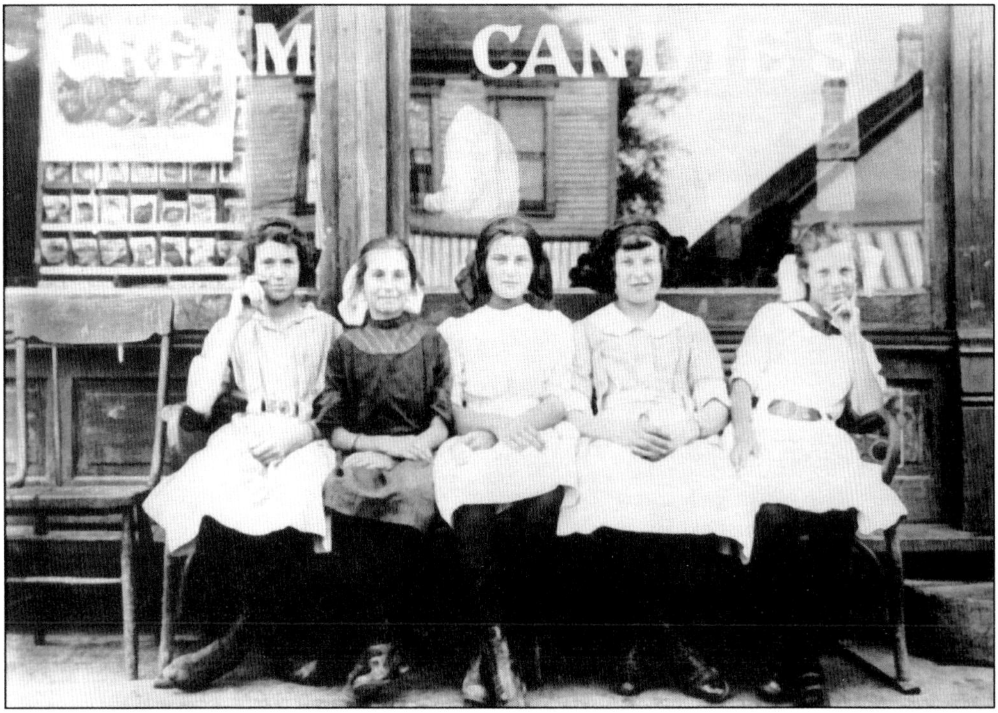

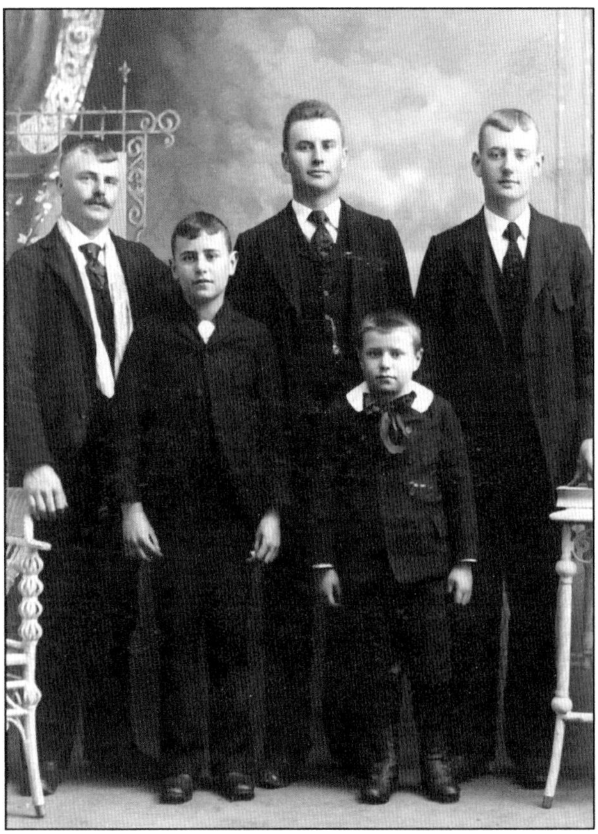

Sitting in front of Theodore Van der Aa's store at 158th Street and South Park Avenue are, from left to right, Agnes Rinkema, Annie De Jong, Josey Van der Aa, Ester De Graff, and Minnie Bardwick. Note the seed packets for sale in the window. (Courtesy of the South Holland Historical Society.)

The five sons of Michael and Johanna (Van Zanten) Van der Aa are, from left to right, Lendert, Theodore, Harry, Nick, and John. Michael Van der Aa (1835–1912) arrived from the Netherlands in 1855 and served during the Civil War in the 51st Regiment, Illinois Infantry. (Courtesy of Cynthia Anderson.)

Tunnis Keesen (1883–1959) married Petronella Margaretha Eenigenburg (1882–1981) on February 26, 1907, in Lansing, Illinois. Tunnis was born in Gano, an area that is now part of Chicago, directly south of Roseland. Gano is approximately bounded by 115th Street, south to 119th Street, and from Wentworth Avenue to State Street. (Courtesy of Marie Eenigenburg Min.)

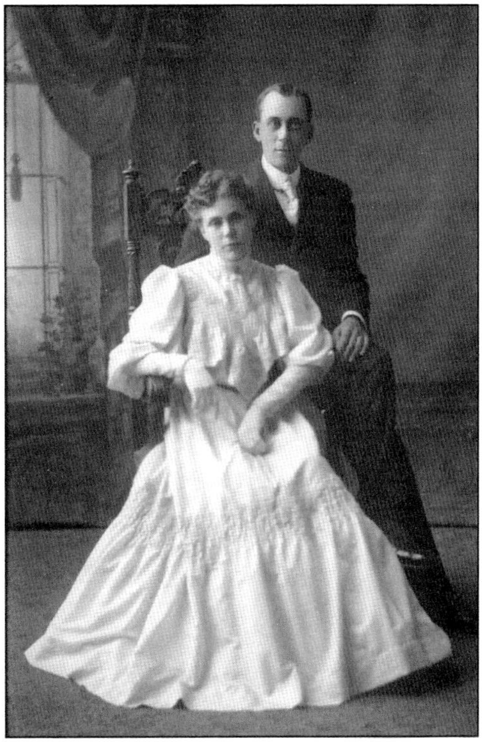

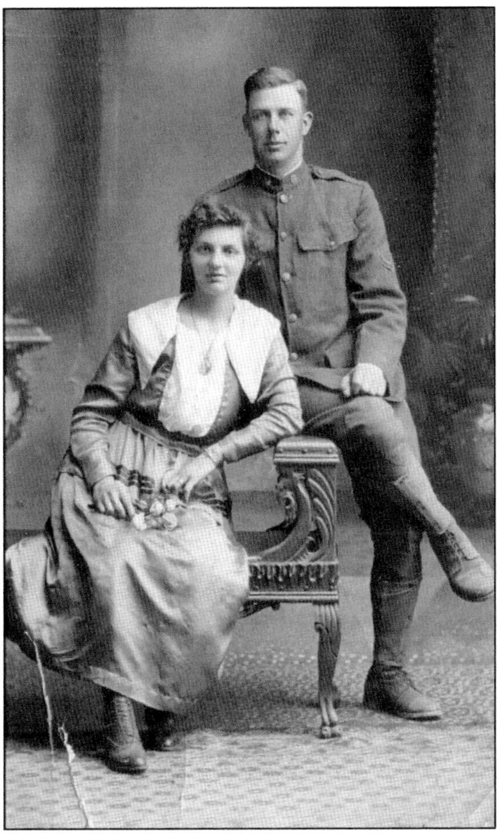

Nicklass Gerrit Eriks (1891–1972) and Suzanne M. Jansen (1899–1982) were married on March 5, 1919, and went on to raise seven children. Note Nick's World War I–era uniform. Suzanne's father, Jan Jansen (1866–1953), was born in Ameide, Zuid-Holland, shortly before his family left for America. (Courtesy of the Eriks family.)

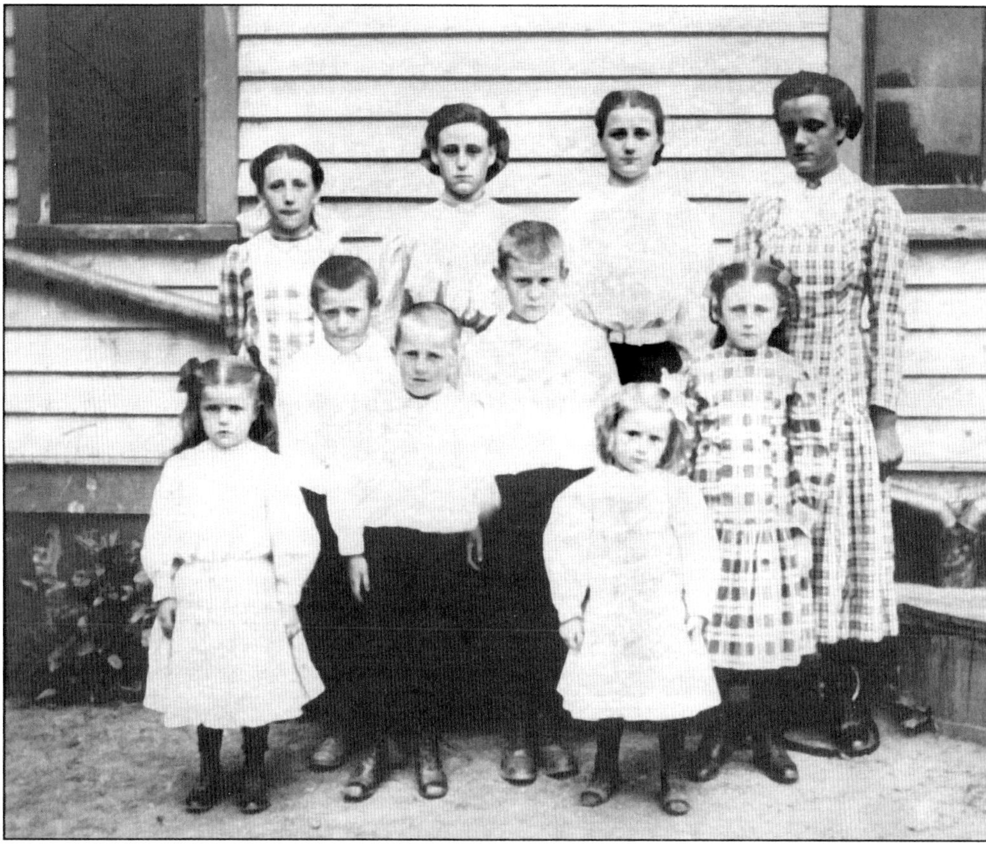

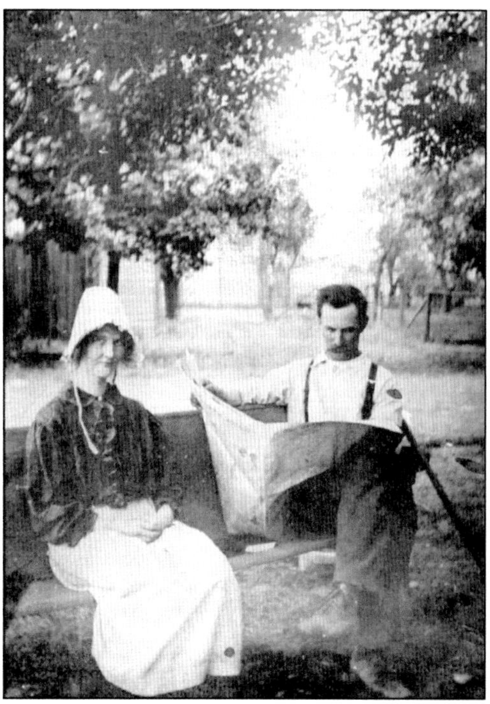

Nicholas Van Heest (1871–1944) married Wilhelmina "Minnie" Van der Aa (1872–1925) on July 12, 1893. This photograph, taken before Mary was born in 1911, includes 10 of their 11 children. Listed by the girls' married names, shown here are Ann Van der Aa, Tillie Swets, Lena De Boer, Johanna Van Drunen, Katie Carr, Gilbert Van Heest, Nickolas Van Heest, John Van Heest, Minnie De Graff, and Nellie Witvoet. (Courtesy of Cynthia Anderson.)

Harry Gouwens (1909–1986) and his wife, the former Margaret De Winter (1908–2002), take a break from chores to relax on their South Holland farm. Harry's family came to the United States from Lekkerkerk, Nederlek, Zuid-Holland, in 1849. (Courtesy of the South Holland Historical Society.)

Kathryn (left) and Jeanette Zandstra pump water on the Zandstra farm in Highland, Indiana. Their father, Bartele Hanzes Zandstra (1867–1939), was born in Oostermeer, Tytsjerksteradiel, Friesland, Netherlands, and married Trijntje Klaases De Ruiter (1875–1939) from Heerhugowaard, Noord-Holland, on February 6, 1893, in Chicago. (Courtesy of the Calvin College Archives.)

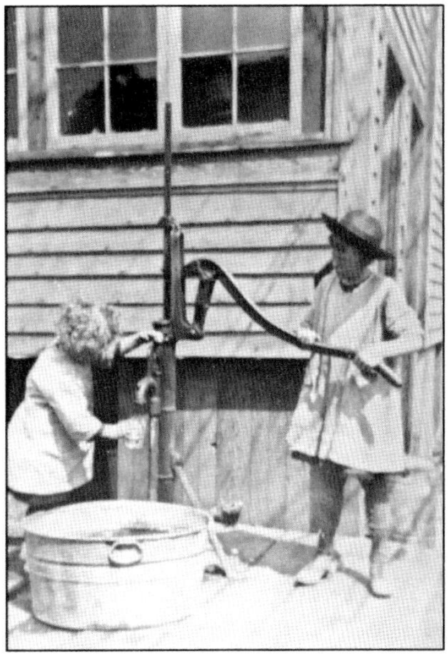

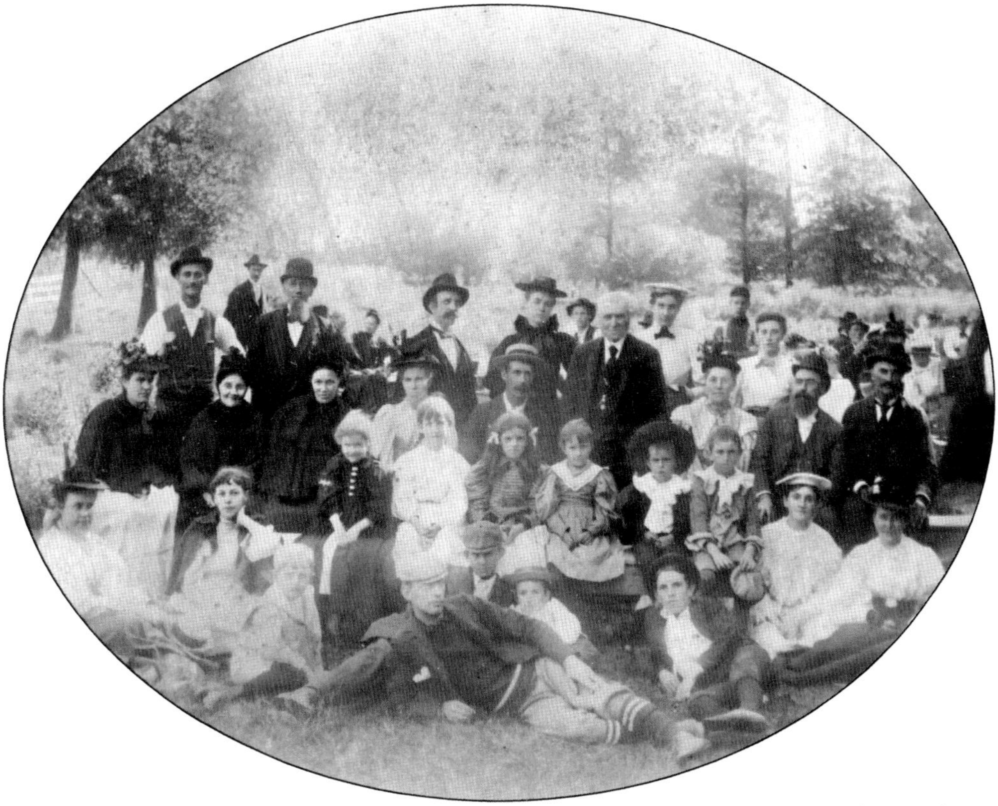

The Madderom branch of the Ton family gathers for a photograph at the second-annual Ton family reunion in 1897. Klaas Nicholas Madderom married Tryntje Ton (1814–1867) in Broek op Langedijk, Heerhugowaard, Noord-Holland, Netherlands, on January 13, 1841. Klaas and Tryntje took over Gerrit Eenigenburg's Roseland home when he moved his family to Oak Glen (Lansing, Illinois). (Courtesy of the Munster Historical Society.)

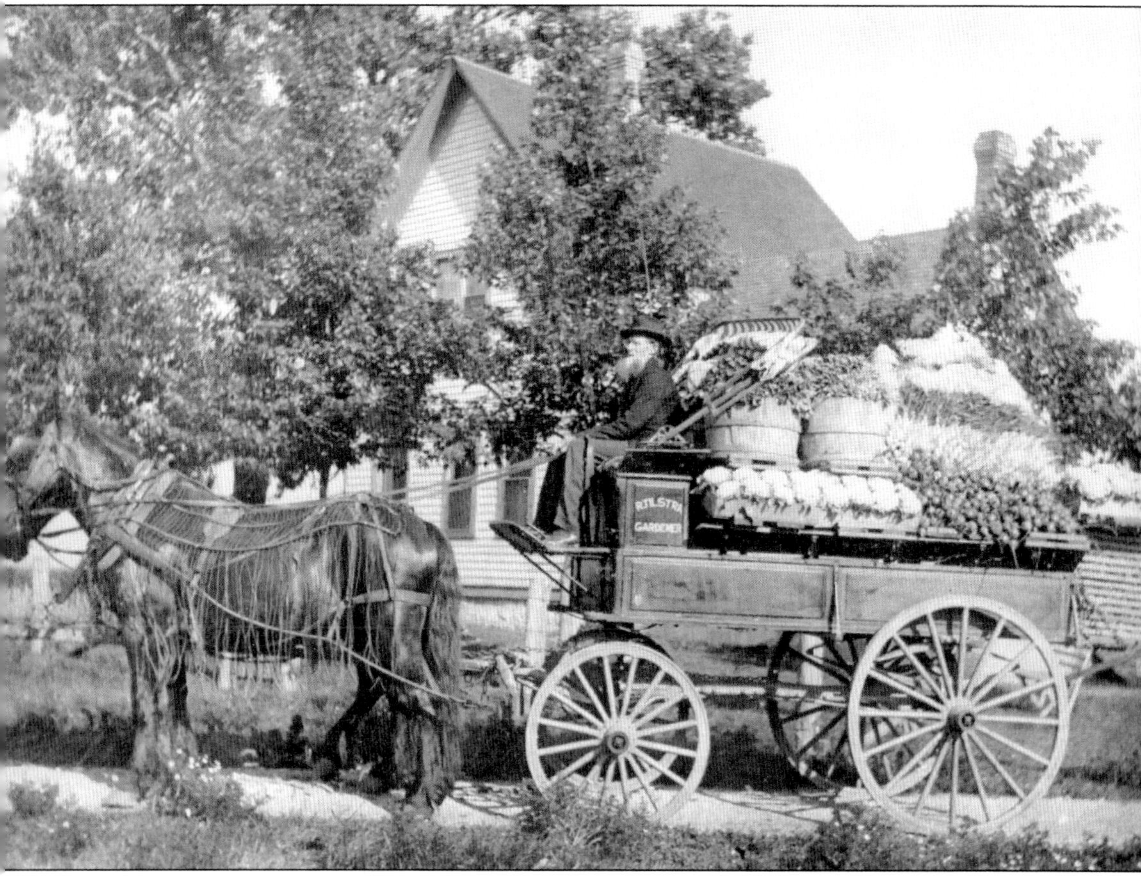

Renze Tilstra (1847–1916) heads off to the South Water Street market in Chicago with a load of garden vegetables. Renze married Baukje Jeltes Stellingwerf (1851–1928) on January 23, 1873, in Menaldum, Friesland, the Netherlands. The Tilstra family emigrated from Schingen in the northwest part of Friesland in 1887. (Courtesy of the South Holland Historical Society.)

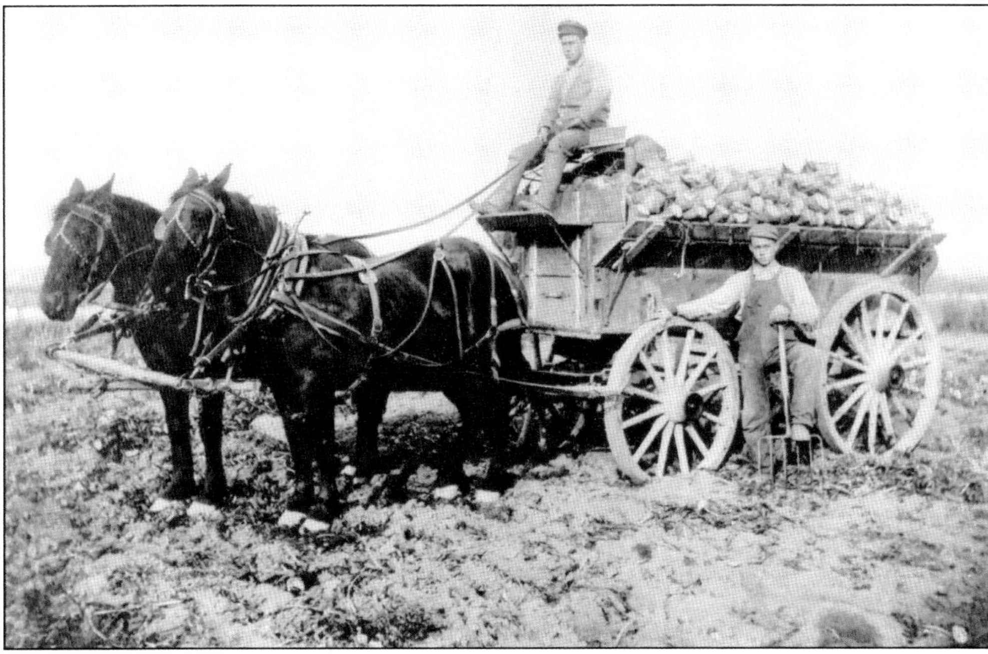

Brothers Issac (1891–1976), seated on the wagon, and William Rietveld (1894–1966) are hard at work with a wagonload of sugar beets. Their father, Cornelius Rietveld (1850–1924), married Maria Van Ostenbrugge (1857–1915) on February 24, 1878, in South Holland, Illinois. Cornelius immigrated to the United States in 1868. (Courtesy of the South Holland Historical Society.)

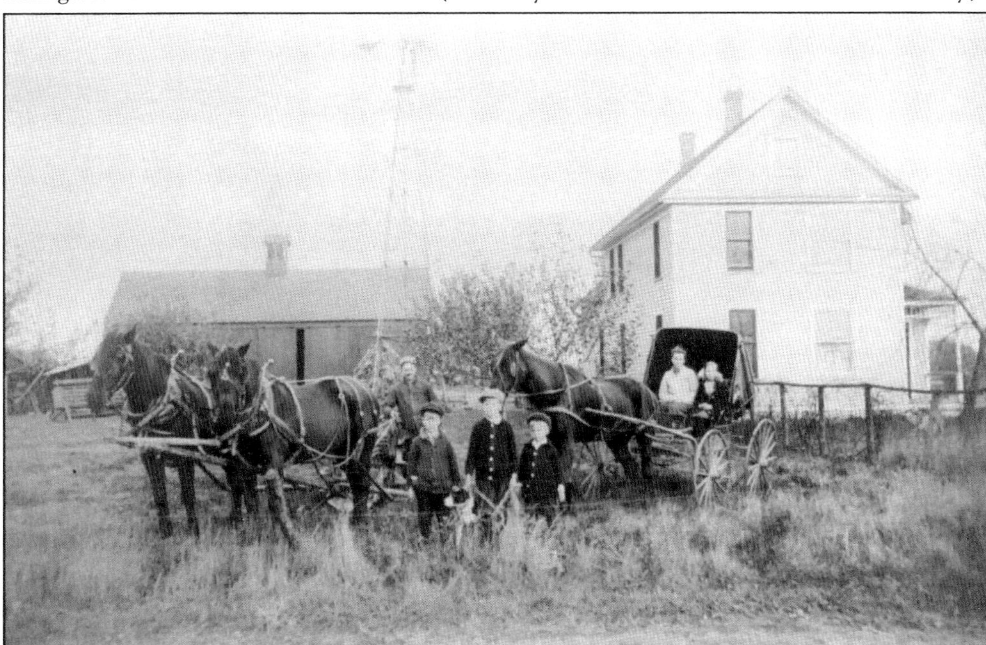

William T. Paarlberg (1874–1960) married Maria Cornelia Hillegonds (1870–1949) on May 3, 1902. They pose here with their four children on the family farm. Shown are, from left to right, William, James, Cornelius, Phillip, Maria, and, Ruth. William was the grandson of the Widow Paarlberg. (Courtesy of the South Holland Historical Society.)

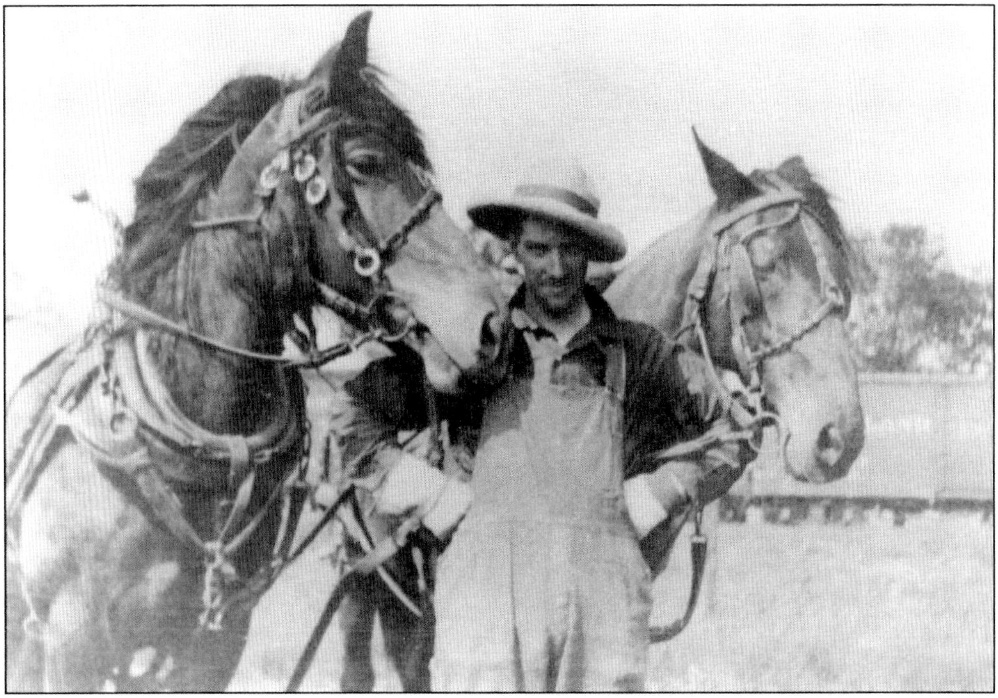

Posing for a photograph with his horses is John Klaas De Jong (1887–1958). He married Helen Van Der Gilssen (1890–1976) on June 20, 1918. John's father, Klaas (1846–1928), traveled from the Netherlands in 1866 and married Johanna Prijs (1846–1939) on April 25, 1872, in Illinois. (Courtesy of the South Holland Historical Society.)

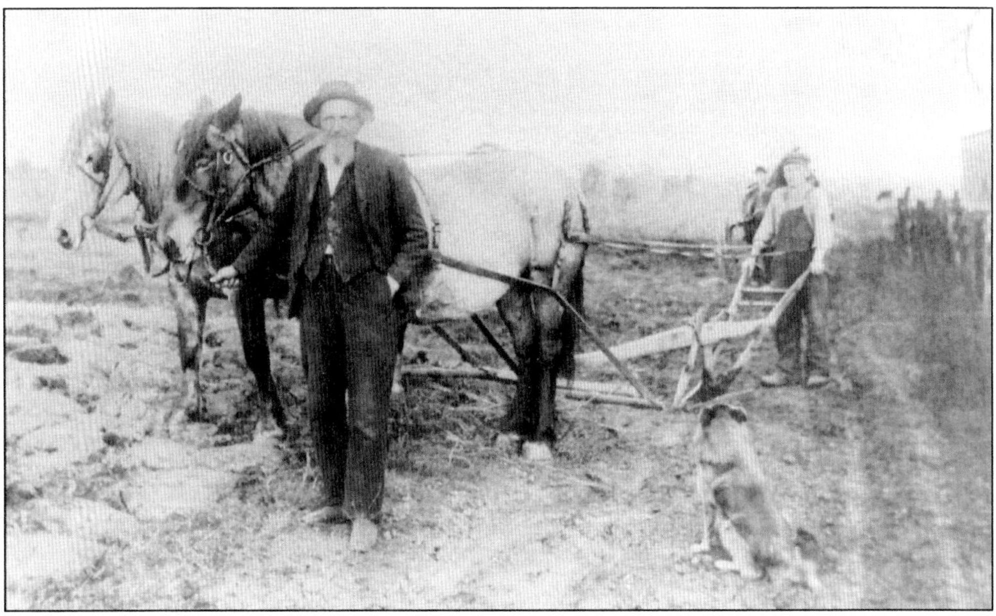

Cornelius Anker (1835–1926) was born in Benschop, which is about 12 miles east of Stolwijk, in the province of Utrecht in the Netherlands. His father, Willem Anker (1797–1889), and his mother, the former Willemijntje van Dam (1799–1882), immigrated to the United States with the rest of the Anker family in 1848. (Courtesy of the South Holland Historical Society.)

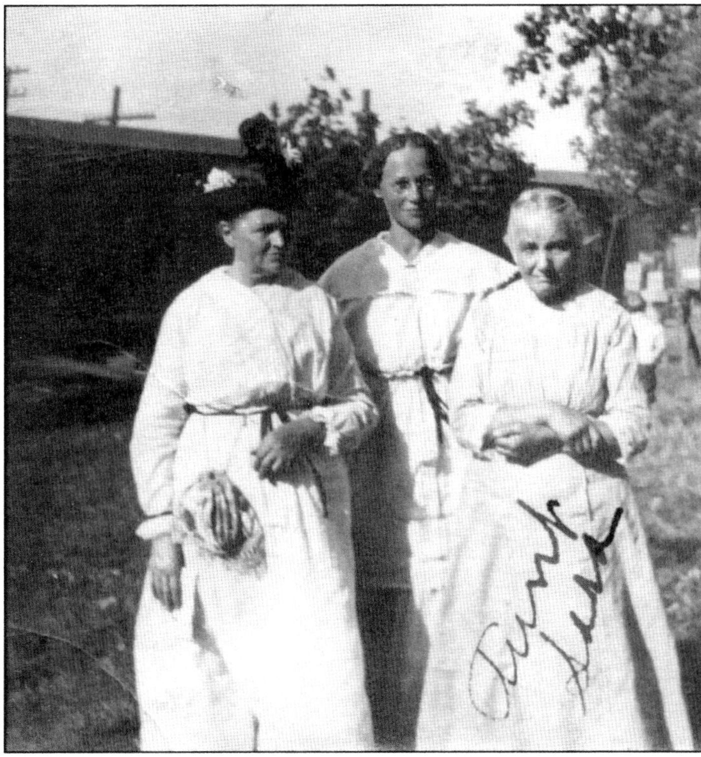

Shown here are, from left to right, Neeltje Bult Eenigenburg, the wife of George Eenigenburg; Maria Eenigenburg Hoekstra (1886–1975), daughter of Jan and Saartje Eenigenburg; and Saartje de Witte Eenigenburg (1851–1931). They are attending a Ton family reunion in the early 1900s. Maria Eenigenburg married Gerban Hoekstra (1886–1960) on August 23, 1906, in Oak Glen, Illinois. (Courtesy of Marie Eenigenburg Min.)

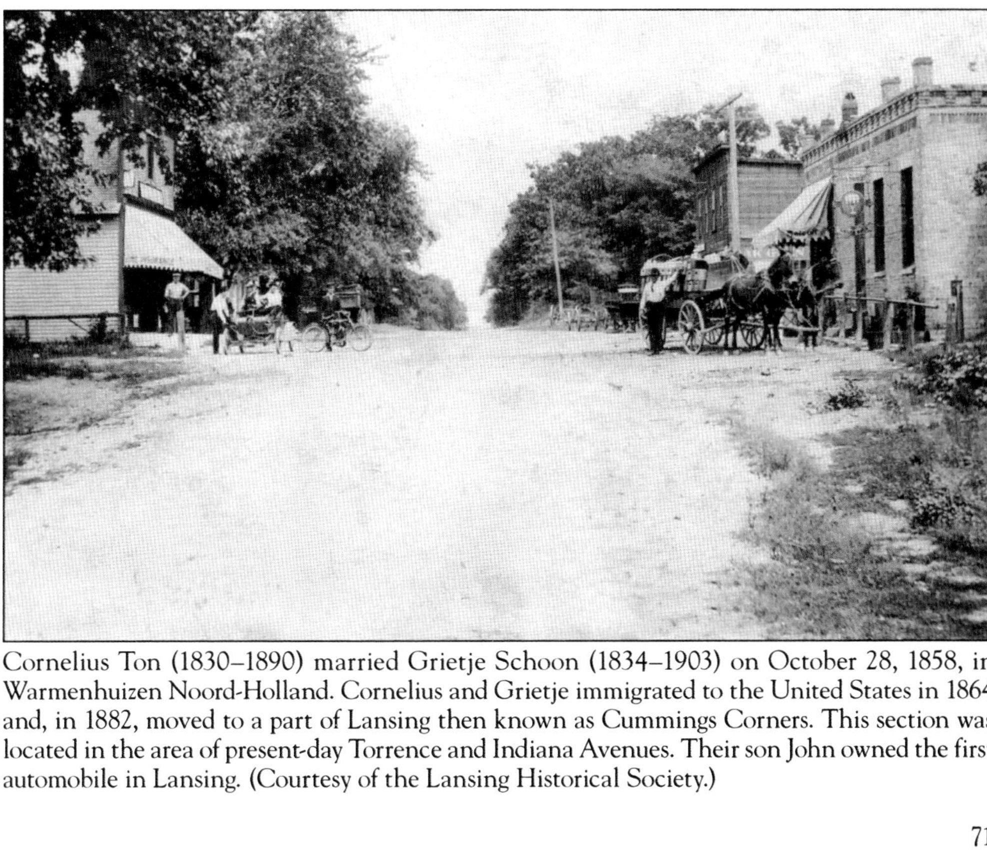

Cornelius Ton (1830–1890) married Grietje Schoon (1834–1903) on October 28, 1858, in Warmenhuizen Noord-Holland. Cornelius and Grietje immigrated to the United States in 1864 and, in 1882, moved to a part of Lansing then known as Cummings Corners. This section was located in the area of present-day Torrence and Indiana Avenues. Their son John owned the first automobile in Lansing. (Courtesy of the Lansing Historical Society.)

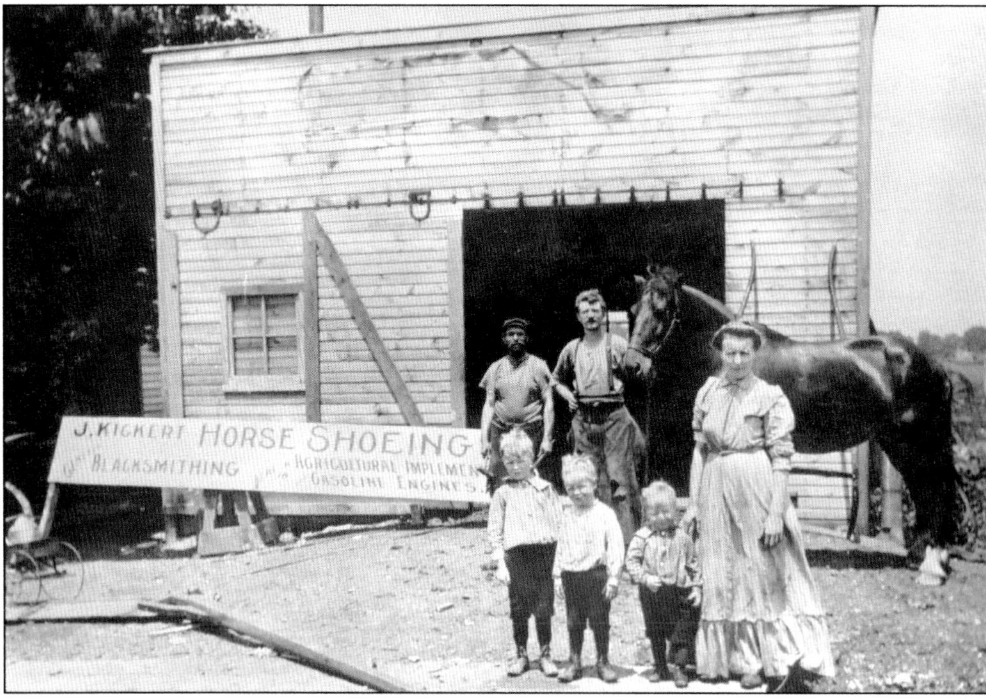

Jan Kikkert (1871–1951) married Fannie "Fenna" Van der Griend (1882–1959) on June 25, 1899. Jan, shown here holding the horse, was a blacksmith who later became an automobile dealer. The Kikkert family came from the Friesland island of Texel in the Wadden Sea. (Courtesy of the South Holland Historical Society.)

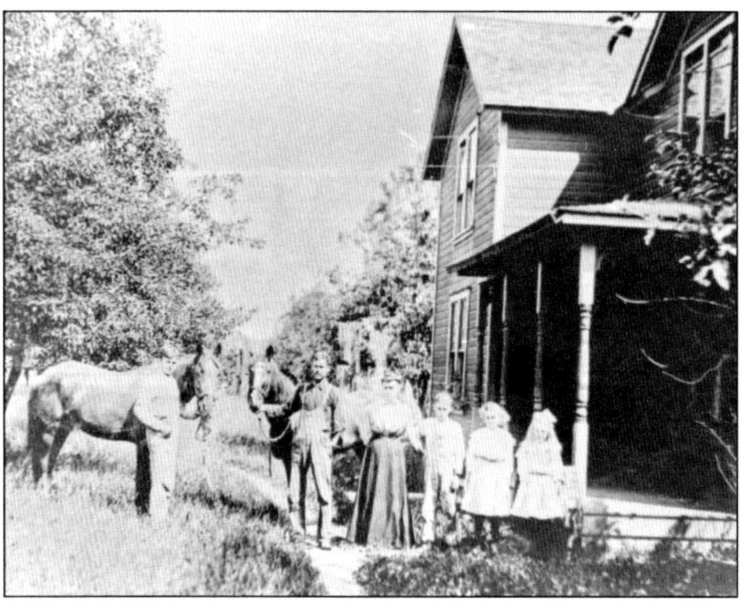

John T. De Jong (1866–1940) married Magheltje "Maggie" Van der Aa (1869–1930) on November 10, 1891, in South Holland, Illinois. The family members are, from left to right, Teunis, John, Maggie, Mitchell, Cora, and Johanna. John's father, Teunis P. De Jong (1839–1920), was born in Charlois, Rotterdam, Zuid-Holland. (Courtesy of the South Holland Historical Society.)

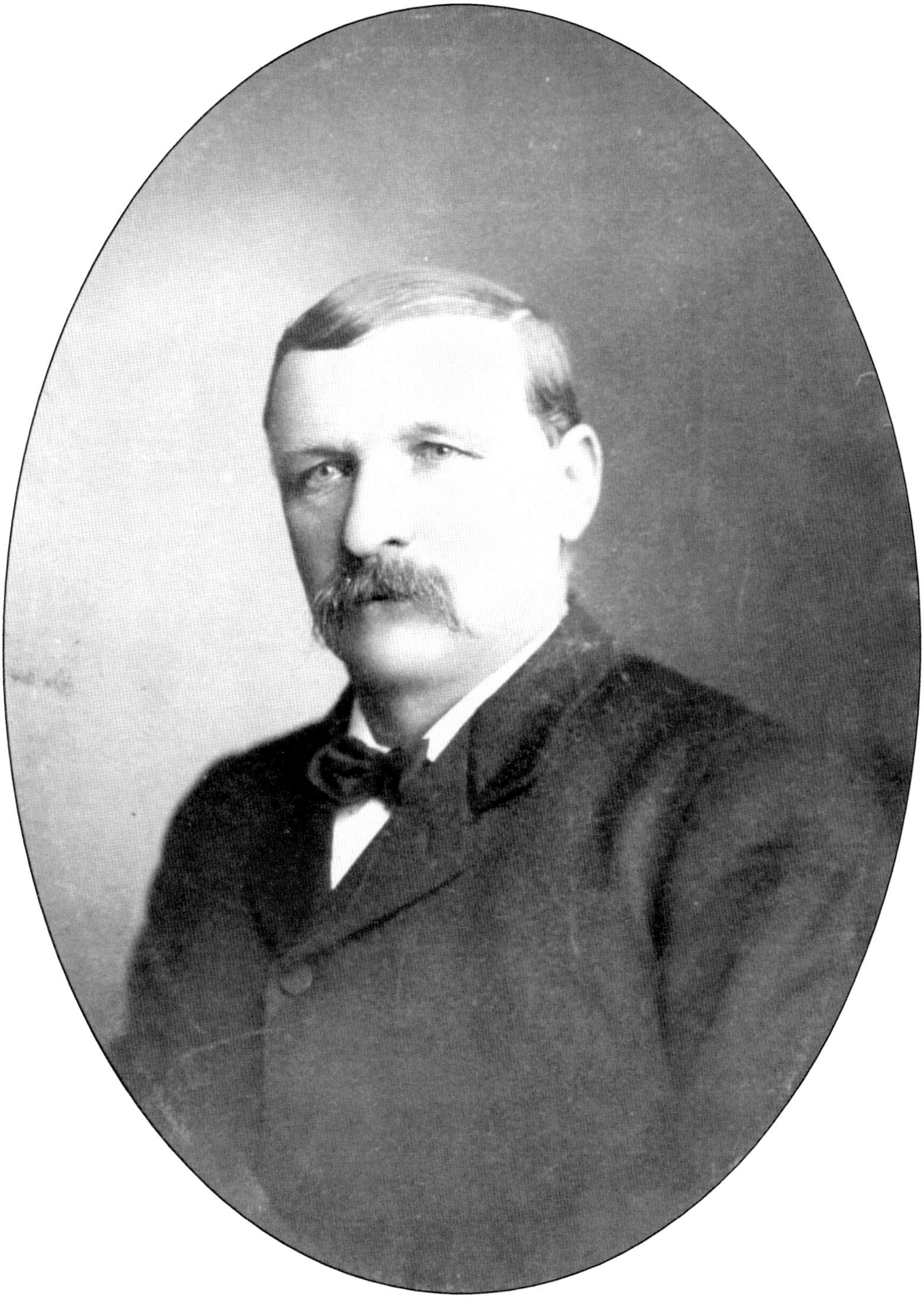

In 1894, South Holland was incorporated into a village under the statutes of the State of Illinois. On May 12, 1894, South Holland's first village board was elected, with Jan Shilling (1851–1924), shown here, as president. Peter Anker was chosen as clerk, and the trustees were Dirk P. De Young, Gerrit Van DeBerg, Roel VanVuren, and Okke VanZanten. (Courtesy of the South Holland Historical Society.)

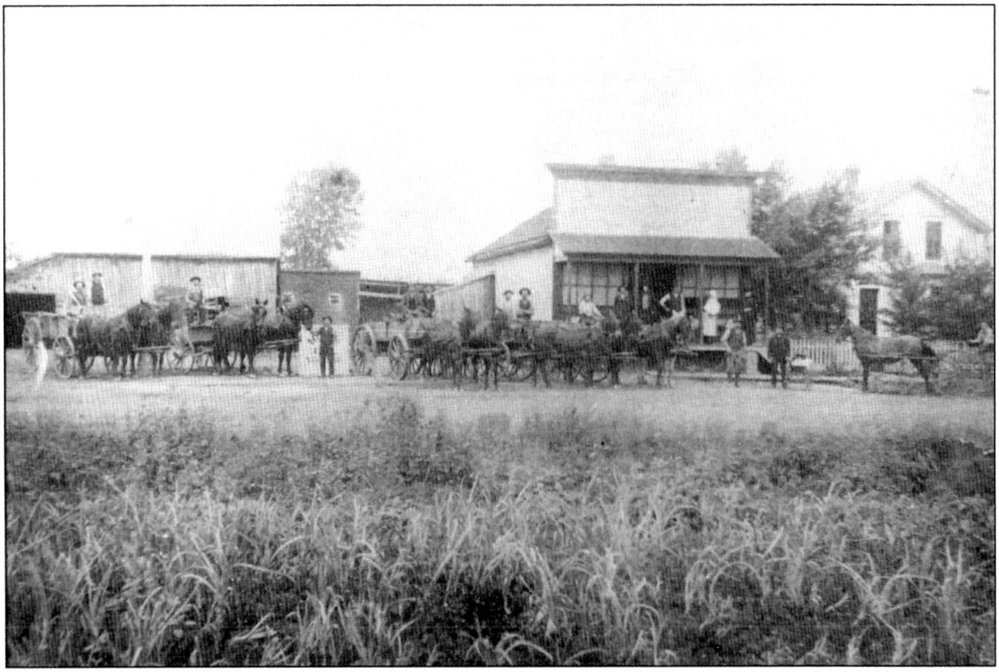

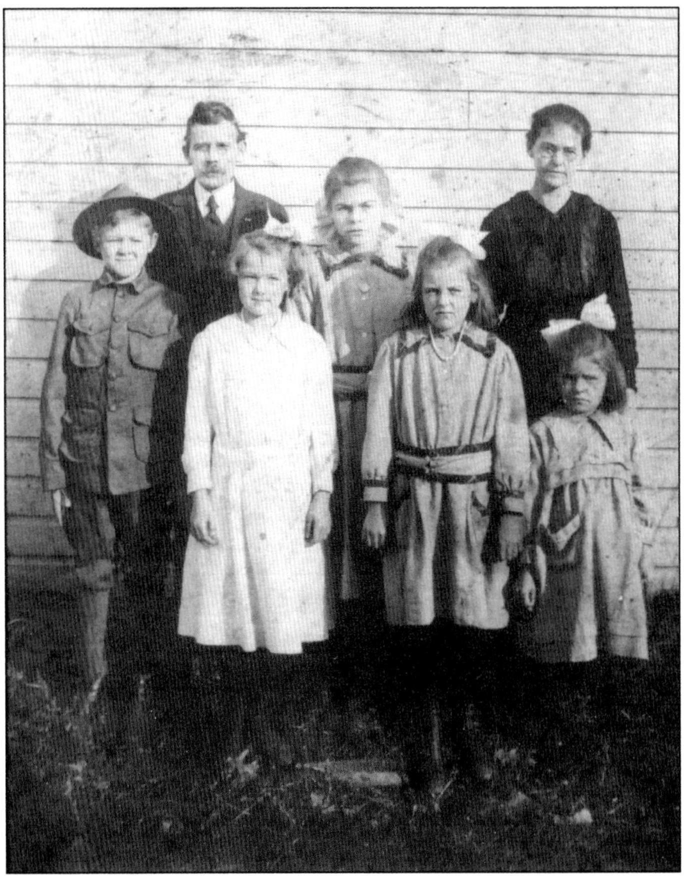

Dirk P. De Young (1868–1940) was born in South Holland to Pieter De Young (1836–1902) and Maaike Schaap (1841–1908). Dirk married Gooltje Santeford (1872–1928) on November 24, 1891, and they had 11 children together. Their son Peter (1894–1918) was killed in World War I. (Courtesy of the South Holland Historical Society.)

John Kortenhoeven (1879–1971) met Nellie Voorn in Roseland, where he was a blacksmith. They moved to Highland after they were married. John became that town's first blacksmith. The couple is shown here with their children, from left to right, Jacob, Marie, Cornelia, Amelia, and Grace about 1918. (Courtesy of the Highland Historical Society.)

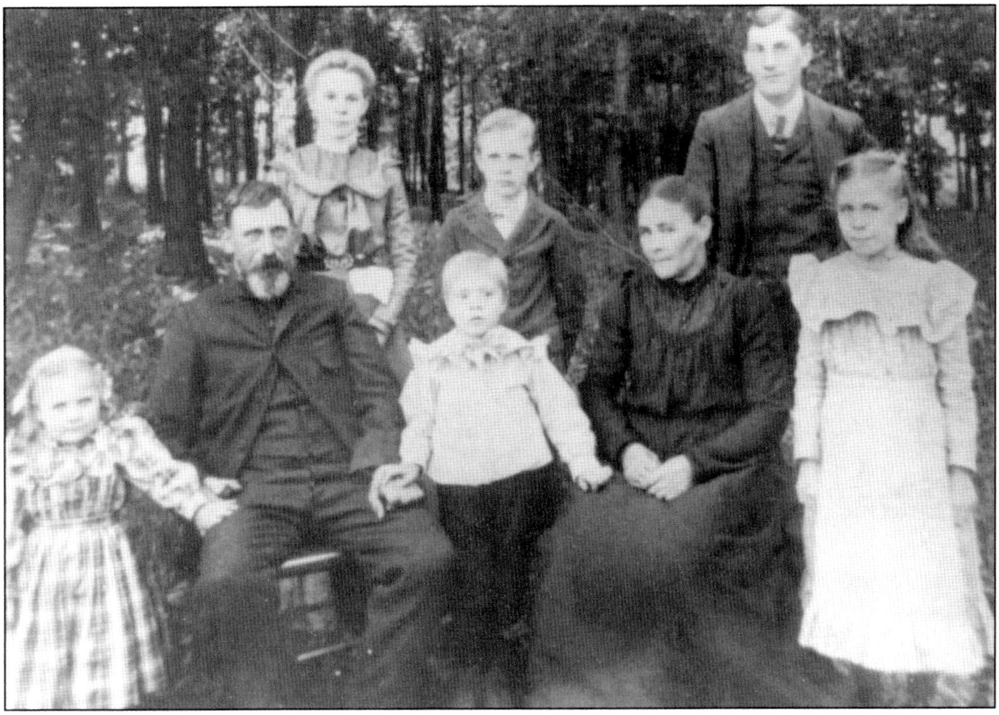

The John and Jane (Kraay) Zyp family is seen here in 1901. The family members are, from left to right, (first row) Beatrice, John, William, Jane, and Gert; (second row) Emma, Art, and Richard. Their farm was located at 3600 Ridge Road, on the south side of the road, in Highland. (Courtesy of the Highland Historical Society.)

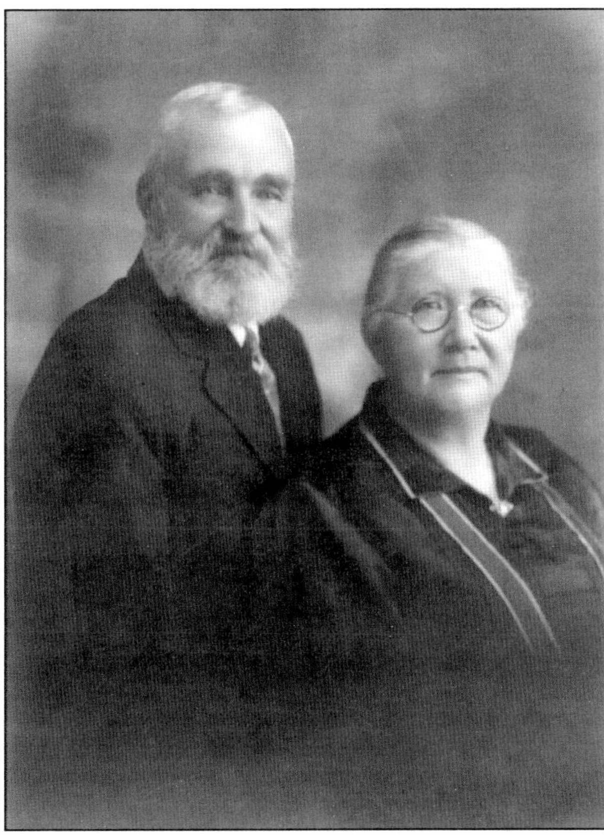

Gerrit Eriks (1854–1928) arrived from the Netherlands on May 9, 1873, and soon found farmwork in Roseland. It was in Roseland that Gerrit met and then married Stientje (Christina) Dyke (1858–1940) on December 26, 1877. After some years in Roseland, Gerrit and Stientje moved to Highland, where they raised seven sons and two daughters. (Courtesy of the Highland Historical Society.)

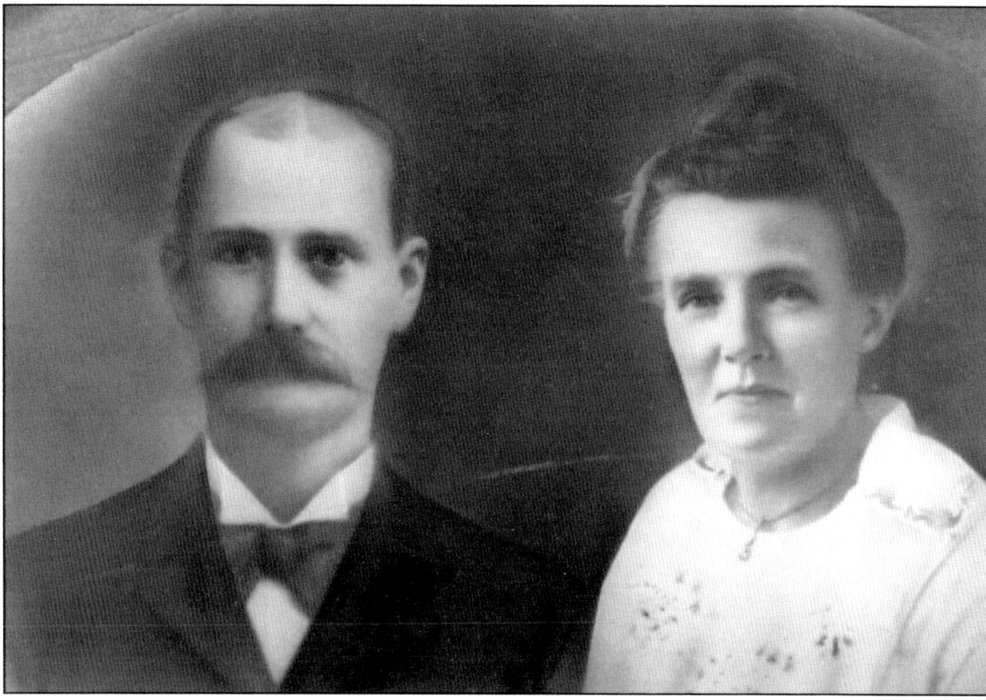

Dirk Pieter Schoon (1858–1913) arrived in the United States on August 13, 1867, aboard the German ship *Tarifa*. On March 8, 1883, he married Dorothy Talsma (1865–1948), who had been born in The Hague, Netherlands. Dirk, along with his father and brothers, dug the Schoon ditch, which runs along Fisher Street in Munster, Indiana. (Courtesy of the Munster Historical Society.)

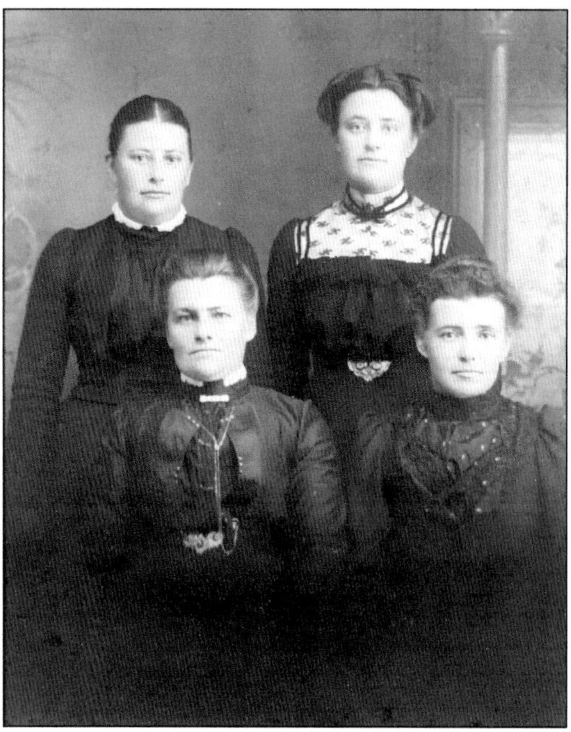

The four daughters of Maghiel and Johanna Van der Aa, listed by their married names, are, from left to right, (first row) Trientje "Kate" Van Drunen (1862–1932) and Maggie De Young (1869–1930); (second row) Wilhelmina "Minnie" Van Heest (1872–1925) and Johanna De Young (1883–1912). A fifth daughter, Helena, died in 1893 at the age of 19. (Courtesy of Cynthia Anderson.)

Baaye Van der Griend (1852–1923) was born in the Netherlands and came to the United States in 1866. He married Johannah Geluk (1861–1914) on April 13, 1879, at the True Dutch Reform Church in South Holland, Illinois. Their eldest daughter, Gerrityte "Carrie" Van der Griend (1880–1955), married Jan Gerrit Witvoet on August 23, 1900. (Courtesy of the South Holland Historical Society.)

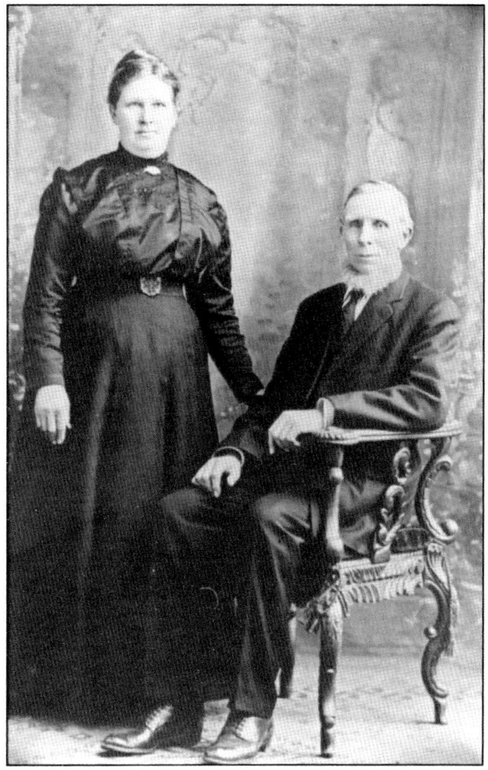

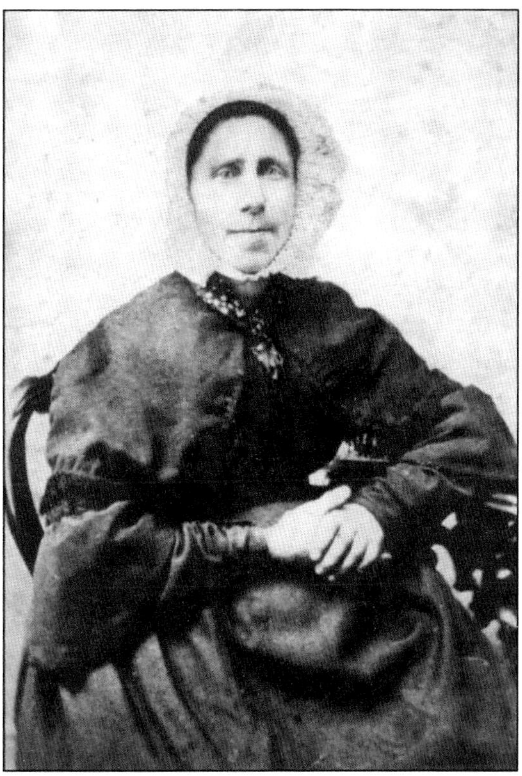

Jannigje Gelderblom was born on June 20, 1819, to Izaak Frederikse Gelderblom and Annigje Vuurens in Schelluinen, Giessenlanden, Zuid-Holland. She married Arie Rietveld (1818–1899) on August 31, 1843, and they had nine children together. She passed away on February 26, 1894, in Cook County, Illinois. (Courtesy of the South Holland Historical Society.)

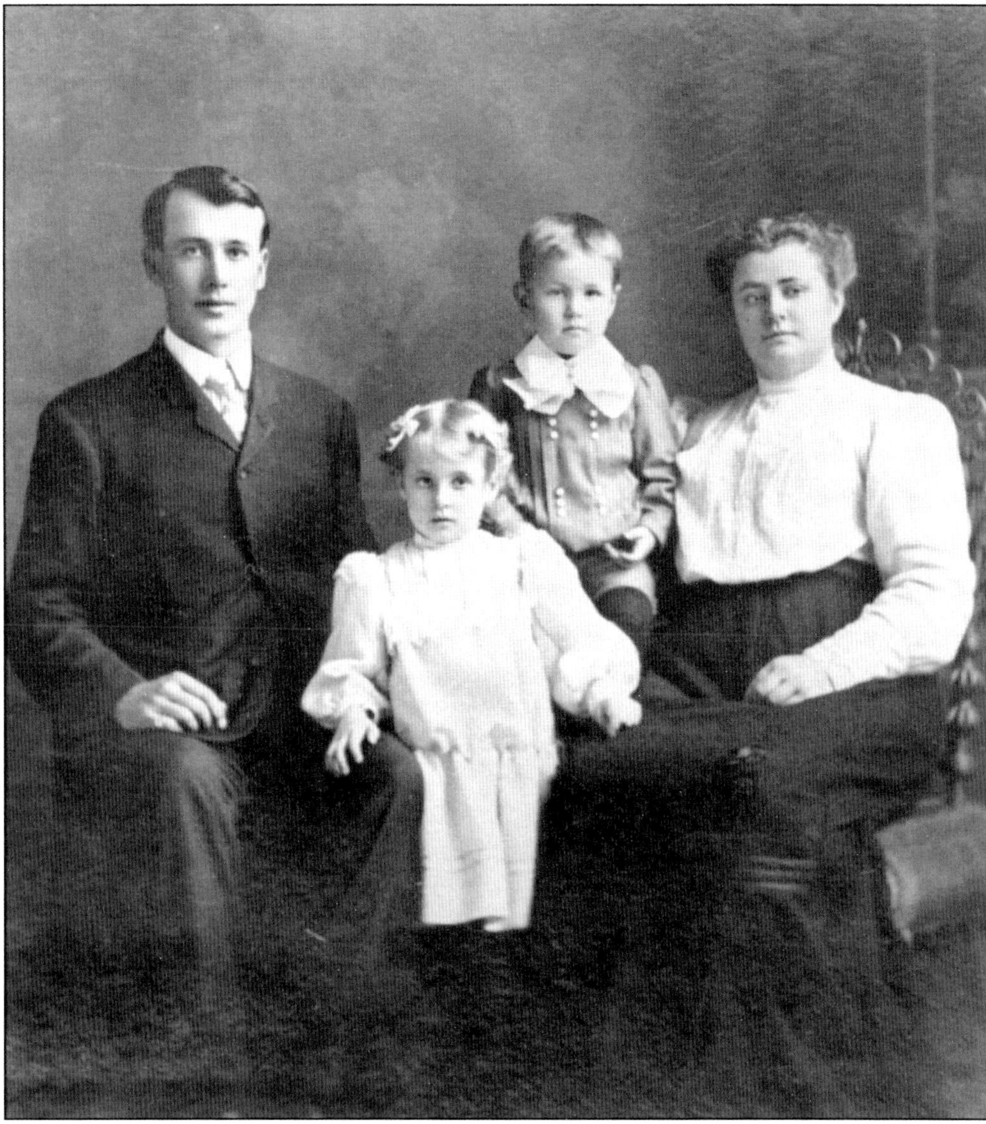

Jacob and Johanna (Van der Aa) De Jong pose here in 1904 with two of their children, Johanna and Peter. On February 10, 1934, while filling in as a bank guard for his vacationing father, Peter was killed in an attempted robbery before the bank opened. Local law enforcement believed it was John Dillinger's gang. When the gang members returned on May 25, Jacob killed two of the robbers inside the bank, and a third was gunned down outside. (Courtesy of the South Holland Historical Society.)

Pieter Paarlberg (1840–1921) married Cornelia Van Oostenbrugge (1847–1927) on October 31, 1870. They pose here with their family. Shown are, from left to right, (first row) Mary and Cornelius; (second row) Eva, Pieter, Cornelia, Ann, and Teunis; (third row) Henry, William, Klass, Jan, and Gerrit. Ann and Mary were nurses in World War I. (Courtesy of the South Holland Historical Society.)

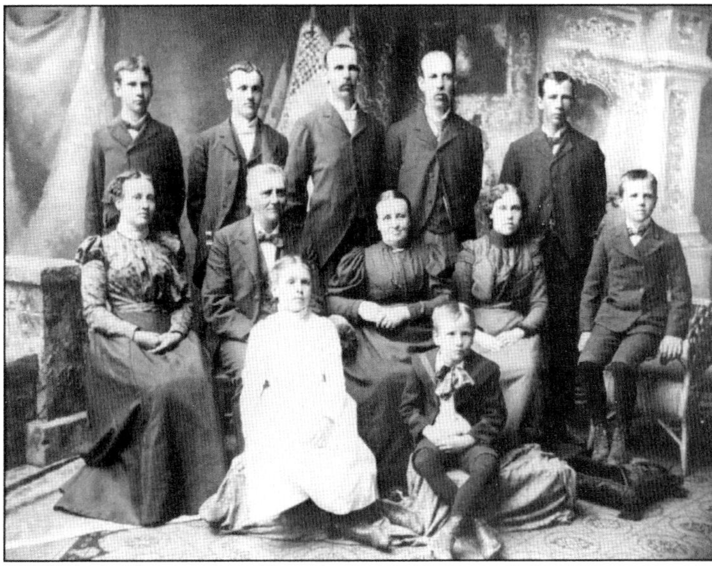

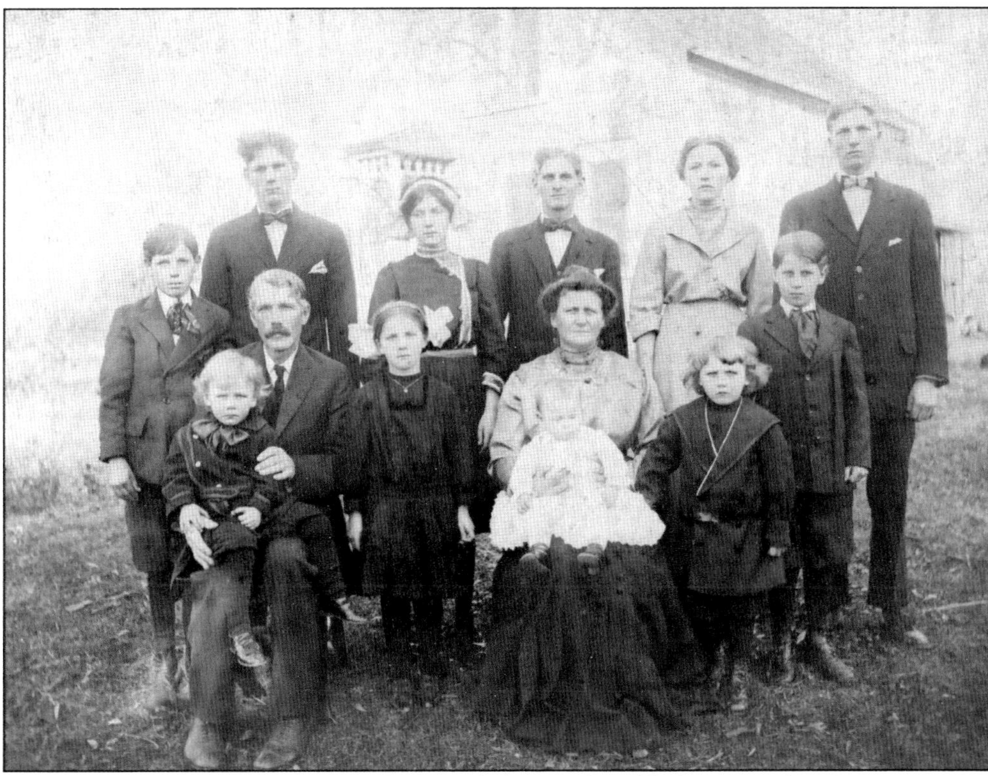

John "Jan" Swets (1868–1944) married Gertrude (Geertje) Bodde (1871–1946) on January 6, 1892, in South Holland. Jan's family came from Hardinxveld, near Rotterdam, in the Netherlands, and arrived in the United States on May 26, 1856. Gertrude's family was from Gouda, Zuid-Holland, and immigrated in 1866. (Courtesy of the Lansing Historical Society.)

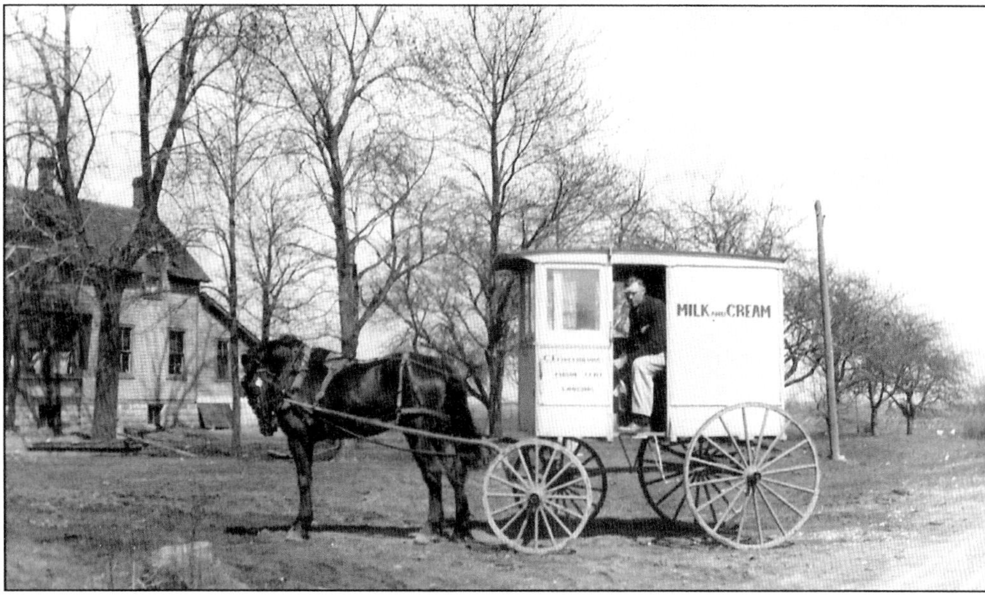

This photograph of Gerrit Eenigenburg was taken by his daughter Edna Eenigenburg (1904–2002) in Lansing, Illinois, in 1924. Edna's grandmother on her mother's side, Adrianna Aderome Molenaar (1854–1927), was born in Langendijk, Rucphen, Noord-Brabant. (Courtesy of Julie Bockheim.)

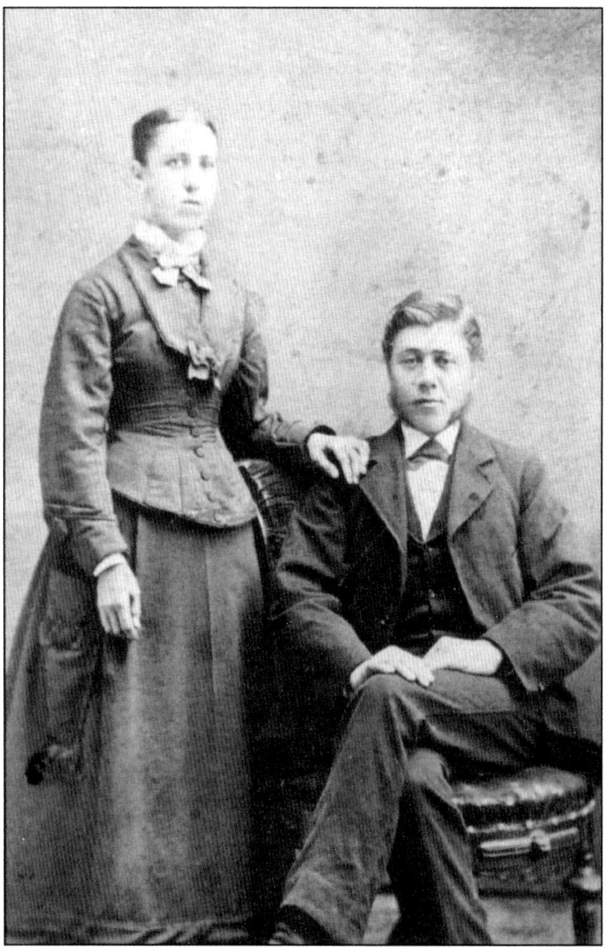

Cornelis A. Rietveld (1850–1924) was born in Schelluinen, Zuid-Holland, and came to the United States in 1868 with his parents, Arie and Jannigje Rietveld. On February 24, 1878, he married Martje Van Oostenbrugge (1856–1915) in South Holland, and they had 12 children together. (Courtesy of the South Holland Historical Society.)

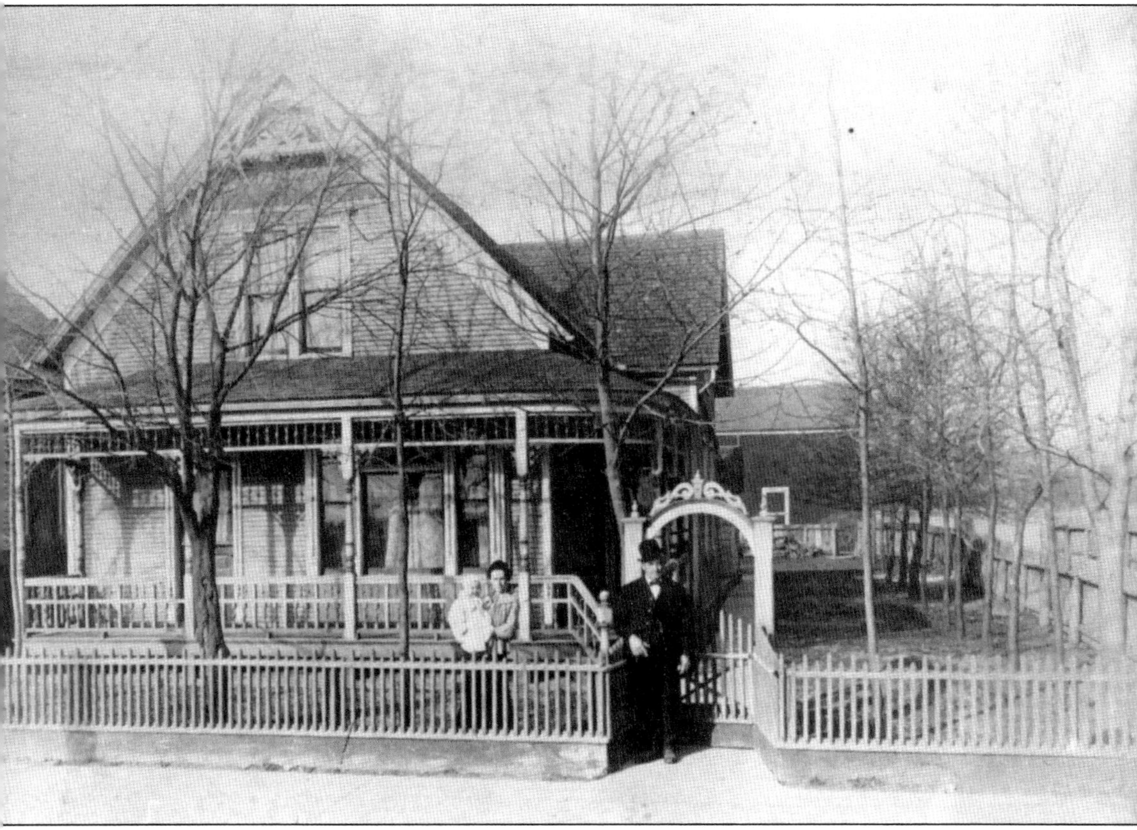

This 1903 photograph shows the home of Theodore M. Van der Aa (1882–1939). He ran an ice-cream parlor for many years at 158 Street and South Park Avenue in South Holland. The man in the photograph is Teddy's father, Michael Van der Aa, and the woman is Teddy's wife, Alice, holding their son Michael. (Courtesy of the South Holland Historical Society.)

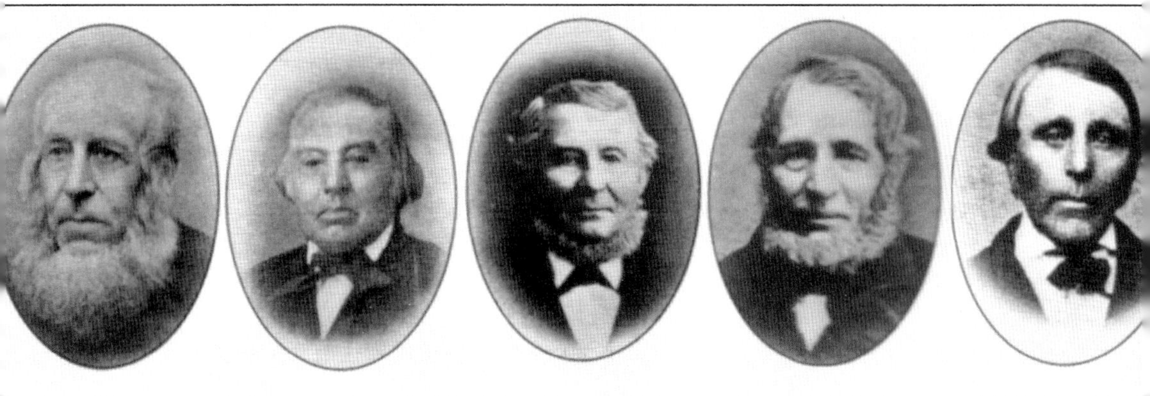

In the 19th century, the journey from the Netherlands to America took about five weeks, if circumstances were good. During that time, the passengers were subject to bad food, damp surroundings, boredom, and rampant sickness, generally spread from one to another due to the close quarters. On the third day that the Roseland families were at sea, Klass Dalenberg's wife and daughter became ill with terrible pains in their stomachs, and it was not long before many more joined them. It was Asiatic cholera. Klass's wife died, as did his father and father-in-law. Somehow, his daughter Trijinje was spared. Among the other founding families of Roseland: Three of Jakob and Geertje De Jong's eight children died. Gerrit and Jannetje Eenigenburg lost three of their four children. Johannes Ambul's wife and child both died. Pieter Oudendijk died, leaving behind a widow and an orphan. Only two of Cornelis and Maartje Kuyper's six children survived the trip to America. A baby girl born to Jan and Pietertje Jonkers just before they set sail never got the chance to grow up in America. Shown here are, from left to right, Johannes Ambul, Jacob De Jong, Cornelis Kuyper, Jan Jonkers, and Klass Dalenberg. (Courtesy of Marie Eenigenburg Min.)

Gwendolyn M. Jonkman (1908–1998) was born in Grand Rapids, Michigan, and attended Calvin College in her hometown. On June 12, 1936, she married Bartel Zandstra (1905–1983) in Highland, Indiana. Gwendolyn retired from the Highland Christian School after 20 years of teaching kindergarten. (Courtesy of the Highland Historical Society.)

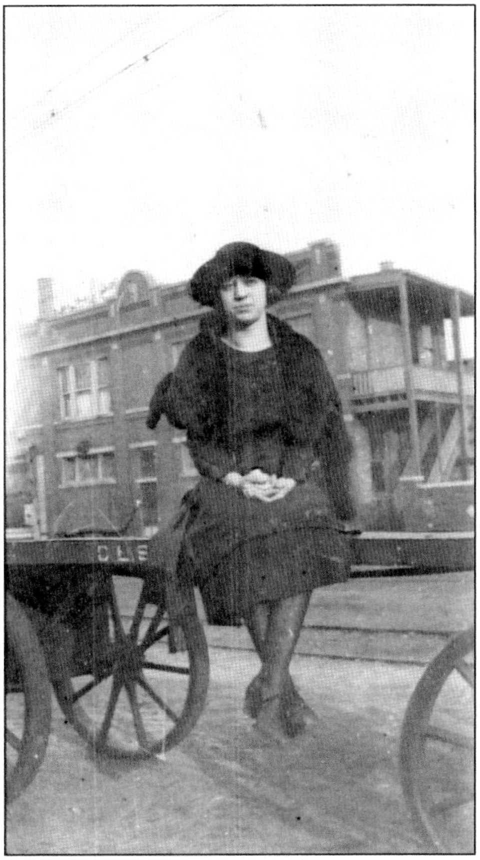

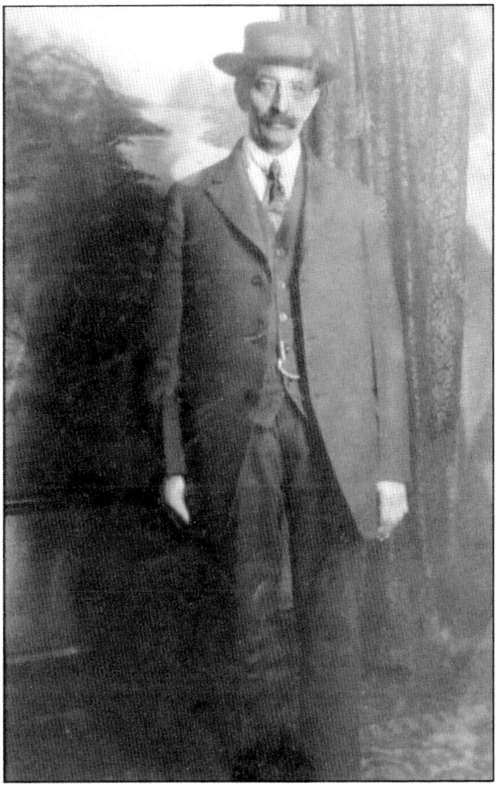

Gerband B. Kikkert (1856–1930) was born on the island of Texel in Noord-Holland and arrived in the United States on May 31, 1881. On March 20, 1884, he married Geeske de Vries in Roseland. He is at rest in Hope Cemetery. (Courtesy of the Highland Historical Society.)

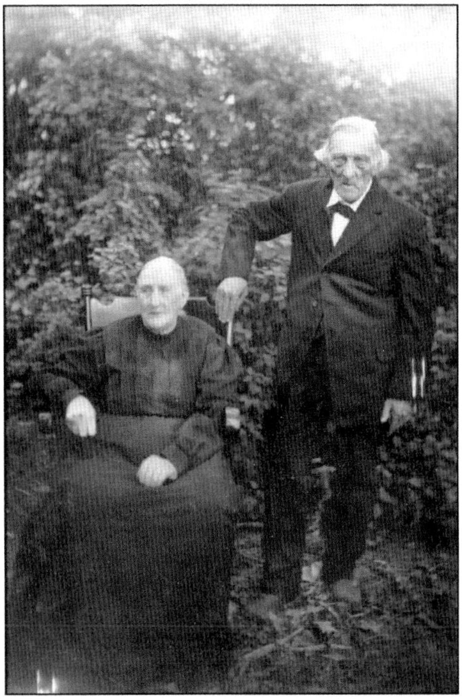

Barend Willem Jansen (1826–1915) was born in Geldermalsen, Gelderland, Netherlands. Pietertje van Sessen (1827–1915) was born in Ijsselham, Overijssel, Netherlands. They were married on January 30, 1854, in Langerak, Gelderland. The couple arrived in the United States with five children in the spring of 1867. Barend and Pietertje, members of the First Reformed Church of Lansing, are at rest in the cemetery next to the church. (Courtesy of the Highland Historical Society.)

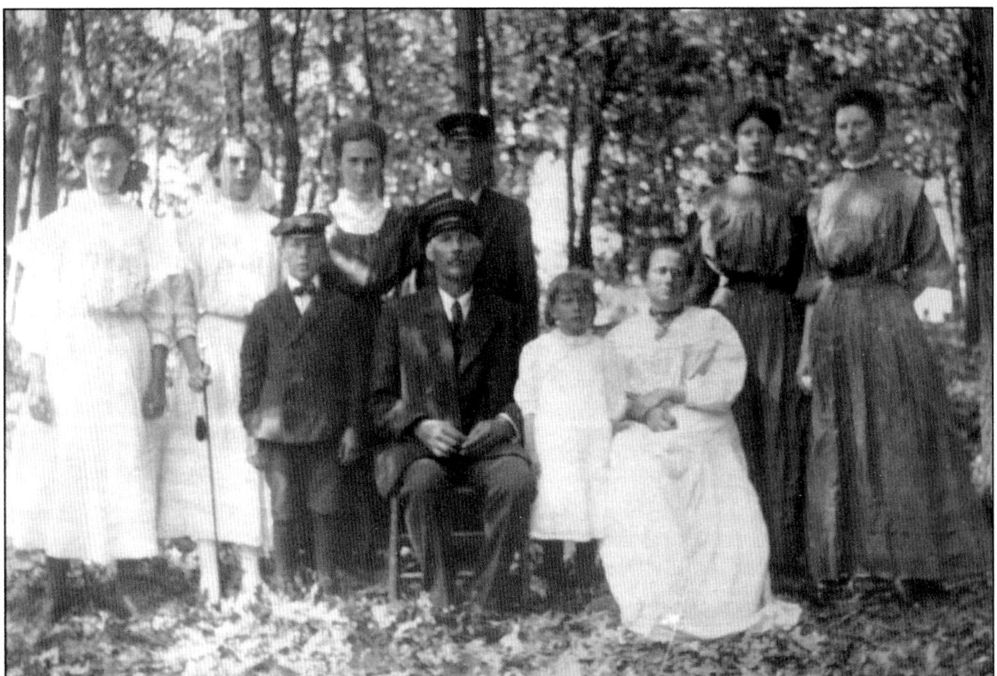

Pieter Jansen (1863–1931) and Iola Johnston (1871–1939) were married on July 26, 1888. This is how their family looked on July 4, 1908. Shown here are, from left to right, (first row) Michael, Pieter, Rhonda, and Iona; (second row) Clara, Carrie, Millie, Percy, Pearl, and Ruby. Another son, Donald, was born three and a half months after this photograph was taken. (Courtesy of the Highland Historical Society.)

This is the wedding photograph of Antonie "Tom" Wouter De Graf (1876–1945) and Annigje "Annie" T. Gouwens (1879–1967), taken on February 11, 1898. Antonie's family came to the United States from the Netherlands in 1856. Annigje's family came over in 1848. Their daughter Ester (1899–1981) married Steven Van Milligan (1895–1963) on May 13, 1920. (Courtesy of the South Holland Historical Society.)

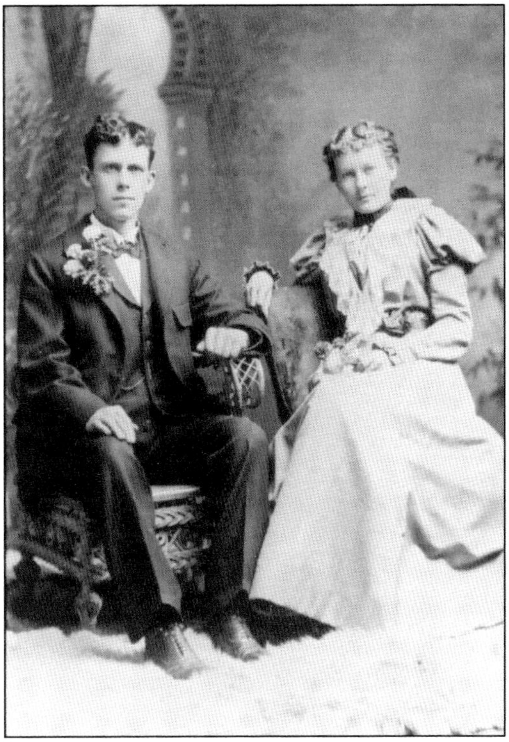

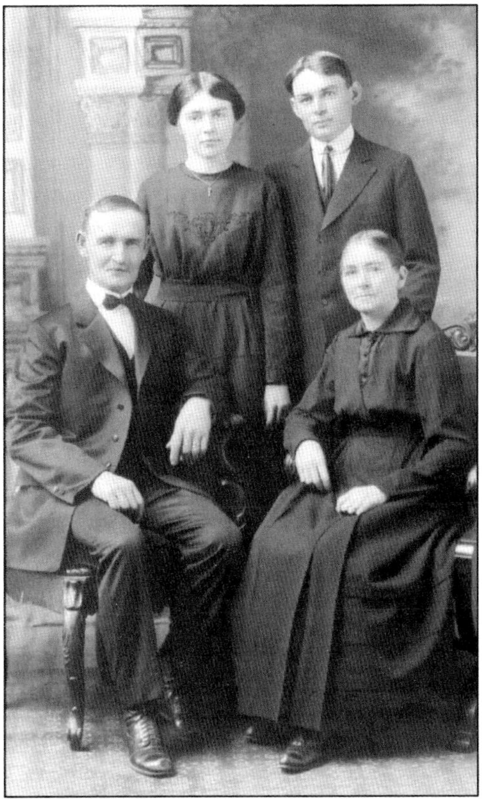

Arie Teunis De Jong (1864–1929) married Jantje Ravenstein (1867–1962) on December 13, 1890. They are shown here with their children Cornelia (1892–1979) and William (1894–1963). Arie's father, Teunis, came from Katendrecht, Netherlands, and spent some time in New Orleans before moving to Keokuk, Iowa, for a while. (Courtesy of the South Holland Historical Society.)

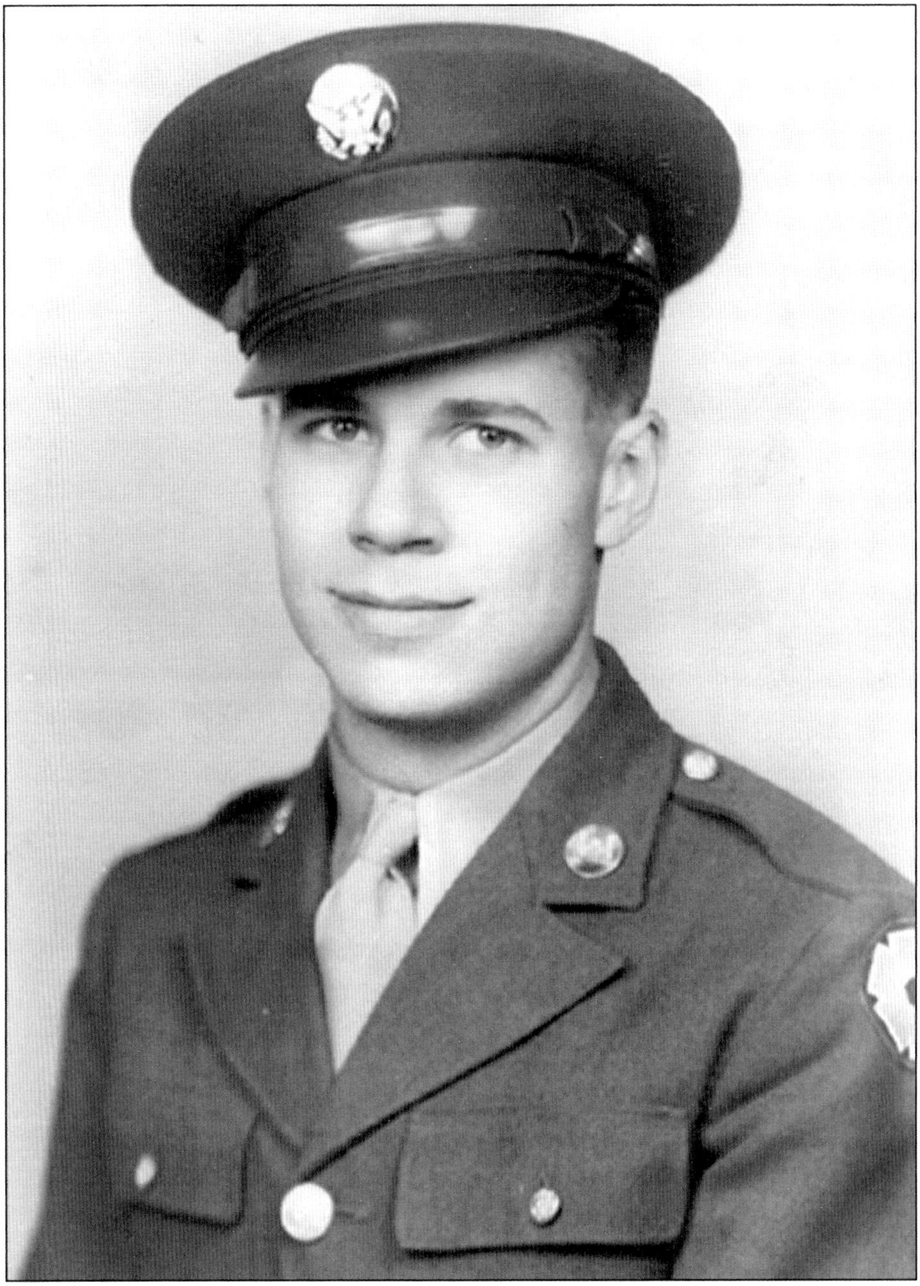

Andrew H. "Bud" Vogel (1924–2011) married Evelyn Van Drunen on June 14, 1944, during his last furlough before going overseas in World War II. Vogel was a graduate of Calvin Christian Grade School in South Holland and Thornton Township High School in Harvey. Before being drafted into the Army, he was a student at the University of Chicago. He became a member of the 96th Infantry Division, which returned to the Philippines with Gen. Douglas MacArthur on October 20, 1944. Vogel later took part in the long invasion battle for Okinawa. He returned home from the Army on February 9, 1946, and continued his education at the American Conservatory of Music in Chicago and Northwestern University in Evanston. (Courtesy of the South Holland Historical Society.)

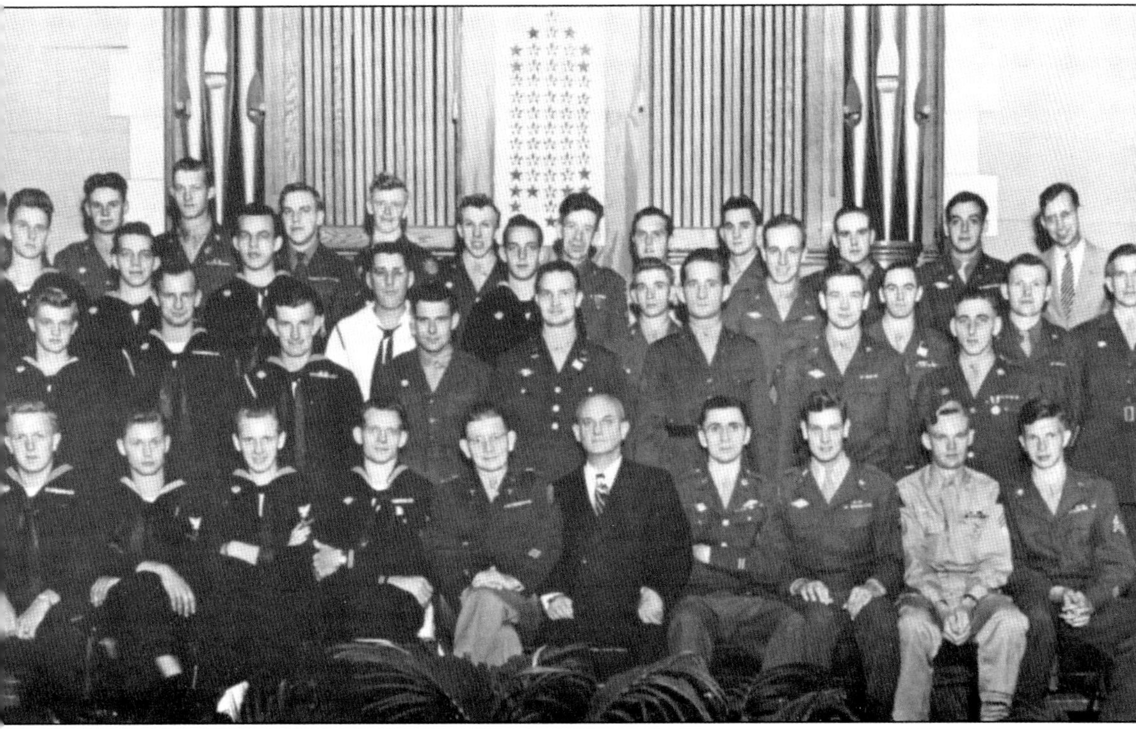

The young men of the Munster Christian Reformed Church did their part in World War II. They are, from left to right, (first row) Melvin Kamstra, Gerald Klooster, Case Dykstra, Ed Huizenga, Chaplin C. Van Schouwen, Rev. J. Monsma, John Doornbos, Fred Klooster, Charles Zandstra, and Arnold Dekker; (second row) Harold Bultema, John Vroom, John Vander Noord, Cornelius Boender, John Dykstra, Jacob Doornbos, Tony Hoekstra, and Bud Meeter; (third row) Harold Scholten, Chester Boender, Peter J. Dykstra, Abel Doornbos, Douglas Boender, Gil Fennema, Peter M. Dykstra, Jake Meeter, Andrew Jabaay, and Harry Rodenburg; (fourth row) Don Klooster, John Harkema Jr., John Dekker, Herb Van Wieren, Joe Norman, Clarence Verbeek, Melvin Jongsma, unidentified, Rich Hoekstra, Bob Ooms, Jim Smit, and unidentified. (Courtesy of the Bult family collection.)

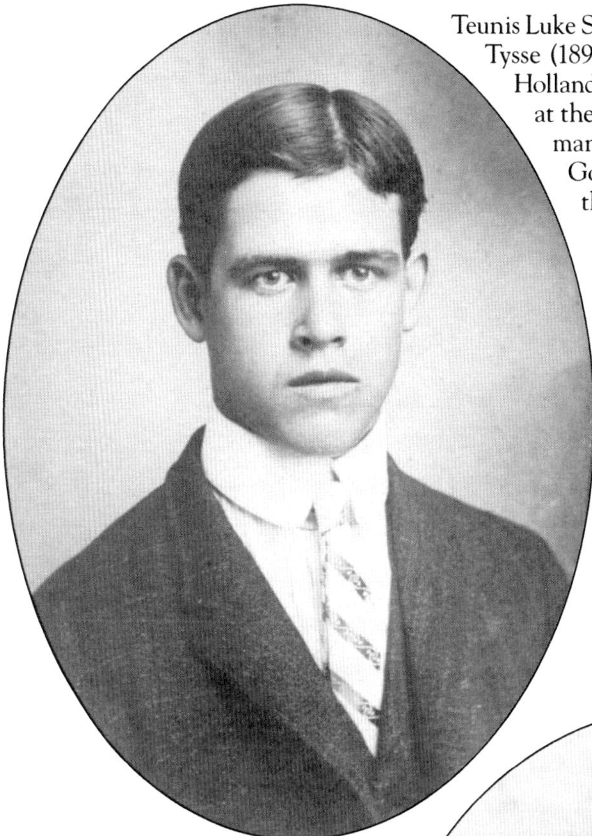

Teunis Luke Santefort (1887–1952) married Henrietta Tysse (1892–1972) on March 12, 1913, in South Holland, Illinois. Teunis worked as the yard boss at the Wausau Lumber & Coal Company for many years. His family came from Ouddorp Goedereede, Zuid-Holland. (Courtesy of the South Holland Historical Society.)

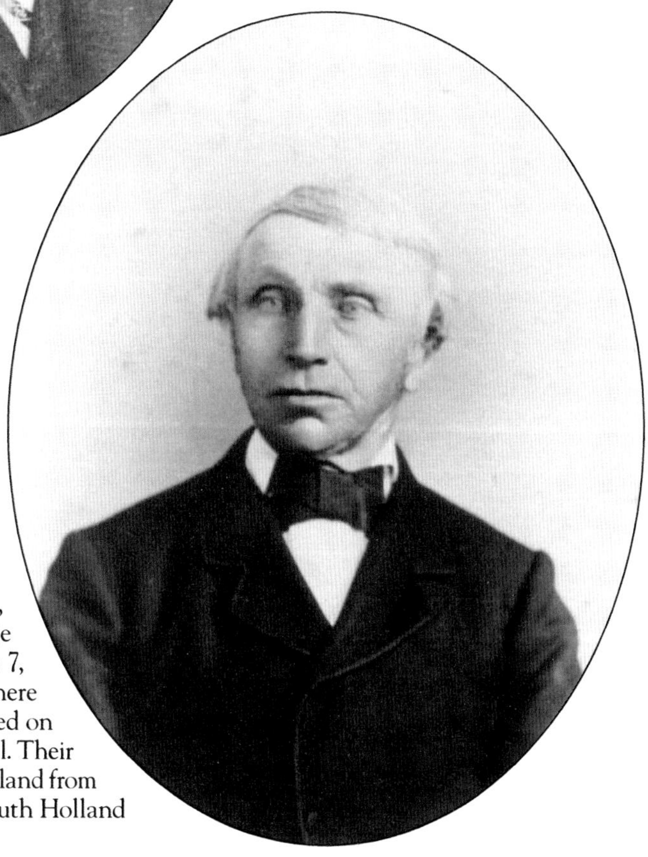

Jan Van Oostenbrugge (1816–1908) was born in Rhenan, Utrecht, Netherlands, and married Evertje Westerveldt (1818–1908) on June 7, 1846, in Barneveld, Gelderland, where Evertje had been born. Evertje died on the very day of her husband's funeral. Their son Gerrit was mayor of South Holland from 1896 to 1898. (Courtesy of the South Holland Historical Society.)

Nellie Van Deursen (1891–1952) came to the United States as an infant and married Pieter Van der Bilt (1884–1921) on May 29, 1909. She would marry Benjamin De Jong (1884–1975) after Pieter's death. Ben's first wife was the former Jennie Medema (1885–1923). (Courtesy of the South Holland Historical Society.)

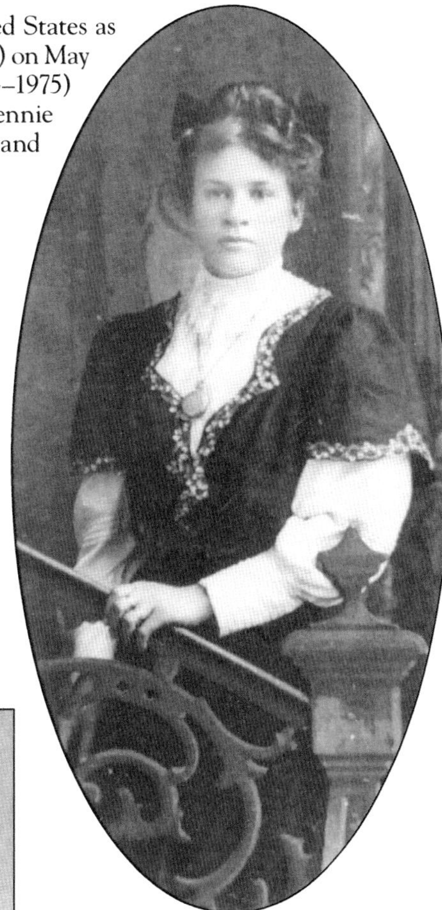

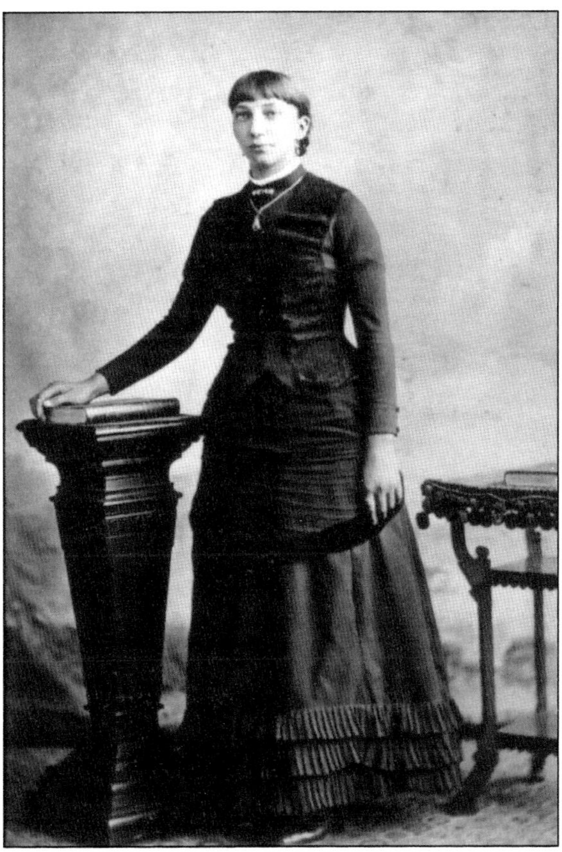

Gerbride Ida Vliem (1868–1938) was born in Staverden, Ermelo, Gelderland. At some point after arriving in the United States, the family name was Americanized to Flym. On April 3, 1888, she married Dingeman Arie Jabaay (1868–1956). Ida was mother to Harry, John, Sarah, Albert, Gertrude, William, and Martin. (Courtesy of the Munster Historical Society.)

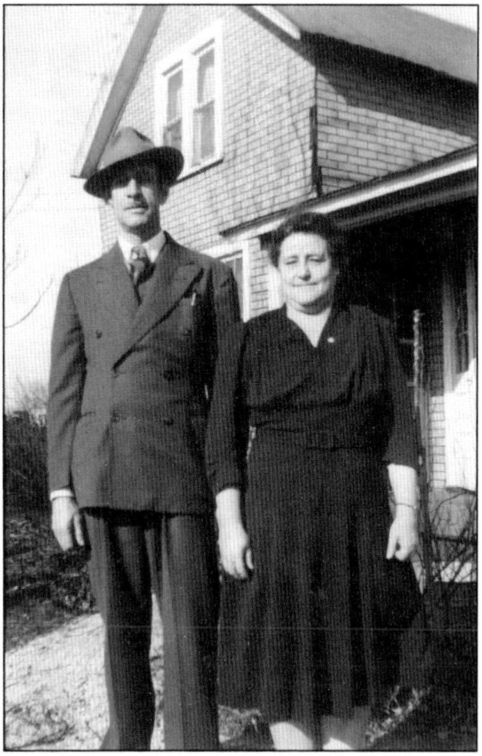

Harry Wouter Swets (1894–1967) married Tillie "Helen" Van Heest (1989–1980) on November 16, 1915, in Lansing, Illinois. Harry's mother, Tryntje "Katie" Mol, was born in Sint Maartensbrug in the northwestern part of Noord-Holland in 1866 and died in childbirth on January 20, 1904. She is buried in the Old Holland Section of Homewood Memorial Gardens in Homewood, Illinois. (Courtesy of Cynthia Anderson.)

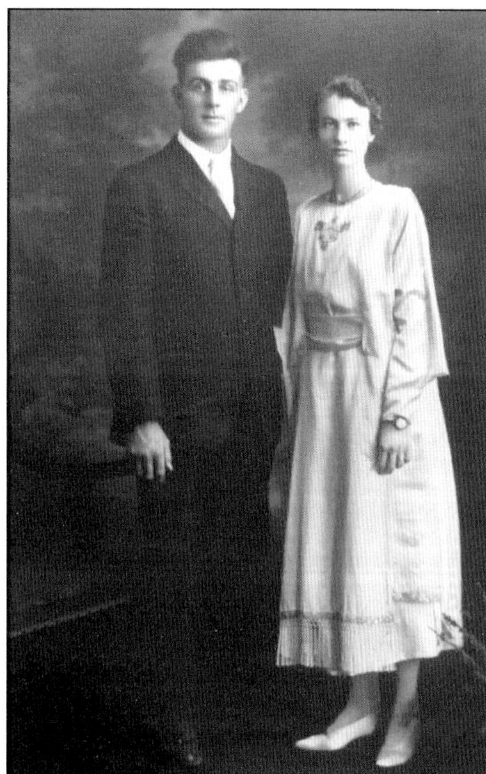

Peter Cornelius Jabaay married Mary D. Schoon (1899–1989) on February 26, 1919. Mary was the daughter of Dirk Pieter Schoon (1858–1913), who was born in Brock Op Lange, Dijk, Netherlands, and came to the United States with his family in 1867. (Courtesy of the Munster Historical Society.)

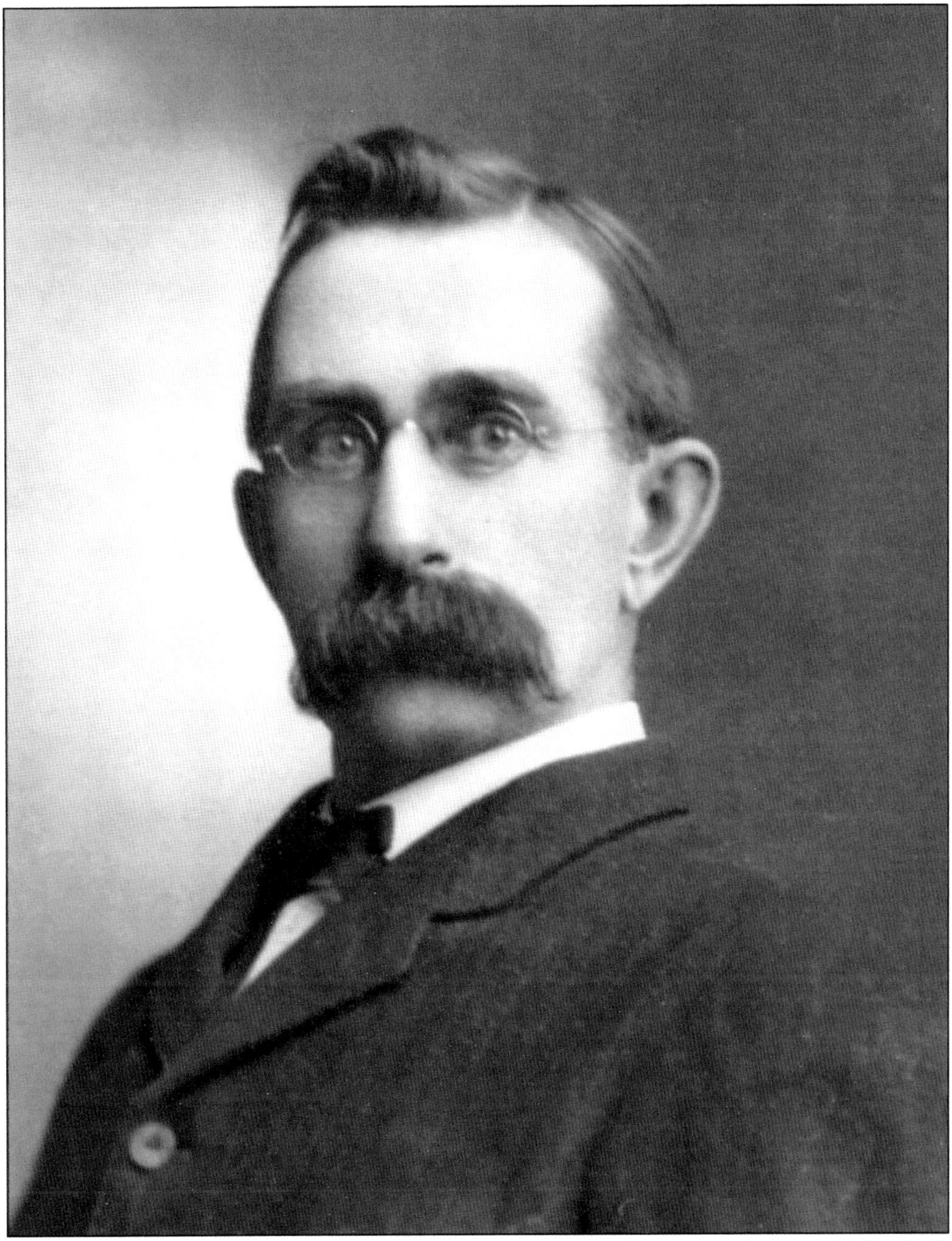

Cornelius Pieter "C.P." Schoon (1861–1941) married Stijntje "Susie" Van Reenen (1866–1949) on August 5, 1891. C.P. served as Munster's first town clerk and as the North Township assessor from 1890 to 1905. (Courtesy of the Munster Historical Society.)

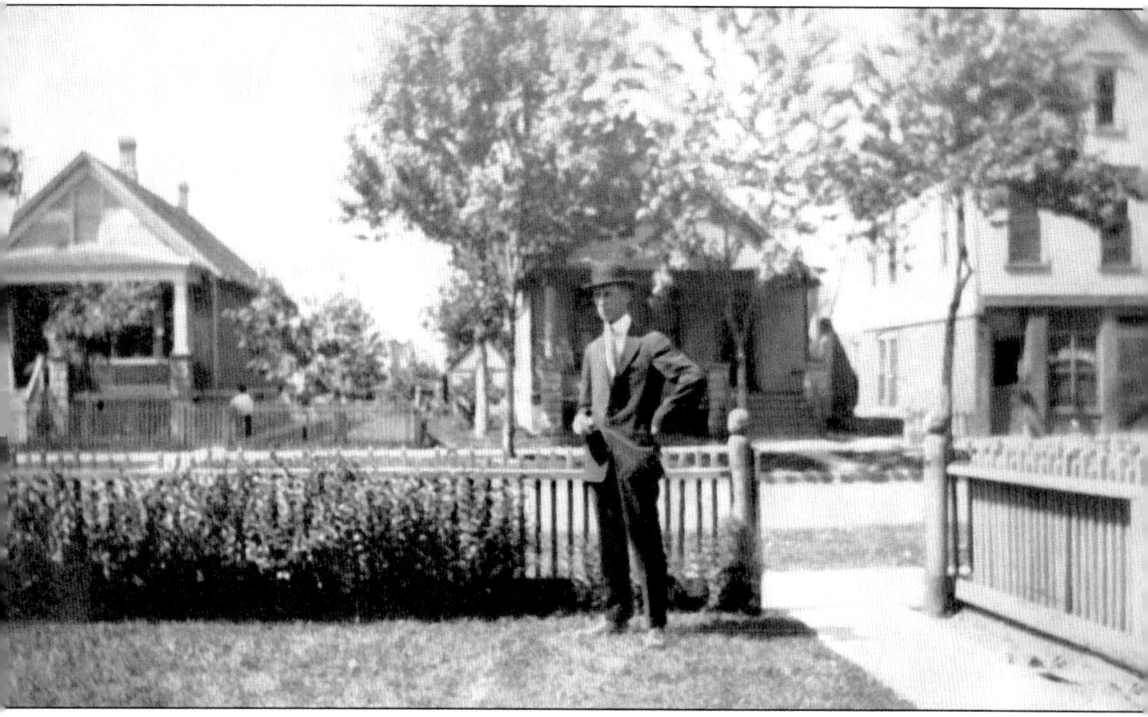

Joseph Eenigenburg Sr. stands in his yard on 109th Street in Roseland. During World War II, five of his sons—Joseph Jr., Theodore, Donald, Philip, and Paul—served in the armed forces. All five of them were employed as roofers at the Standard Roofing Company before the war interrupted their lives. Joseph Sr. served four years in the Navy before the outbreak of World War I. (Courtesy of Marie Eenigenburg Min.)

Three

Places and Things

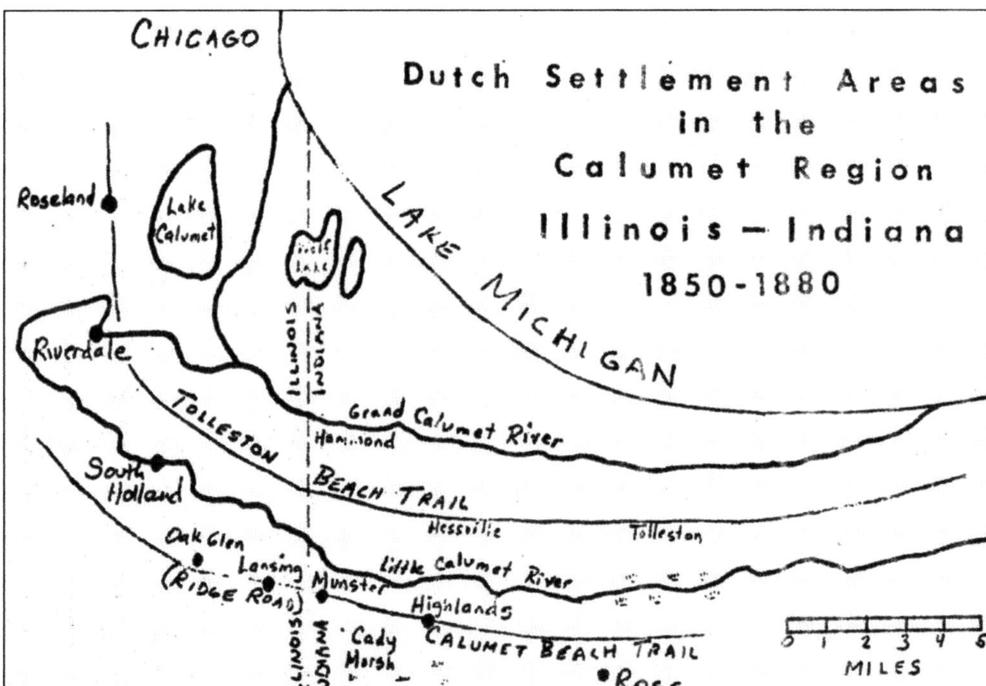

The Calumet region was settled by the Dutch in the 19th century. The area's loose boundary runs from what today is part of Chicago's South Side, to the western border of Griffith, Indiana, forming a Dutch crescent along the southern edge of Lake Michigan that includes the communities of Roseland, South Holland, Lansing, Munster, and Highland. (Courtesy of Kenneth J. Schoon.)

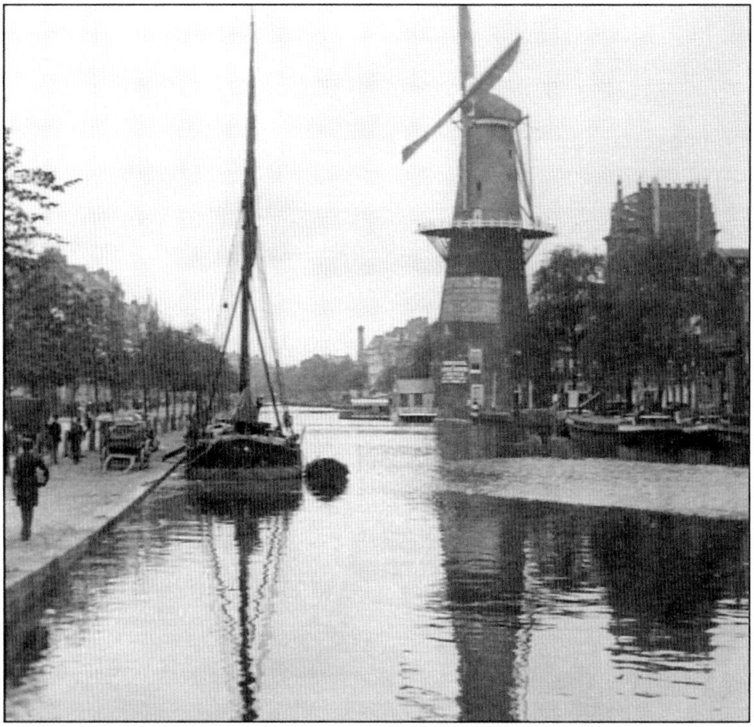

The travelers who would soon become the founders of Roseland, Illinois, loaded their belongings onto a Frisian barge on April 14, 1849, in preparation of the first leg of their journey to America. Being that the 15th was a Sunday, the group attended church and then boarded the barge to prepare for the early-morning start down the Dutch canals. (Courtesy of the Bult family collection.)

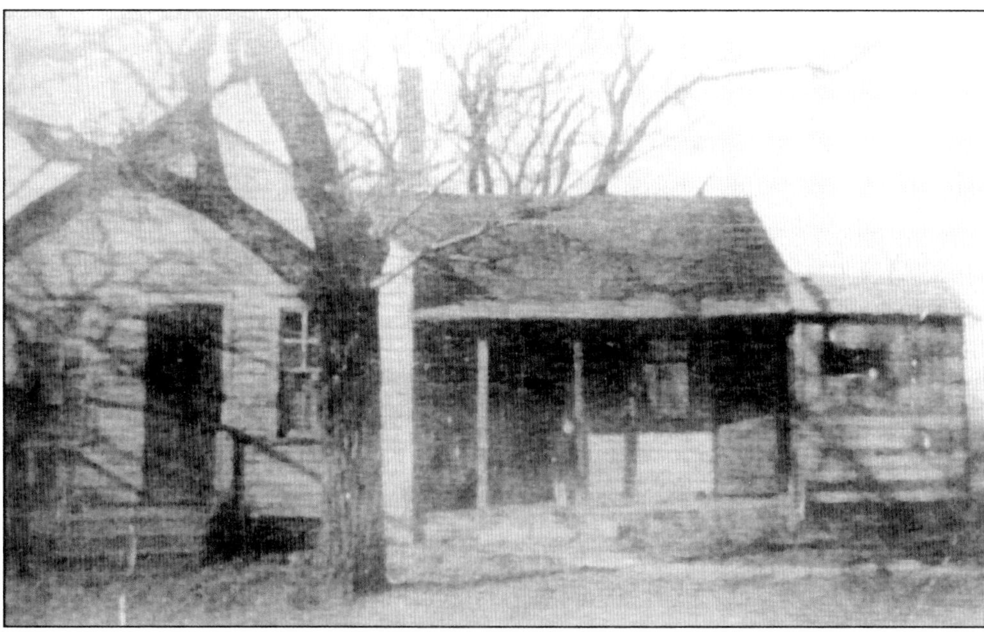

Hendrick De Jong's daughter, Engeltje, once recalled how her father had to walk in front of their oxcart as they made their way from Chicago to their new home, in order to break a path through the tall prairie grass. It has been said that the De Jong home (pictured) was built close enough to the river so that one could fish from the front porch. (Courtesy of the South Holland Historical Society.)

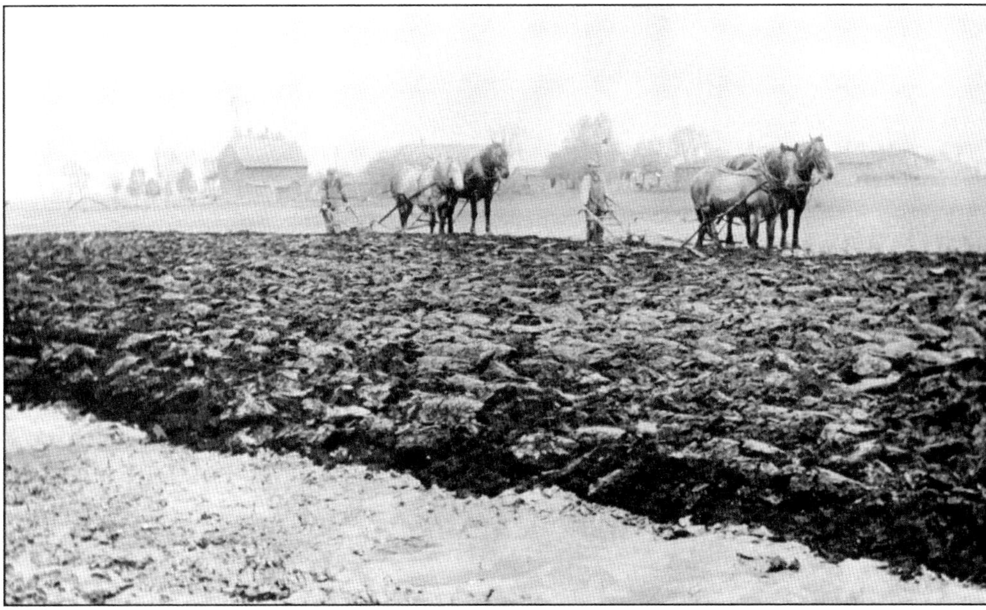

South Holland farms of 160 acres or more were hard to work and, as a result, were broken up into more manageable sizes, to be divided among the sons. A plot of 20 to 40 acres was the perfect size for truck farming. When there were no more parcels to be handed out, many Dutch sons moved east to Lansing and Munster. (Courtesy of the South Holland Historical Society.)

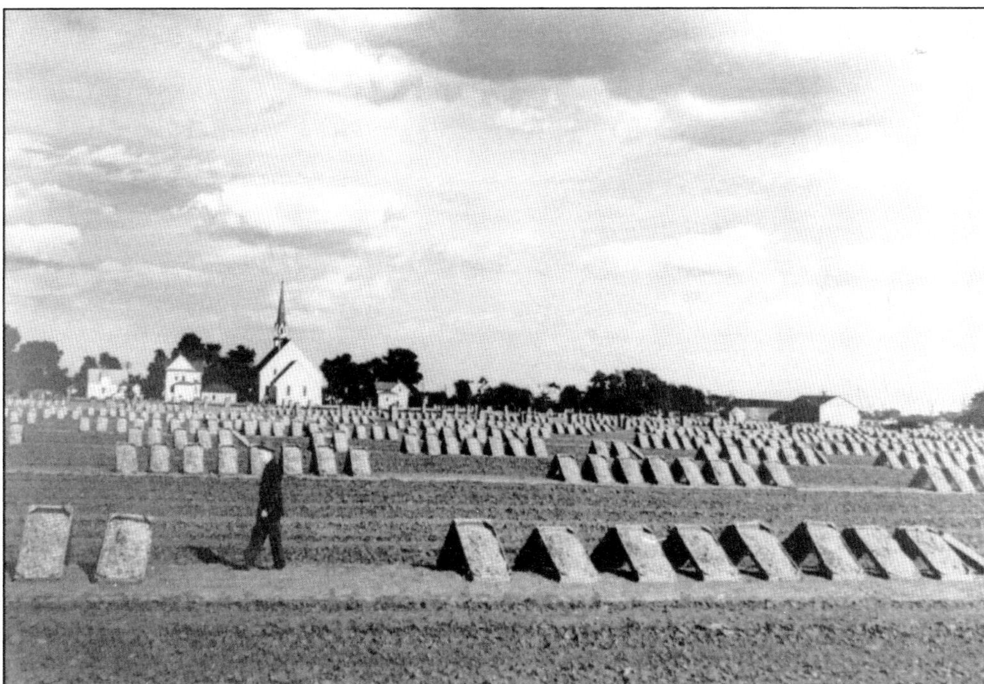

In this view looking east from the present-day site of South Holland's library, a crop of onion sets has been harvested and arranged to dry. South Holland was surrounded by onion fields for years. In the distance is the First Christian Reformed Church of South Holland, Illinois. (Courtesy of the South Holland Historical Society.)

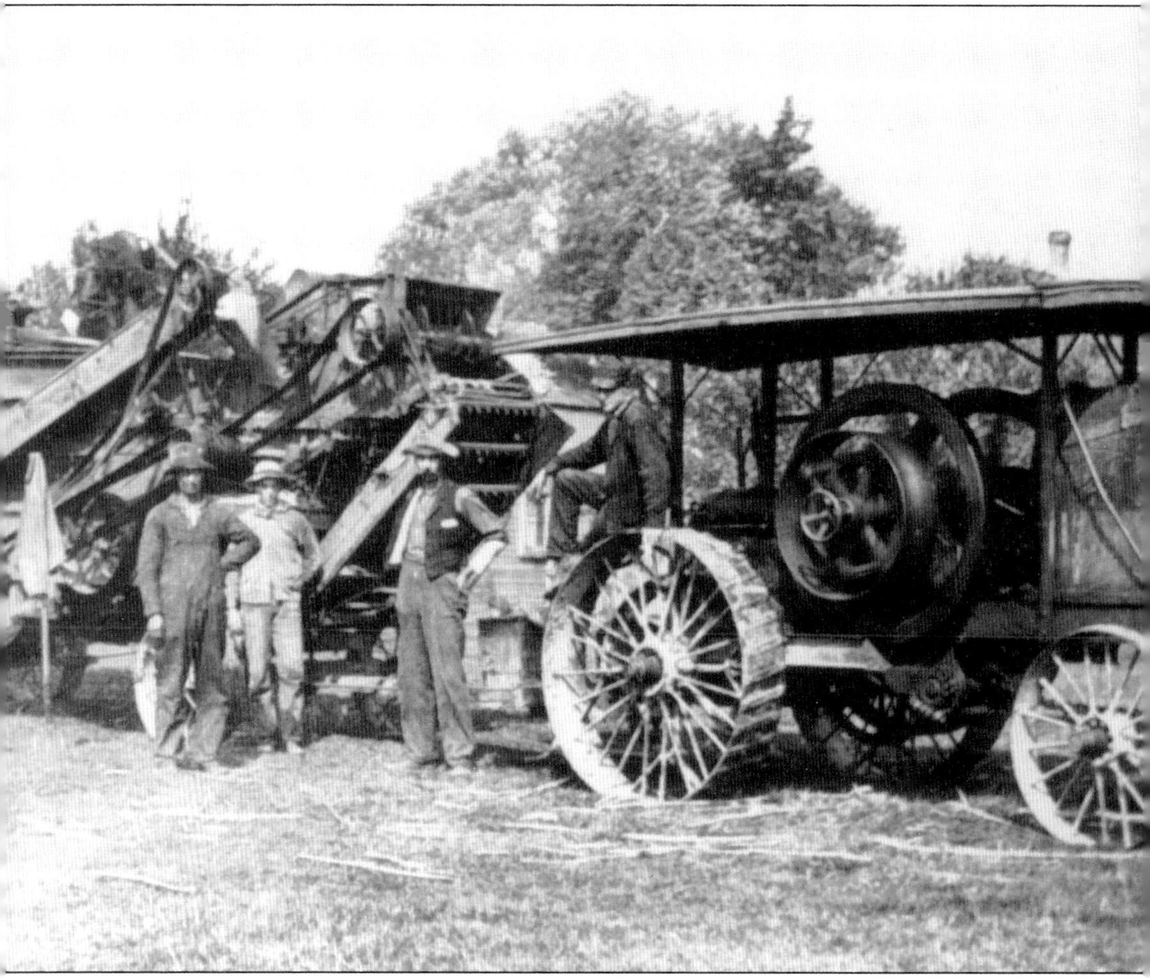

Roseland, Illinois, Pella, Iowa, and Holland, Michigan, along with South Holland, all started out as Dutch farming communities at about the same time. The first three communities became more industrial-based much earlier than did South Holland. The church, a unifying factor within South Holland at this time, is a major part of its unique history. (Courtesy of the South Holland Historical Society.)

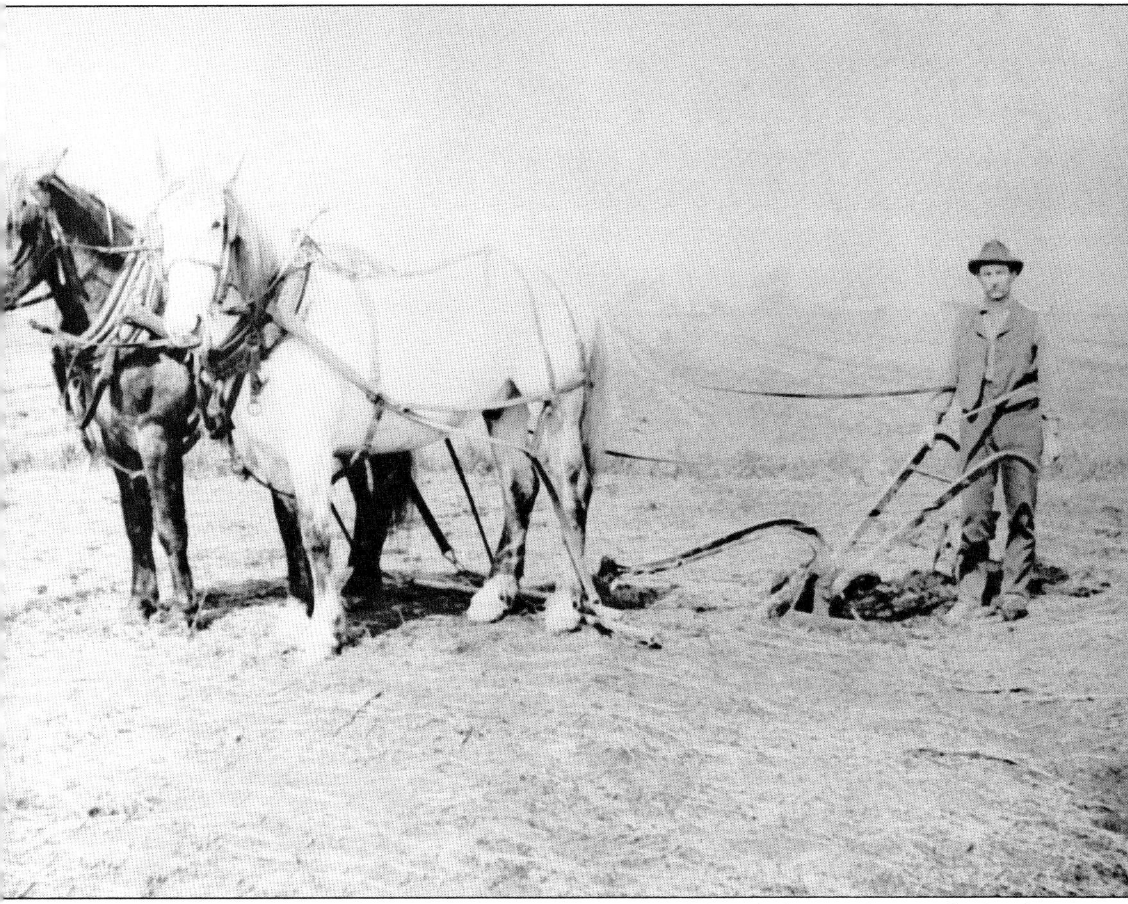

For the Holland colony that Albertus van Raalte (1811–1874) founded in Michigan, the land needed clearing before it could be farmed. Much of the Calumet region, however, was ready for the plow. Teams of oxen were used at first, but they were later replaced with horses. It seems that the oxen did not understand Dutch. (Courtesy of the South Holland Historical Society.)

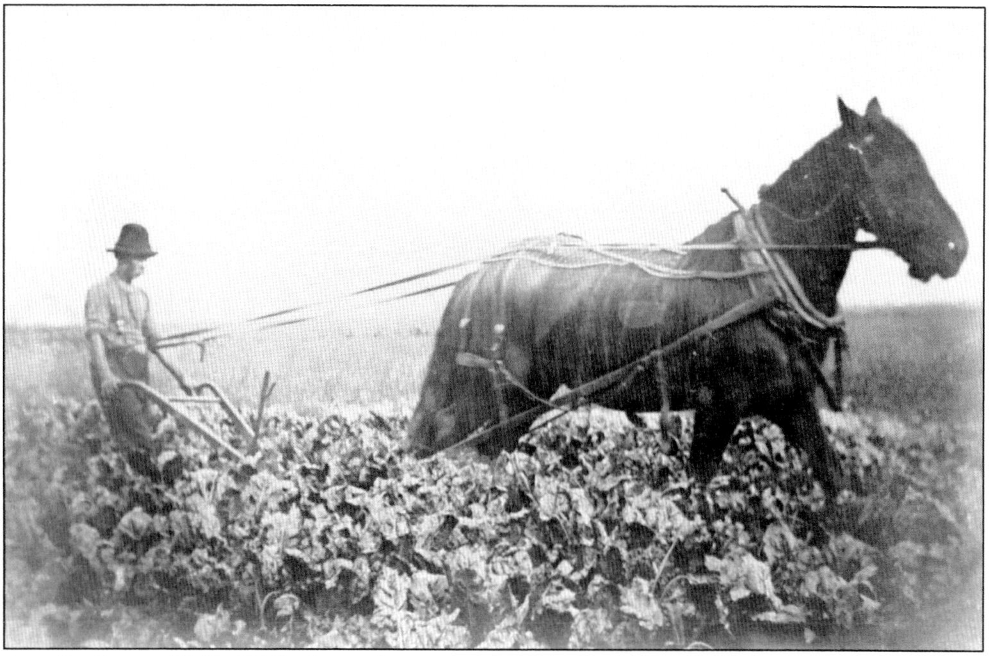

Arie De Ruiter (1858–1942), shown here at work on his South Holland farm, married Jannegje Rietveld (1860–1936) on October 5, 1880. His parents were among the group that came from Giessendam, Zuid-Holland, in 1848 with Rev. Willem Coenran Wust. Also accompanying Reverend Wust to Illinois were the families of Jakob De Vries and Roel Van Vuren. (Courtesy of the South Holland Historical Society.)

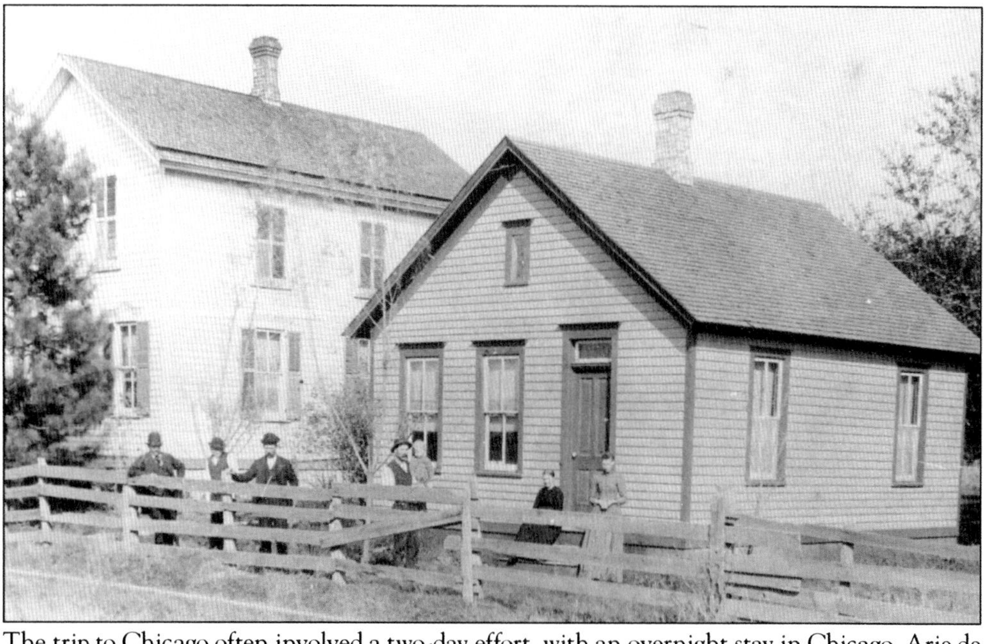

The trip to Chicago often involved a two-day effort, with an overnight stay in Chicago. Arie de Ruiter, whose home is shown here, became confused as to what day of the week it was and arrived back in South Holland as his neighbors were going to church. As can be imagined, this did not sit well with the church elders. (Courtesy of the South Holland Historical Society.)

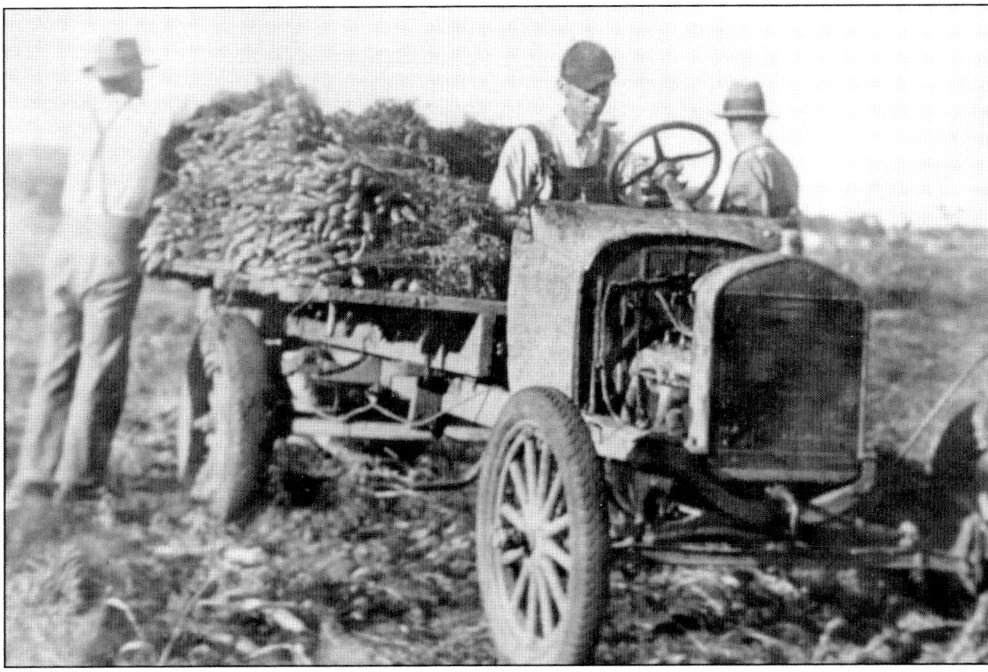

E.K. Leep (1876–1958), seen here at left, harvests carrots on his farm in Highland, Indiana. E.K. was born in Sint Annaparochie, Friesland. He was the second of eight children of Klaas Leep and Klaaske Prins. He came to the United States in 1893 and married Jennie Devries (1879–1924) in Chicago on May 8, 1902. (Courtesy of the Calvin College Archives.)

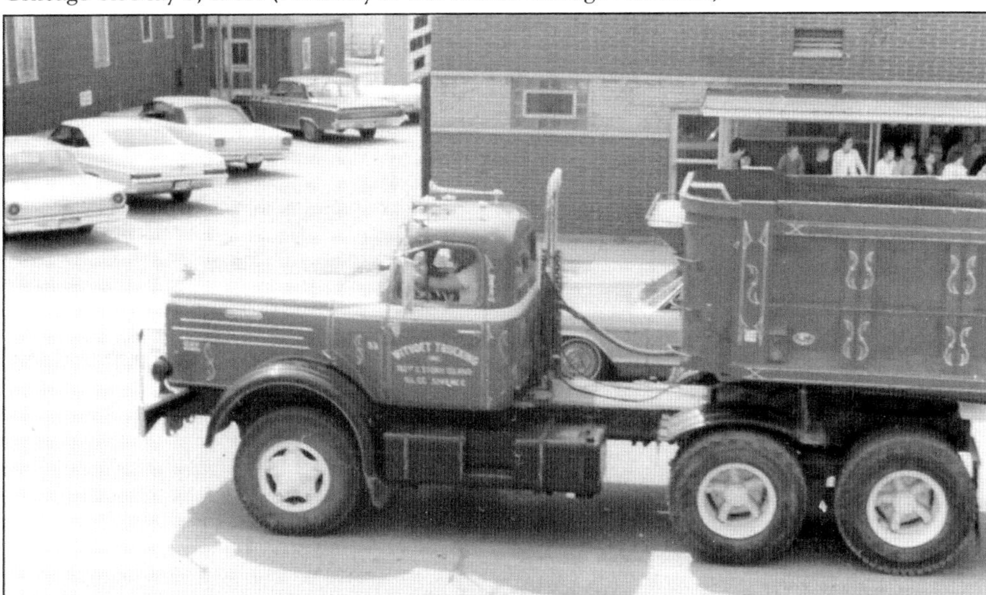

A truck from the Witvoet Trucking fleet rolls down Torrence Avenue in Lansing during a parade. Witvoet Trucking was started by brothers Gerrit (1901–1989) and Boyd Witvoet (1905–1993) in 1946. Gerrit met his wife, Irene Mossell (1904–1994), on the Hoxie Farm, where both of their families were living at the time. Boyd married Sadie Ooms (1910–1976) on August 29, 1929. (Photograph by Donald Henry Bult.)

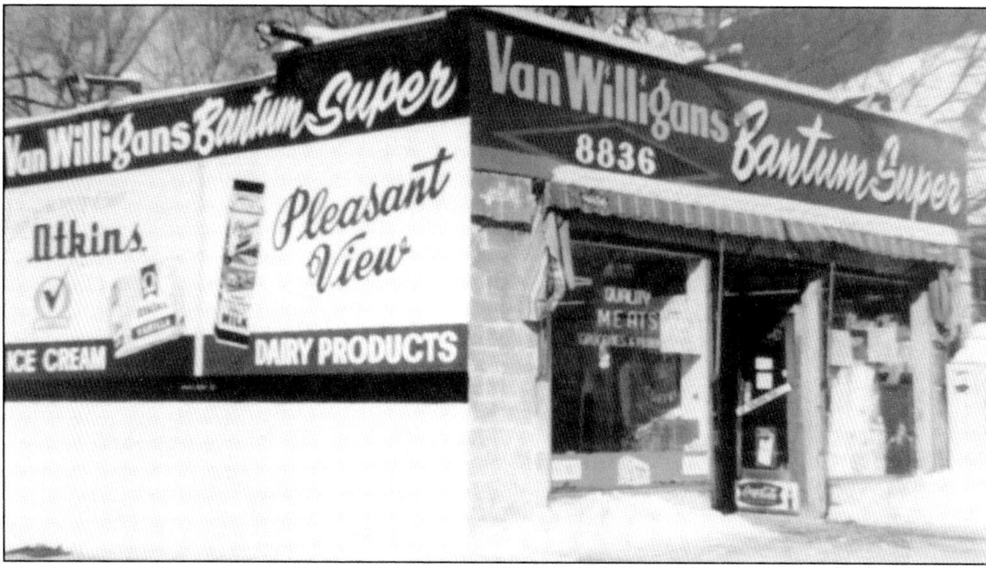

The Van Willigans Bantum store was built in 1947 by John Van Willigan (1911–1970) and his brother-in-law Martin Elzinga (1908–1996). It stood on the corner of Lincoln Street and Kennedy Avenue in Highland. This photograph, taken in 1963, shows the rebuilt storefront that was necessary after a 1958 fire. (Courtesy of the Highland Historical Society.)

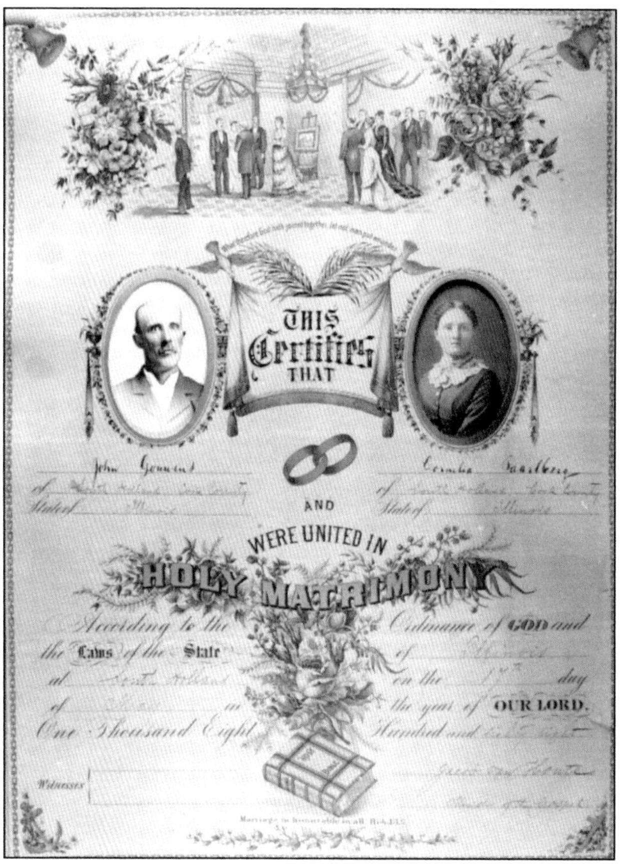

John Gouwens (1864–1945) and Cornelia Paarlberg (1866–1934) were married on May 19, 1888. John's father, Cornelis Pieters Gouwens (1827–1891), arrived in New York from Lekkerkerk, Nederlek, Zuid-Holland, on July 5, 1848, and made his way to South Holland, Illinois, where he met and married Cornelia Ravesloot (1833–1901). (Courtesy of the South Holland Historical Society.)

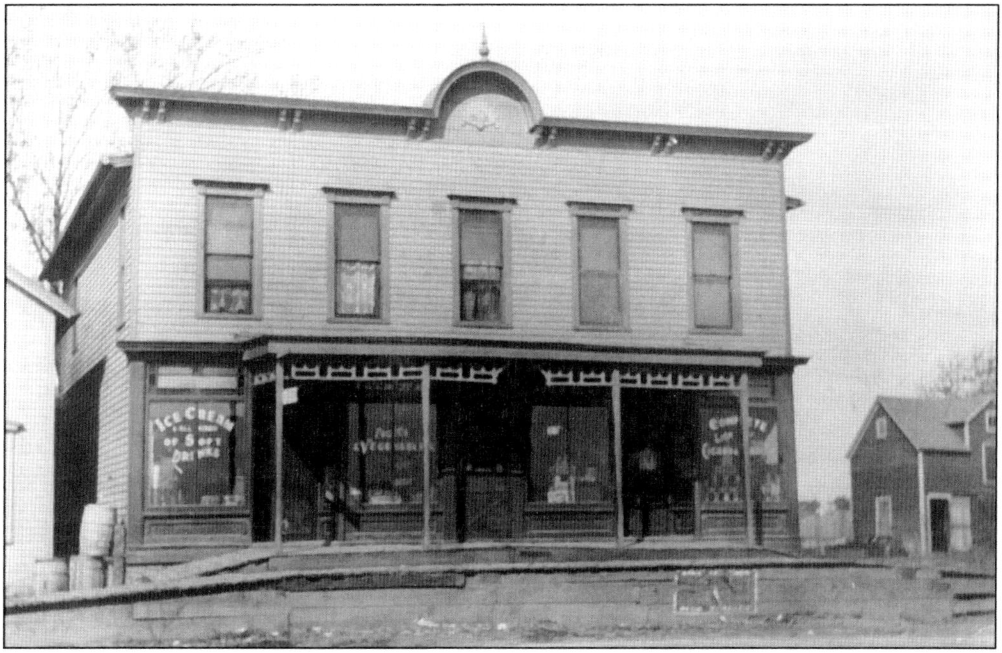

On September 10, 1873, Arie Baardwijk (1840–1915) obtained a grocer's license; the store he opened, Baardwijk's, remained in business until 1946. This photograph shows the Baardwijk store as it looked in the early 1900s. Arie was married to the former Jannigje Jonker (1842–1926). (Courtesy of the South Holland Historical Society.)

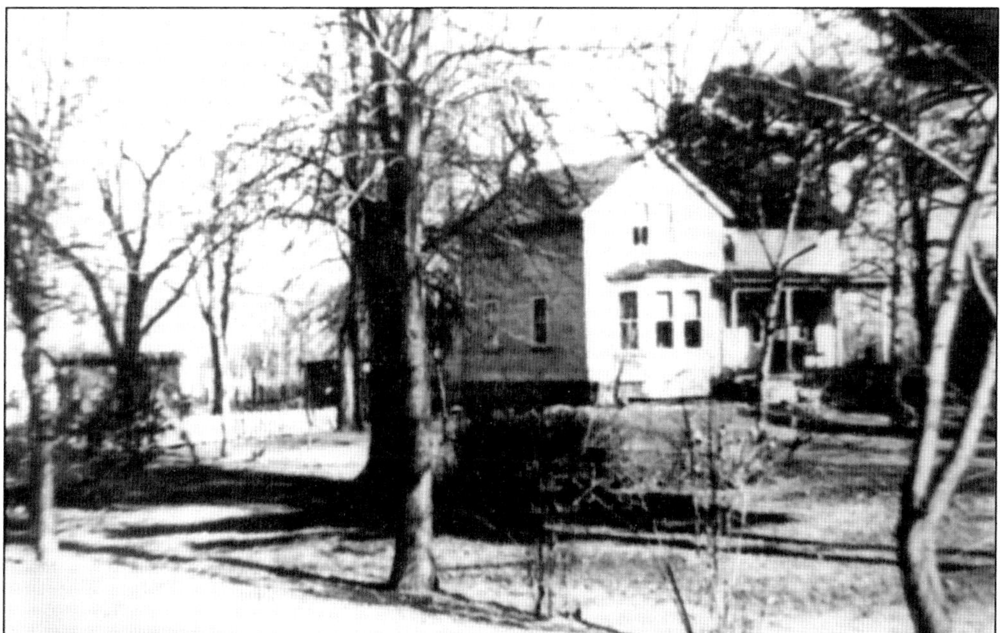

Eldert Monster arrived from the Netherlands on July 5, 1855, with his second wife, Neiltje, three children from his first marriage, and his new in-laws, Antonie and Jannigje Bouman. In 1860, the Monsters Americanized their name to Munster. Shown here is the Munster home, which was located on Ridge Road. (Courtesy of the Munster Historical Society.)

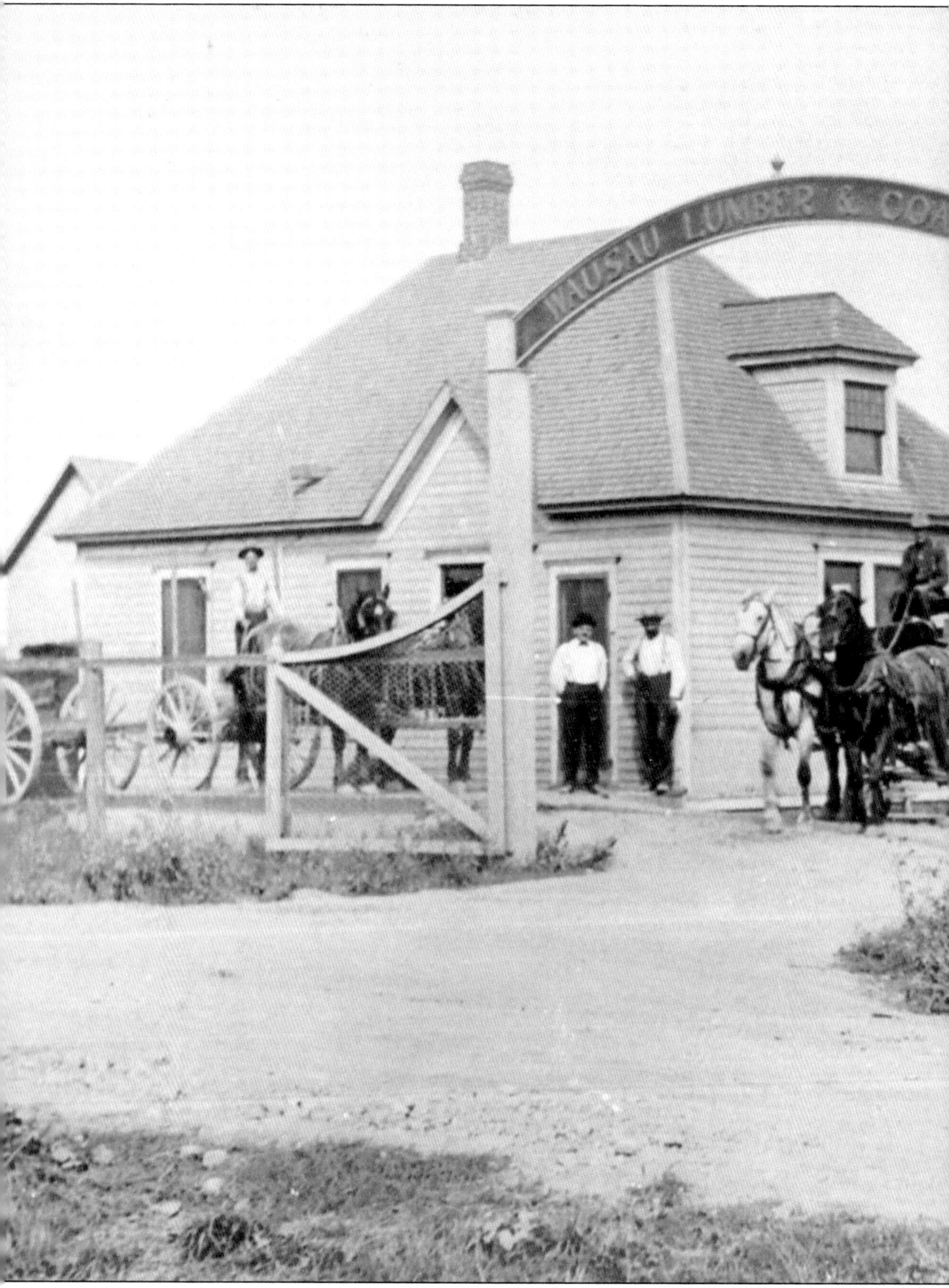
WAUSAU LUMBER & COA

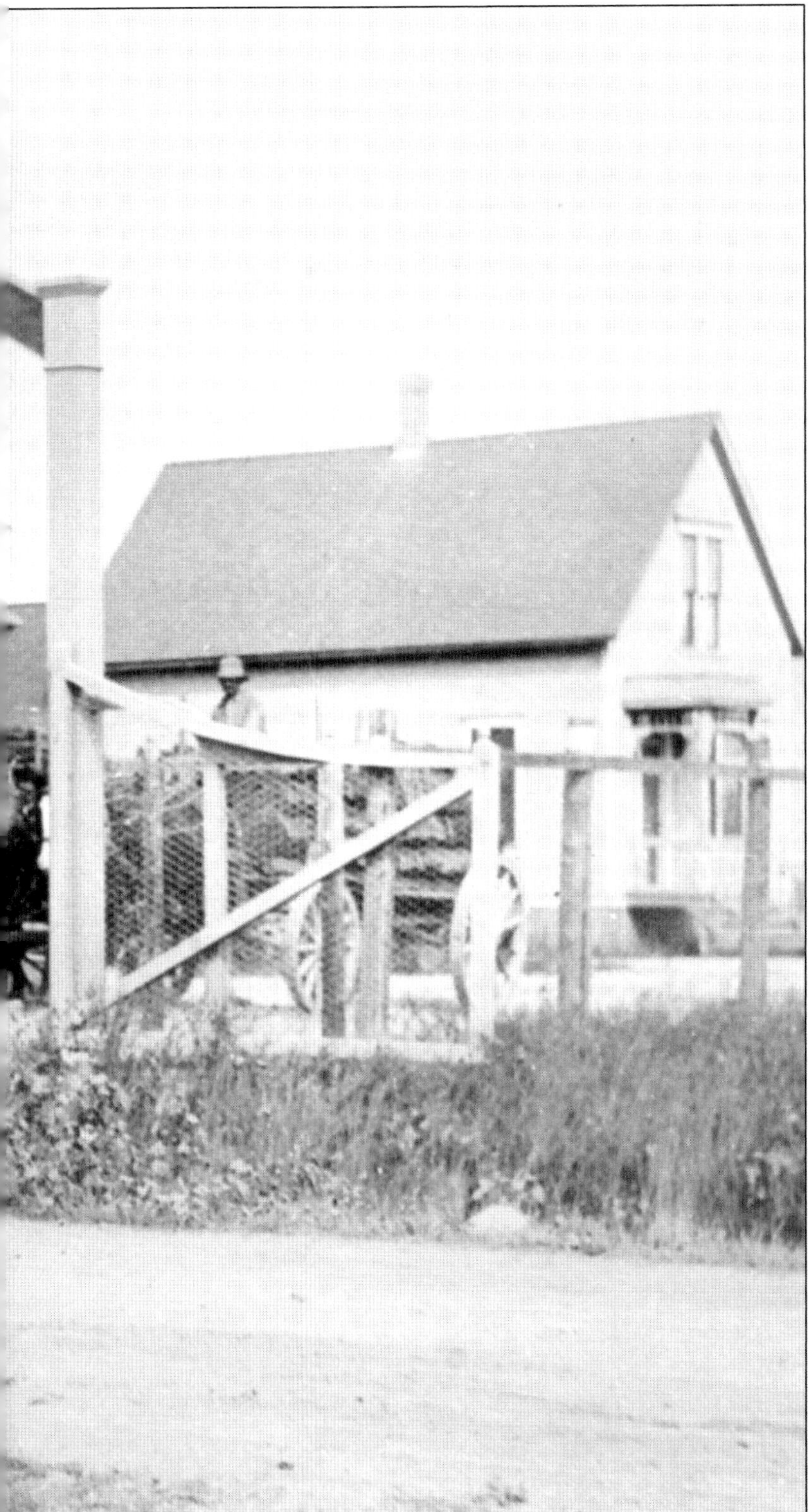

Wausau Lumber & Coal was founded in 1882 as the John Schilling Lumber Company by a group of South Holland investors. In 1895, John L. Vinke founded his coal company, and the two companies merged in 1900 under the Schilling name. In 1902, the Wausau Lumber Company of Harvey, Illinois, was purchased, and the name was changed to Wausau Lumber & Coal. In 1905, the Harvey yard was sold to the Chicago-Riverdale Lumber Company. In 1917, John L. Vinke bought the controlling interest from his associates. Wausau Lumber & Coal is still in business in South Holland, at 236 East 161st Place. (Courtesy of the South Holland Historical Society.)

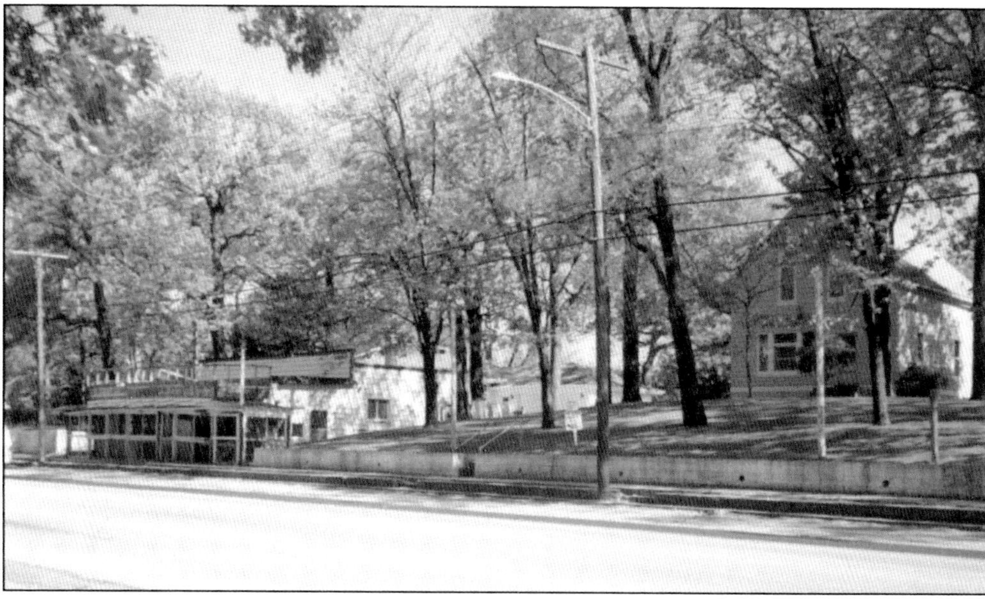

The Vander Molen homestead and farm stand was located at 2024/26 Ridge Road, across from Wicker Park in Highland. David and Jeanete Vander Molen originally lived there; later, Reinder and Kate Vander Molen bought the house and lived there. They operated the farm stand in the summer and sold Christmas trees seasonally. (Courtesy of the Highland Historical Society.)

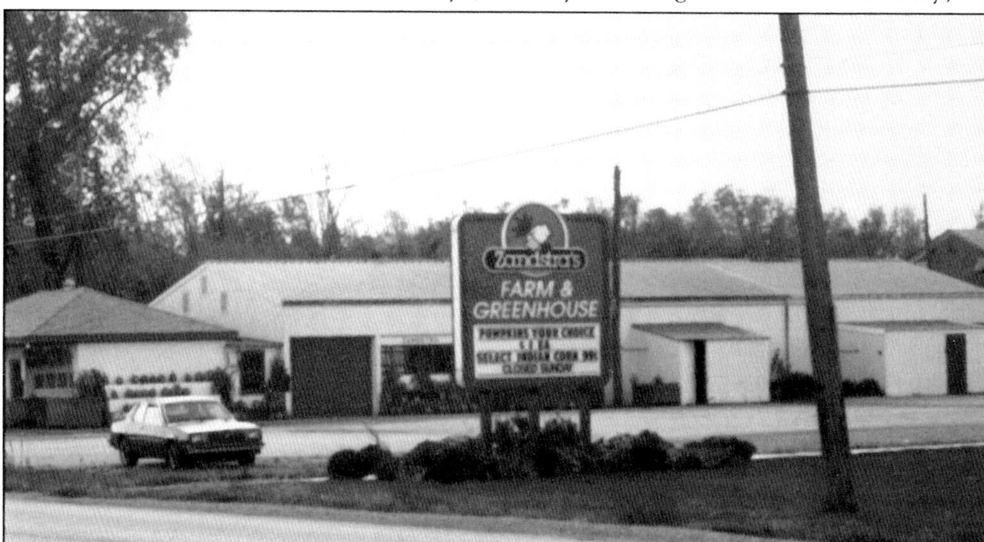

Bartel Hanzes Zandstra arrived from Friesland, the Netherlands, on March 21, 1889. After living for some time in Roseland and then in Thornton, Zandstra began farming vegetables in Highland. Today, Zandstra's Greenhouse, located at 10202 Kennedy Avenue in Highland, is run by his descendants. It has one of the largest greenhouses in Northwest Indiana, with more than two acres of space. (Courtesy of the Highland Historical Society.)

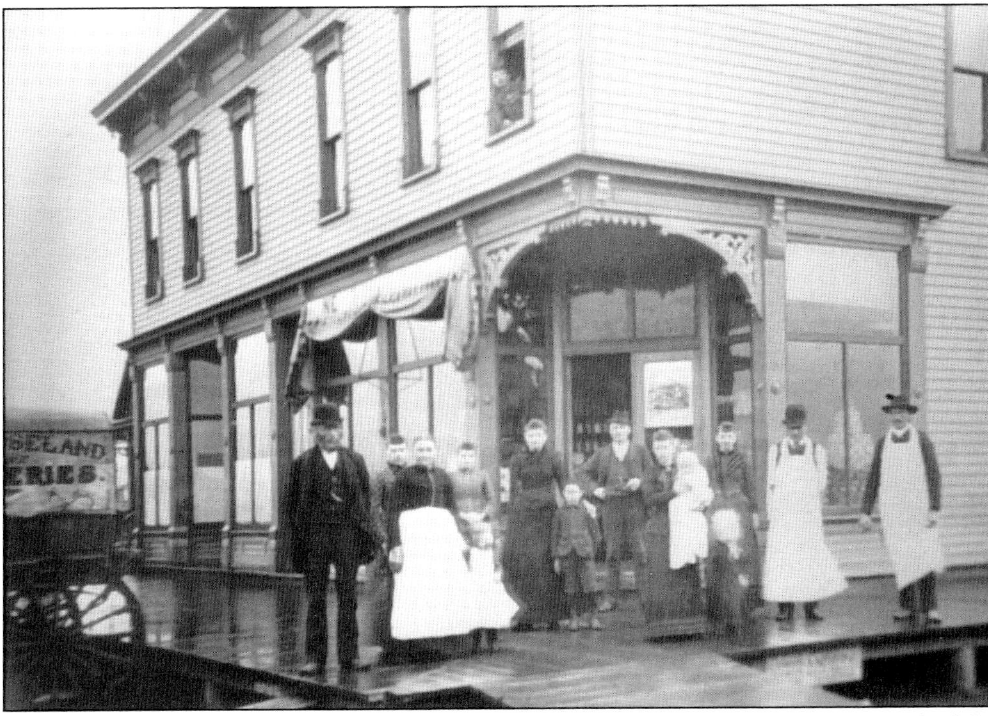

The West Roseland Grocery Store, located at Wentworth Avenue and 109th Street, was built by Pieter Bult and his sons. Seen in this photograph, two of his sons, Henry (far right) and Frank (second from right), worked as butchers in the store. The upstairs apartments were occupied by members of the family, including Pieter and his wife, Petronella, their daughter Diwertje "Delia," and her husband, Alla Van Alsberg. Also living there were Henry and his wife, Hillegonda "Alice," and their small child Petronella, who would marry Peter Boonstra in 1911. (Courtesy of the Bult family collection.)

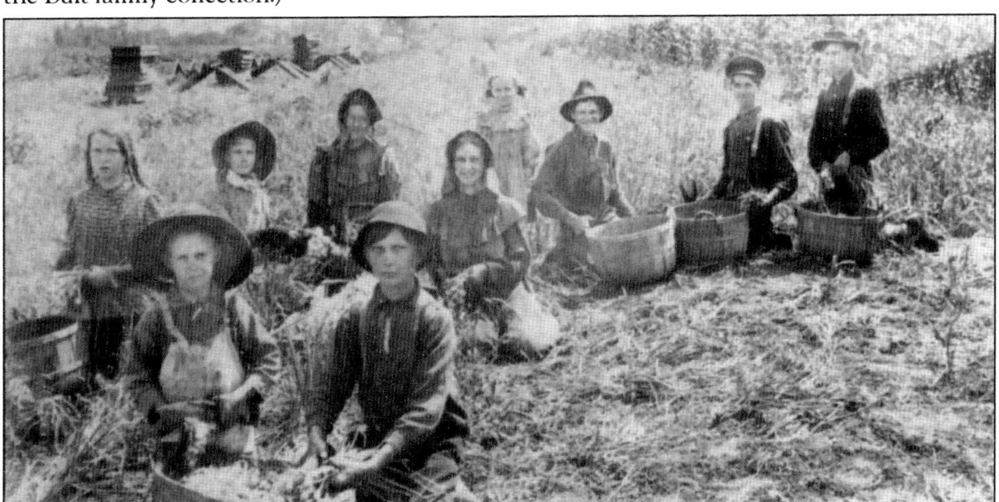

The founders of Munster built their houses on the ridge and farmed the land between the ridge and the Little Calumet River. Many garden crops were grown, especially cabbage and onions, the smell of which was common to the region well into the 20th century, as the Schoon and Jansen children shown here could attest. (Courtesy of the Munster Historical Society.)

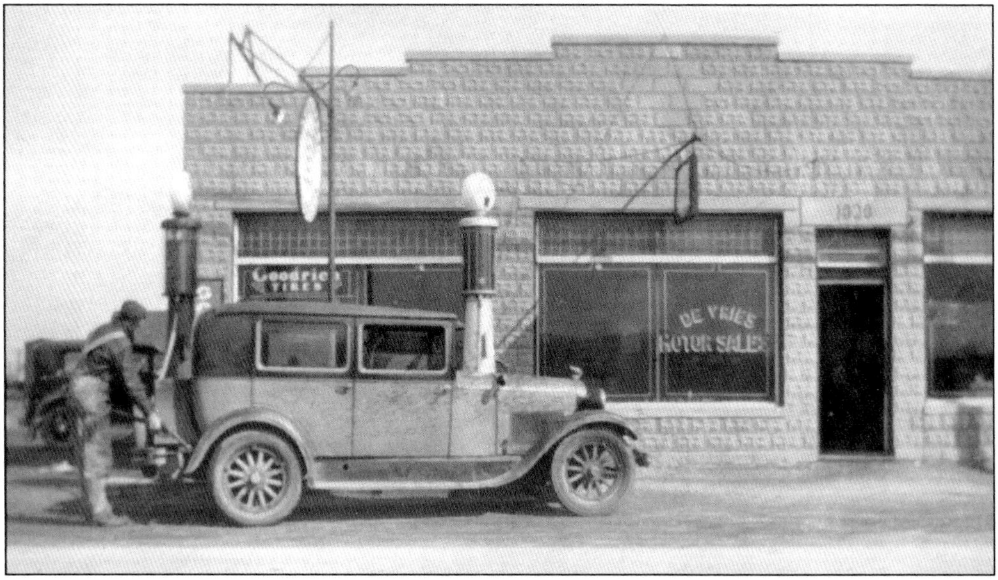

This building, housing De Vries Motor Sales, was built in 1928 by Harry Olthoff and Henry Rietvelt. It was located on 159th Street, just east of the Chicago & Eastern Illinois Railroad tracks. (Courtesy of the South Holland Historical Society.)

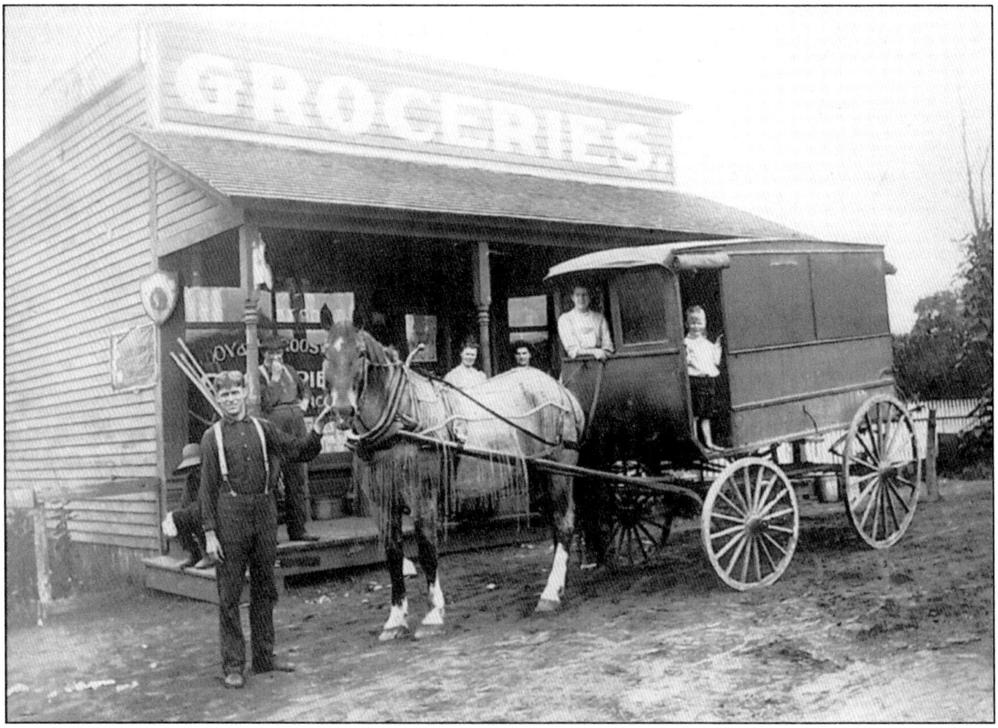

In this c. 1905 photograph, Peter J. Kooy stands in front of the grocery store he built in 1904. The building is still located at 2813 Jewett Street in Highland, Indiana. It later became the Cloverdale Grocery and, as of 2014, was still in use as the Primitive Peddler Gift Shop. Peter's grandparents, Peter and Gertrude Kooy, settled in the region in 1855. (Courtesy of the Highland Historical Society.)

This store was owned by Peter De Young and, later, his son Henry (pictured). It was located near present-day 16000 South Park Avenue. The building was later moved to Route 6, west of 16000 South Park Avenue, and was known as Speyer's Store. (Courtesy of the South Holland Historical Society.)

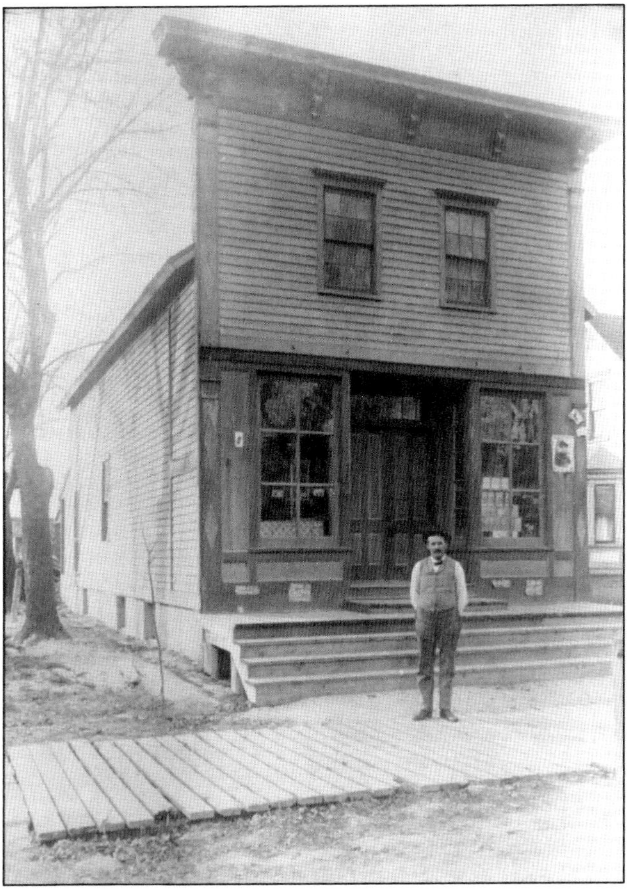

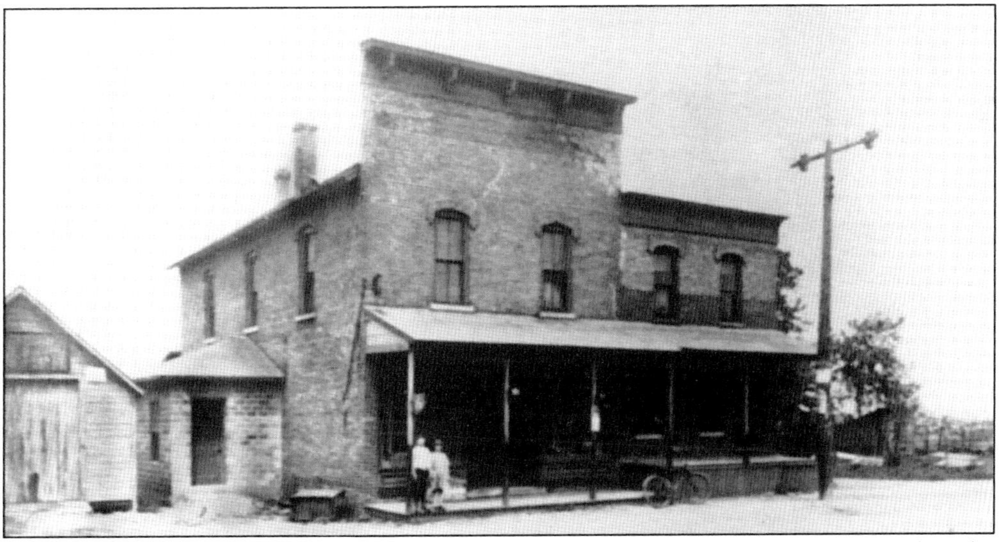

The Klootwyk General Store is shown here as it looked in 1905. The business was located on the left side, and the Klootwyk home is on the right. The Klootwyk children, Peter and Mary, can be seen standing in the front of the store. As of 2014, the building was still standing at 619 Ridge Road in Munster, Indiana. (Courtesy of the Munster Historical Society.)

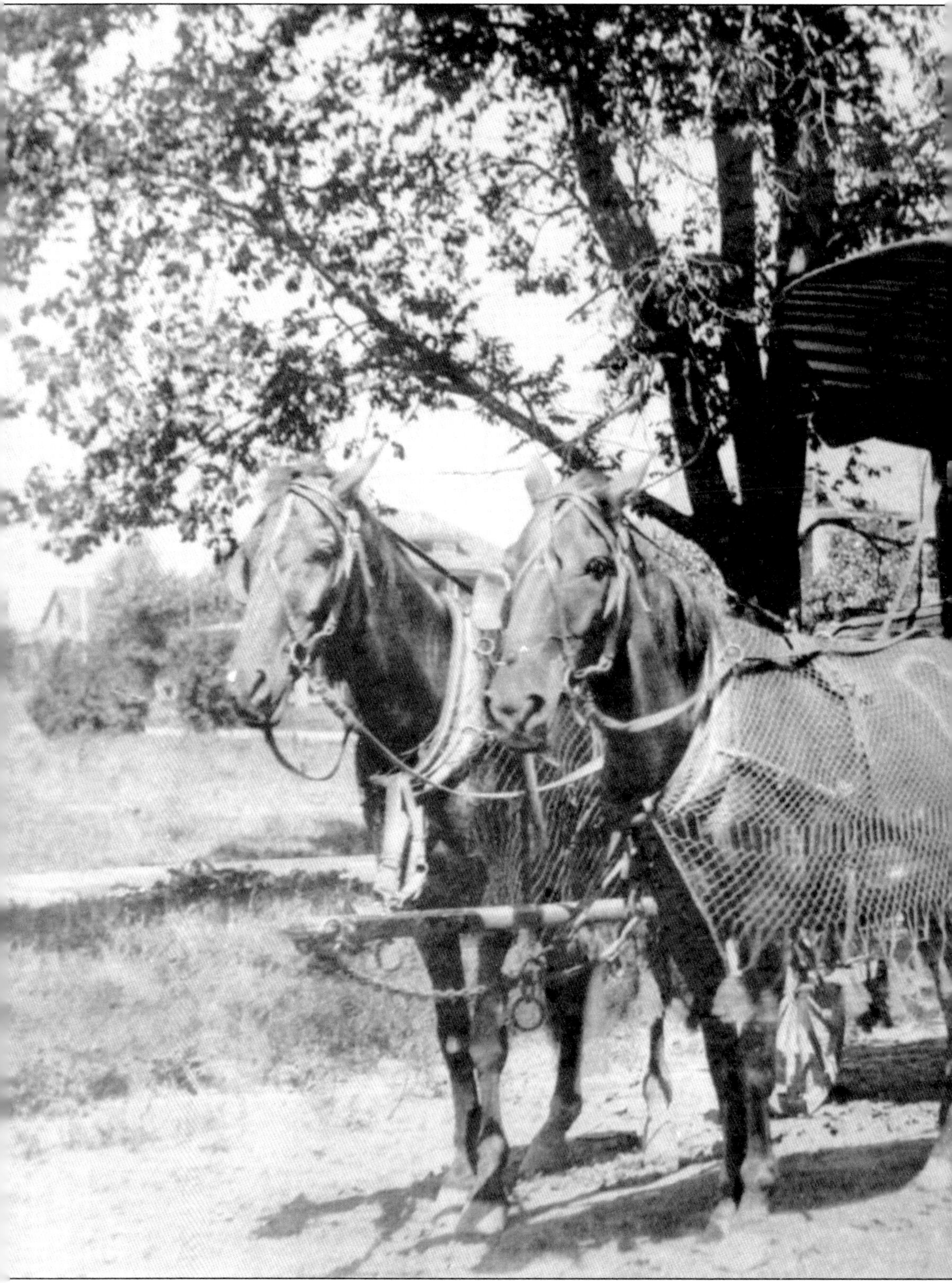

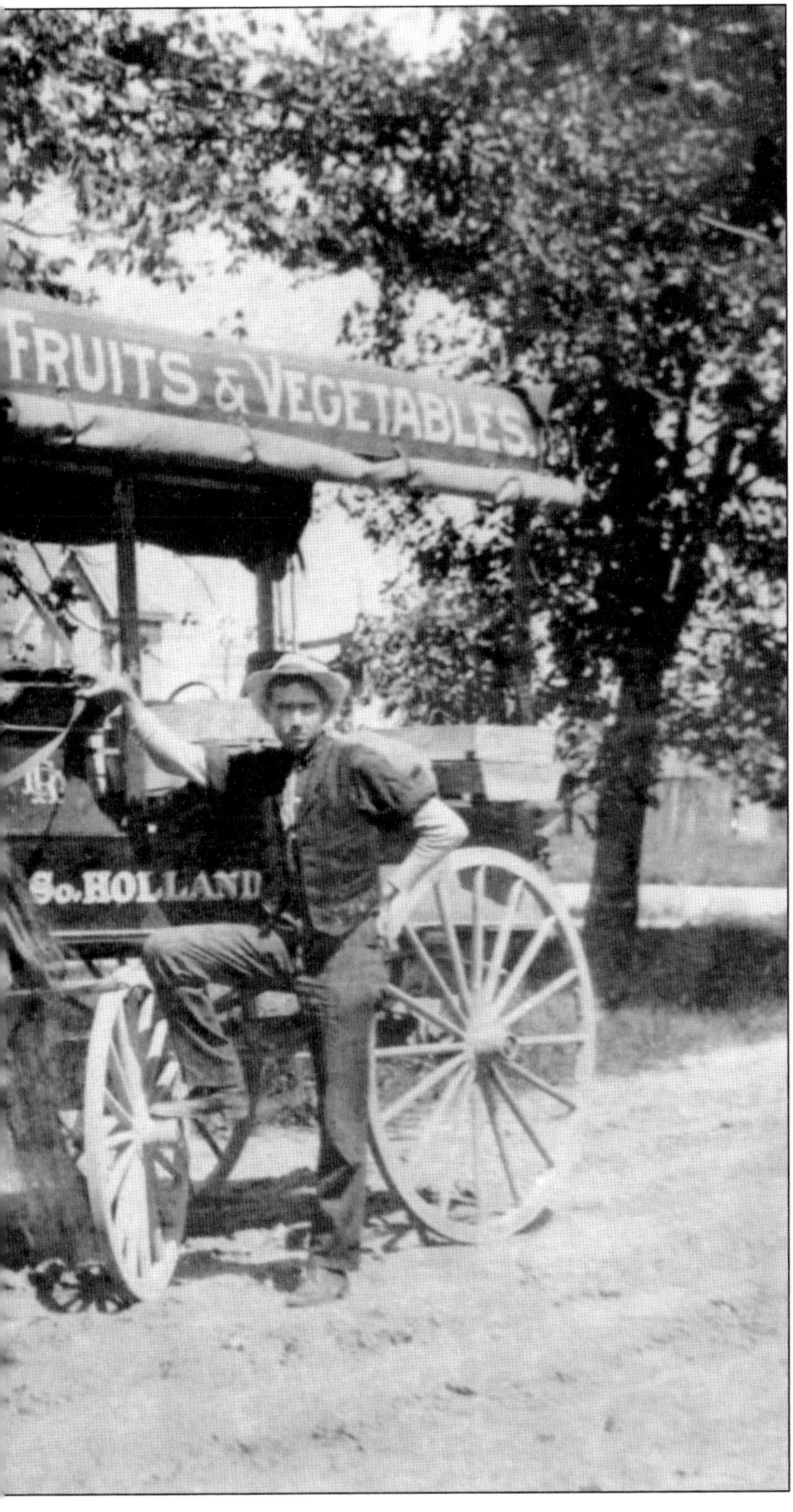

Dave Rinkema is ready for a day of peddling fruits and vegetables in the industrial towns south of Chicago. Note the fly nets on the horses. As the horses walked, the tassels moved, chasing the flies away. (Courtesy of the South Holland Historical Society.)

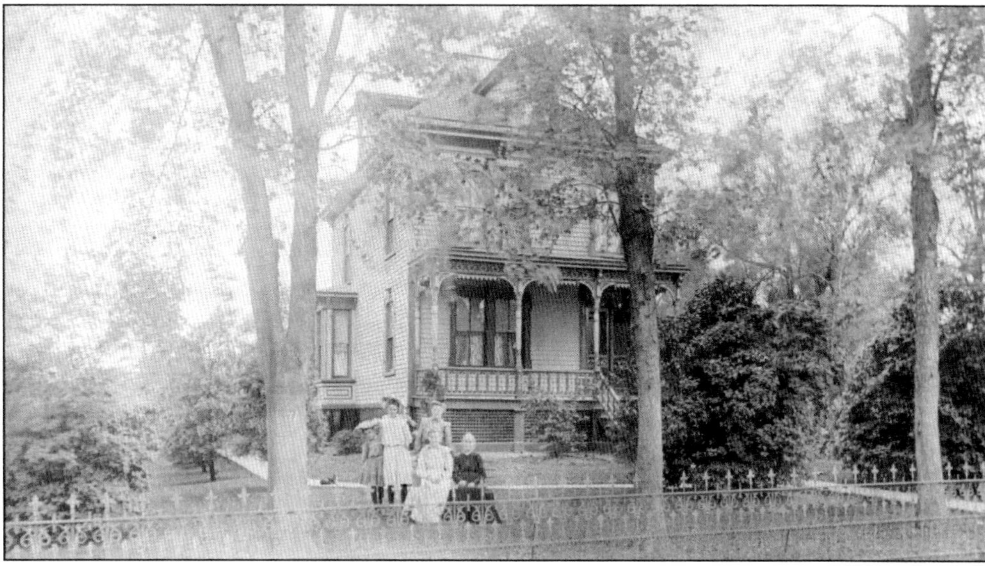

The home of Goris Van der Sijde (1828–1909) was located on the southwest corner of 111th and State Streets in Roseland. Goris was born in Numansdorp, Zuid-Holland, and came to the United States with his family in 1849. In 1860, the area's first post office opened in his store. (Courtesy of the South Holland Historical Society.)

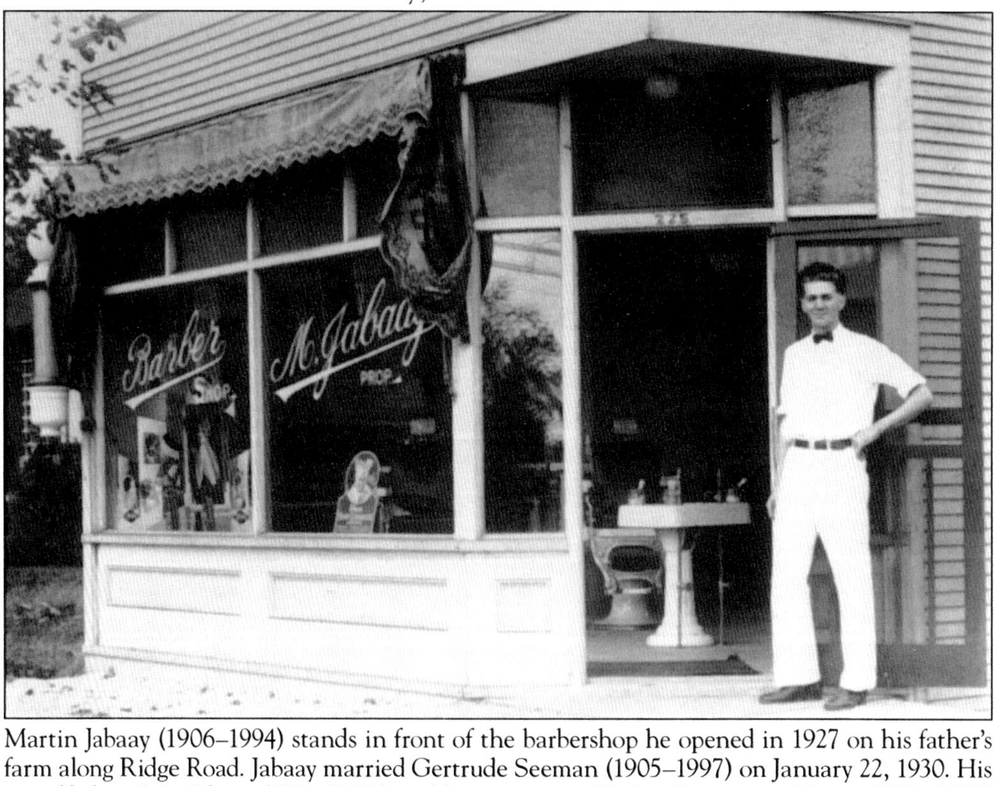

Martin Jabaay (1906–1994) stands in front of the barbershop he opened in 1927 on his father's farm along Ridge Road. Jabaay married Gertrude Seeman (1905–1997) on January 22, 1930. His grandfather Arie Jabaay (1818–1900) and his great-grandfather Dingeman Jabaay (1796–1872) were among the first of Munster's Dutch settlers, in 1855. The original Dutch spelling of their name was Jabaaij. (Courtesy of the Munster Historical Society.)

Much of Munster was swampland before real estate speculator Aaron Hart discovered the art of ditch digging. Hart had acquired 20,000 acres of wetlands property in and around present-day Munster. With hand shovels and a plow, Hart and his crew dug a ditch from the swampland south of the ridge, through the ridge, to the Little Calumet River, which drained the marsh and created some of the best farmland in the region. Hart's Ditch still flows along Munster's eastern edge. (Courtesy of the Munster Historical Society.)

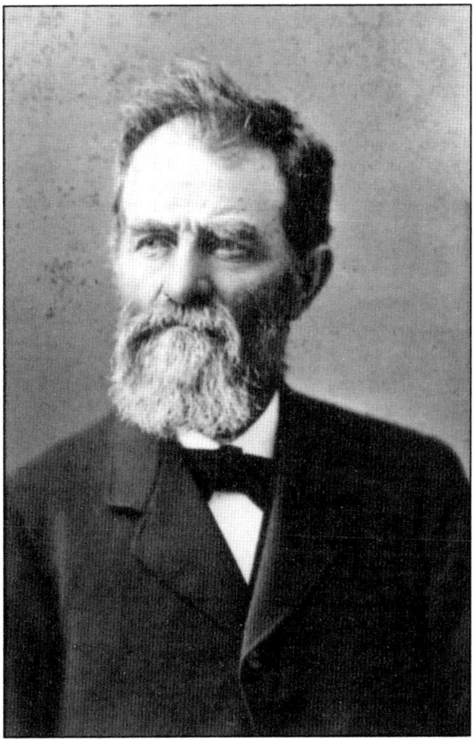

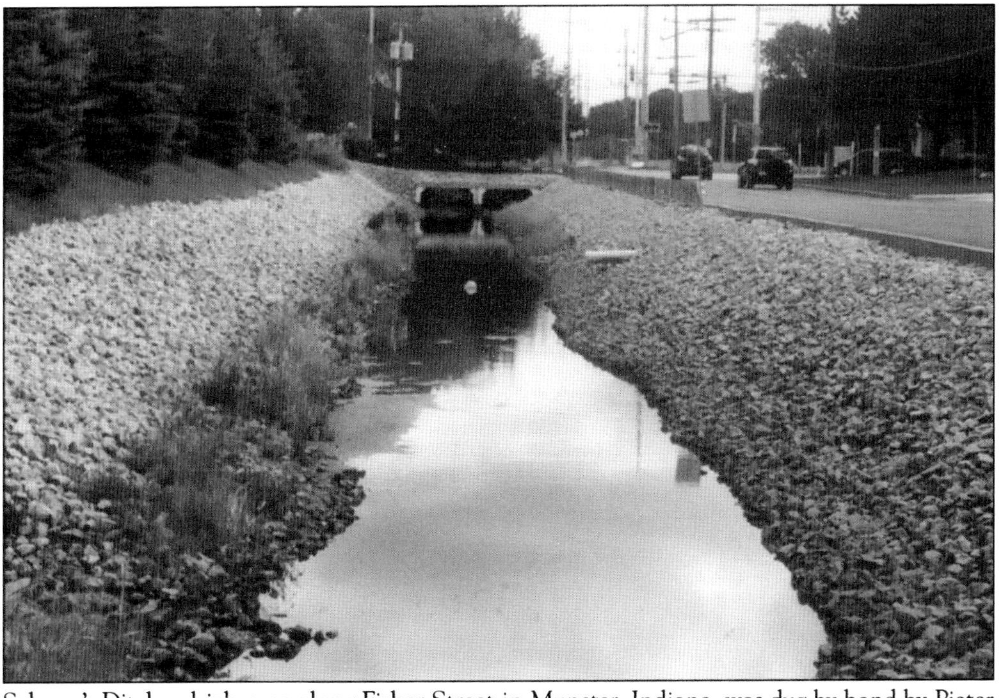

Schoon's Ditch, which runs along Fisher Street in Munster, Indiana, was dug by hand by Pieter Schoon and his sons. Going north, the ditch connects with Hart's Ditch. Schoon's Ditch still drains much of southwestern side of Munster today, including the land occupied by Munster High School and the hospital. (Photograph by the author.)

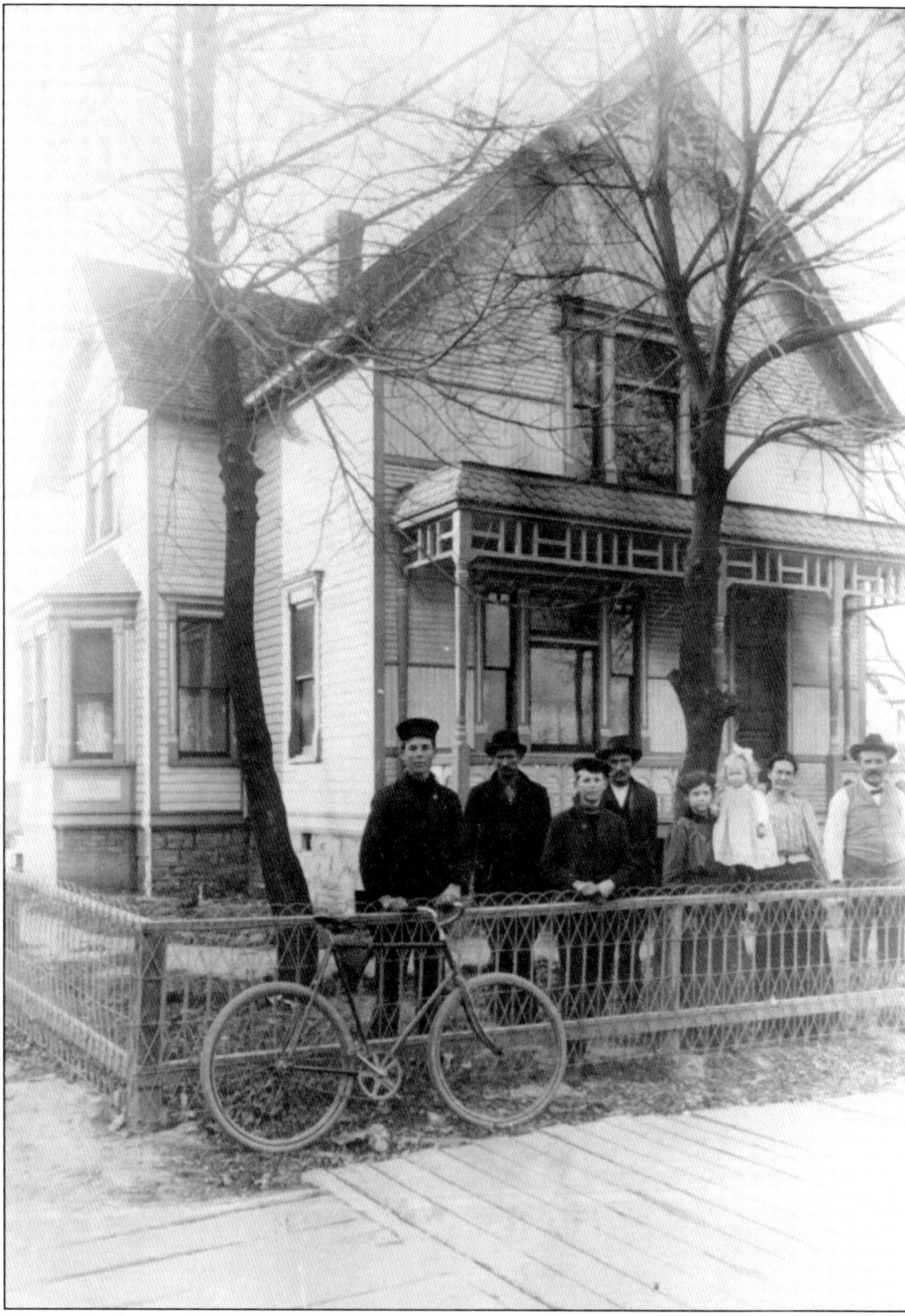

This is the home of Mr. and Mrs. Henry P. De Young. Henry (1865–1914) married Johanna Cornelisdr Tanis (1865–1939) on April 8, 1886. The couple is standing on the far right in this photograph. Their son Peter is on the far left, and son Dirk is third from the left. (Courtesy of the South Holland Historical Society.)

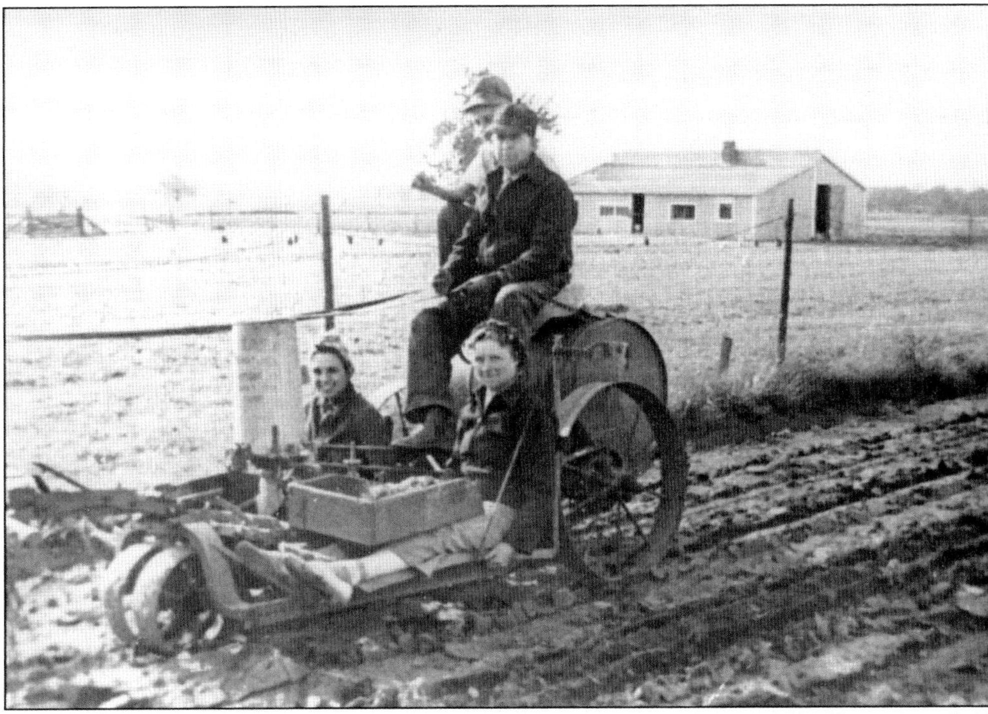

Peter Van der Griend (1886–1952) is planting tomatoes with son Robert and daughters Cora (left) and Carrie (right). Peter married Maaike "Maude" Van Deursen (1891–1971) on June 15, 1910. (Courtesy of the South Holland Historical Society.)

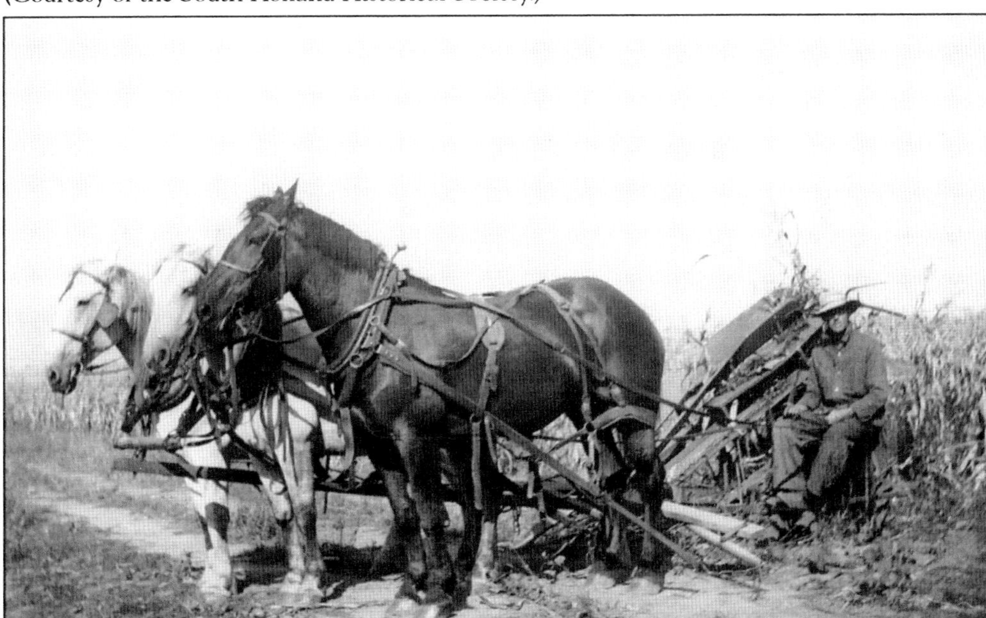

The process of binding corn is illustrated on Reinder Van Til's farm about 1930. Reinder (1882–1966) was born in the village of Grootegast, in the Dutch province of Groningen. His first wife, Lamke van der Velde (1882–1918), was born in the village of Lucaswolde in Groningen. She is at rest in Hope Cemetery in Highland. (Courtesy of the Calvin College Archives.)

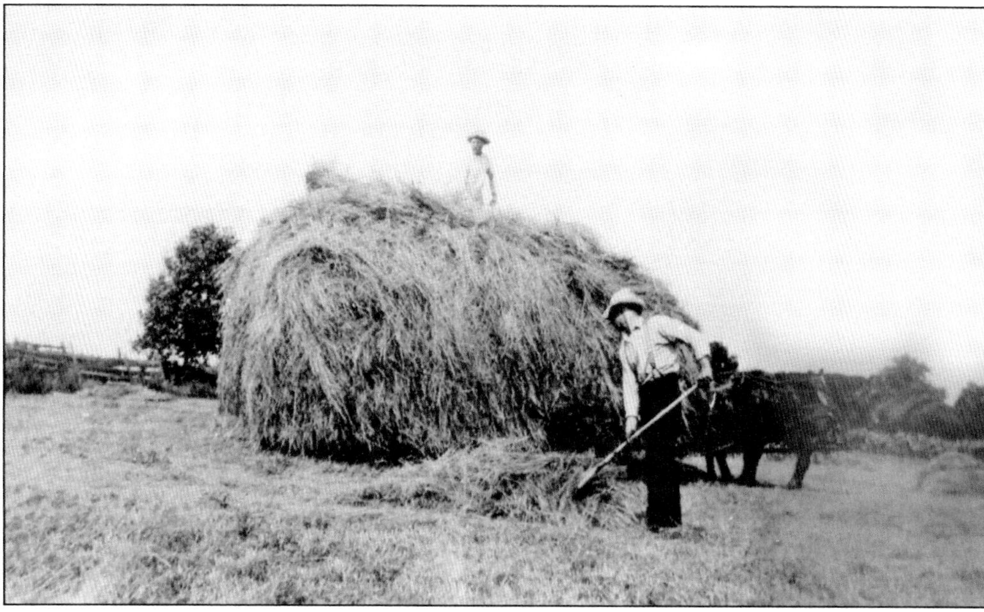

Hay was a necessity of life for the early Dutch settlers. The hay had to be cut with a scythe and loaded by hand. This was only one of the labor-intensive jobs that were a normal part of everyday life on the farm. (Courtesy of the South Holland Historical Society.)

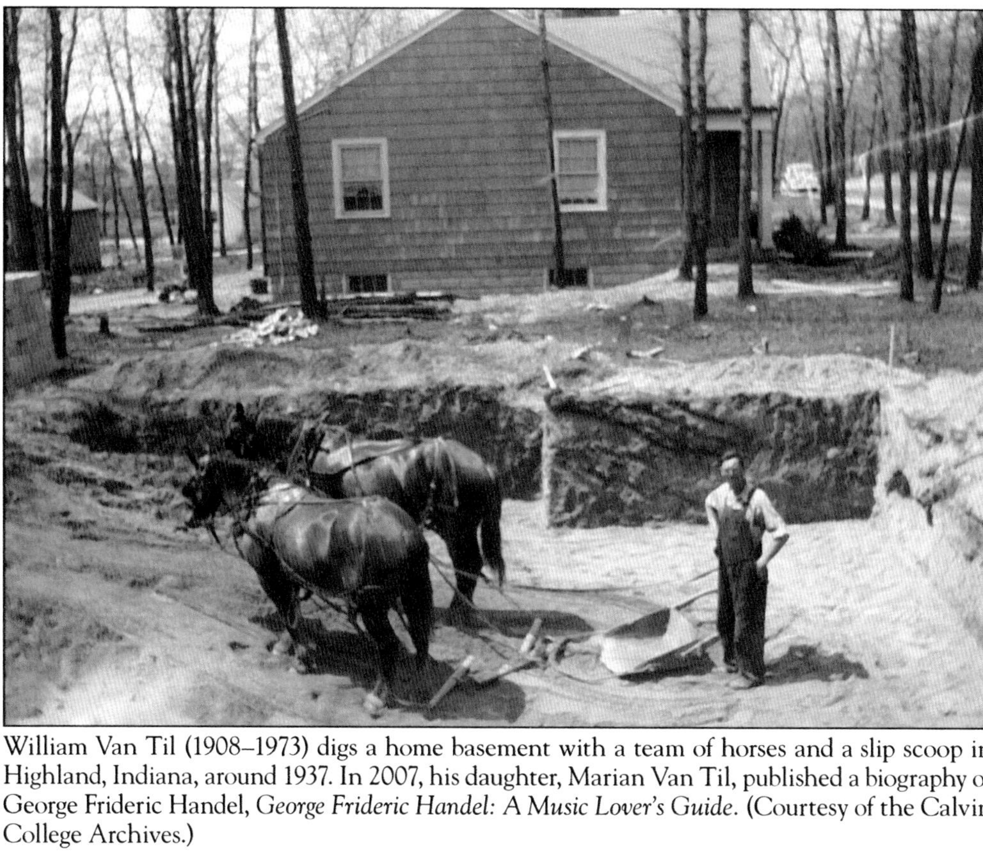

William Van Til (1908–1973) digs a home basement with a team of horses and a slip scoop in Highland, Indiana, around 1937. In 2007, his daughter, Marian Van Til, published a biography of George Frideric Handel, *George Frideric Handel: A Music Lover's Guide.* (Courtesy of the Calvin College Archives.)

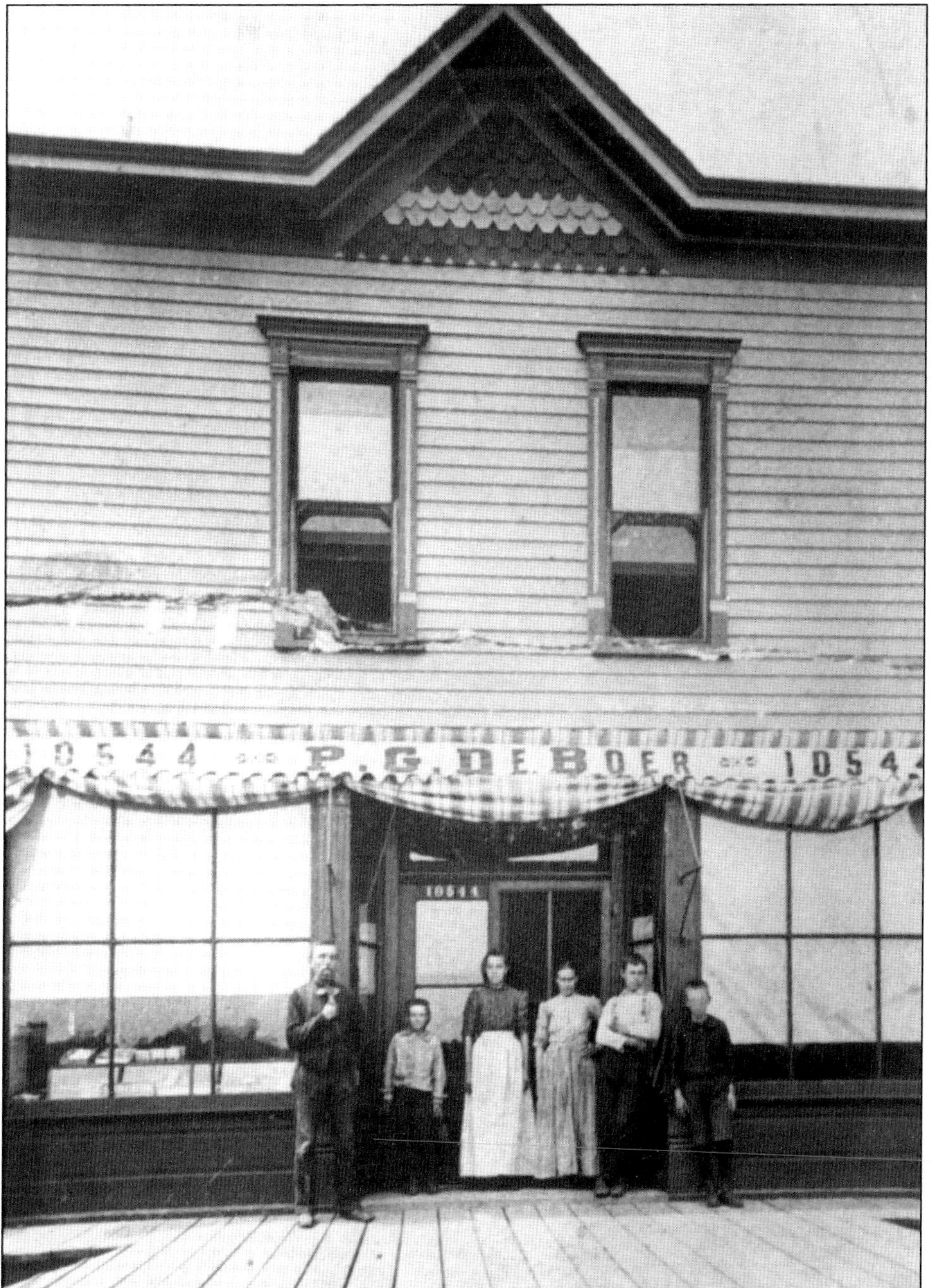

Peter G. De Boer (1850–1921) stands with his wife and children in front of the family grocery store at 10544 Wentworth Avenue in Roseland. Shown are, from left to right, Peter, Harry, Elizabeth (1852–1920), Annie, Govert, and Gerrit. Peter married Elizabeth Brennema in 1876, and they came to America in 1887. They are both at rest in Mount Greenwood Cemetery in Chicago. (Courtesy of the Calvin College Archives.)

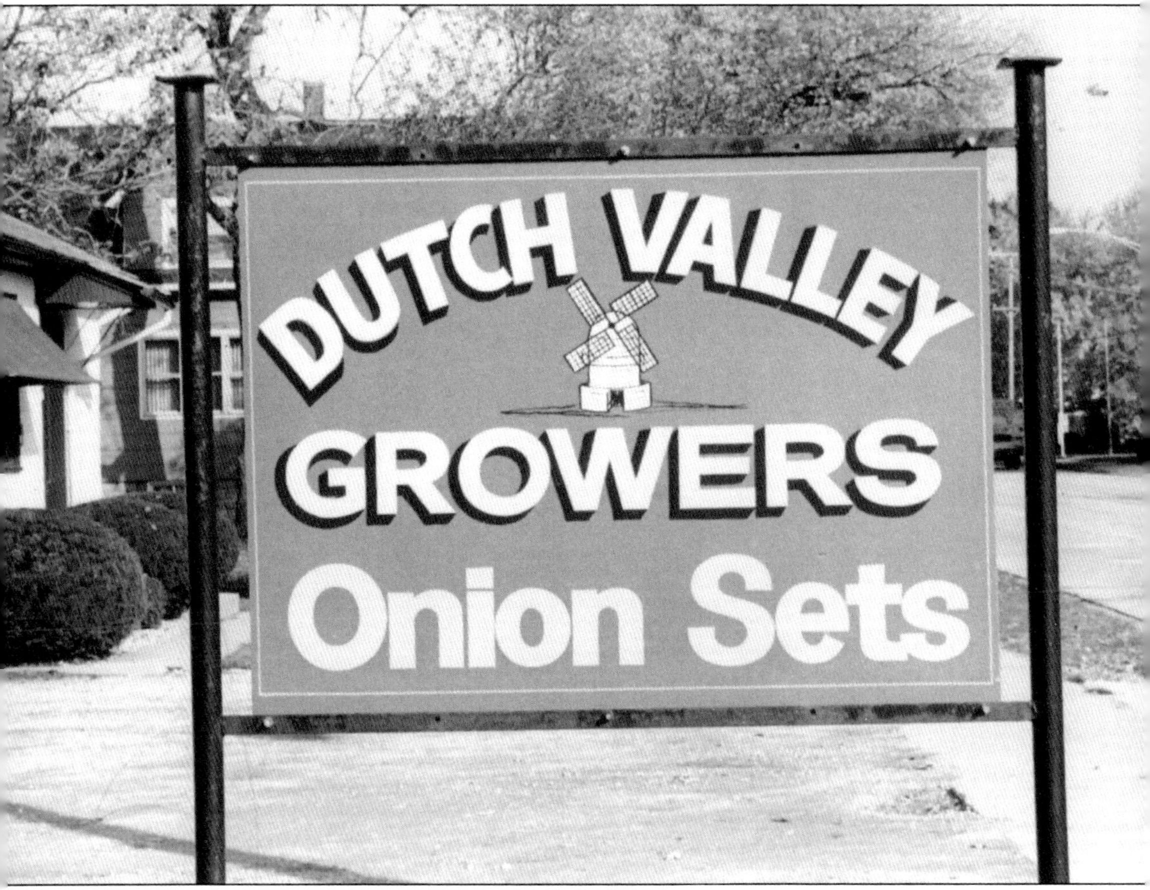

The Dutch Valley Growers was a group of South Holland onion-set farmers that formed a cooperative in 1933. Their motto remains to this day "Dutch Pride in Every Bag." Walter De Graff, Ted De Graff, William Gouwens, Howard Pals, and Arnold Dalenberg were among the organizers. (Courtesy of the South Holland Historical Society.)

The J.P. De Young Store, run by Jacob De Young and located at 158th Street and Chicago Road, was home to the town's post office for a while. The area formerly known as De Laage Prairie become South Holland when the post office was installed in Pieter De Young's store in 1869. Pieter was Jacob's father. (Courtesy of the South Holland Historical Society.)

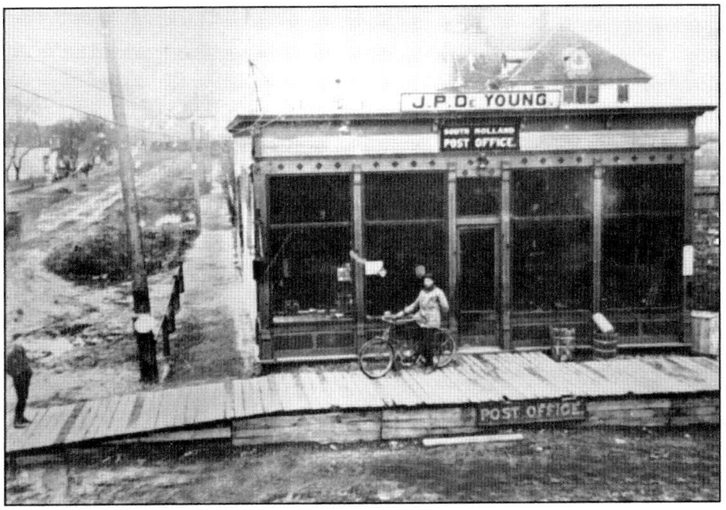

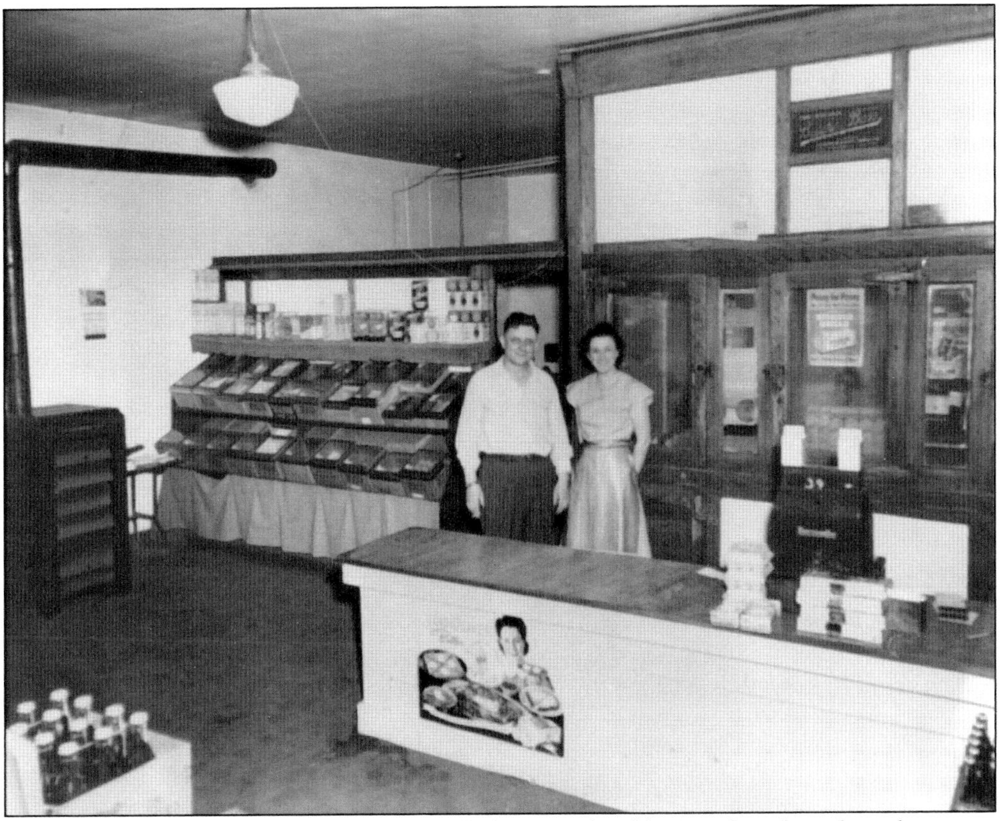

Pleasant View Dairy got its start when Nicholas E. and Hilda Leep bought a dairy farm near Lowell, Indiana, in 1928. Today, the Pleasant View Dairy operates out of a 30,000-square-foot plant on Highway Avenue in downtown Highland. The dairy sells most of the milk it processes to the Strack & Van Til stores. Behind the counter are Bud Leep and Betty Van Dyke. (Courtesy of the Highland Historical Society.)

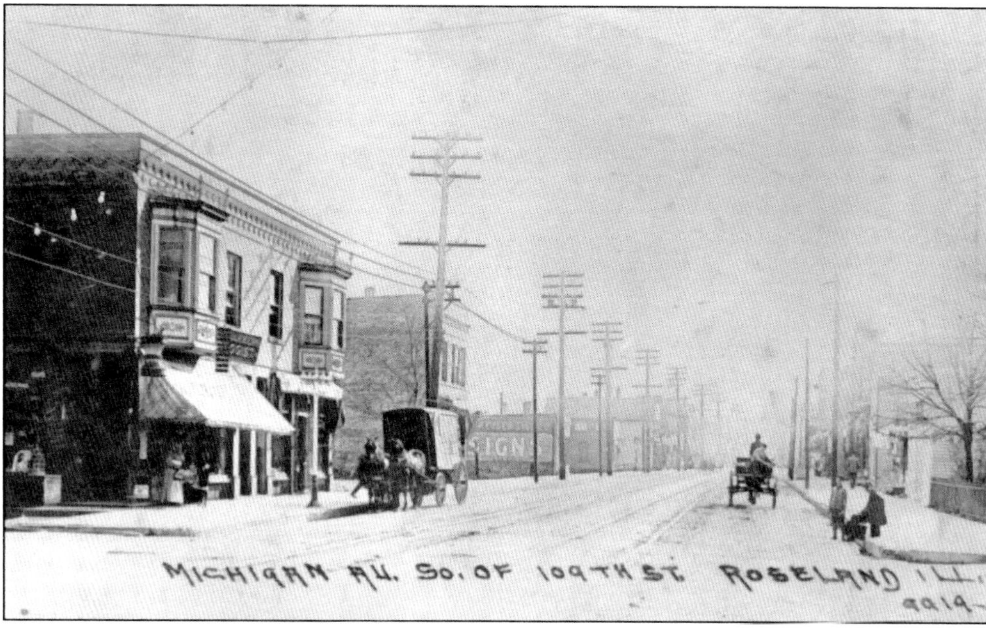

Roseland began as de Hooge Prairie (High Prairie), then it became Hope. Finally, it was named Roseland in 1873 at the suggestion of James H. Bowen, president of the Calumet and Chicago Canal & Dock Company. (Courtesy of the Calvin College Archives.)

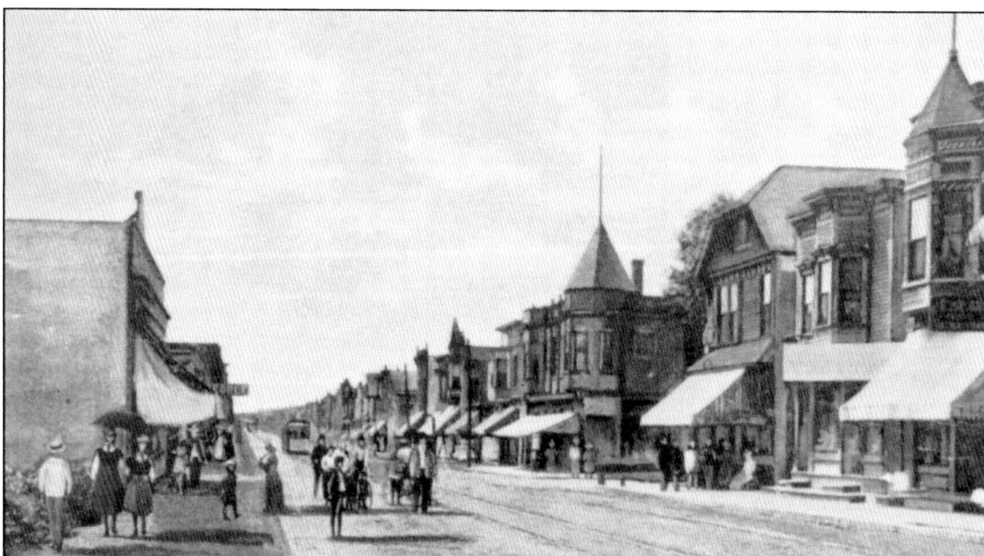

The original Dutch settlement comprising 160 acres stretched east from State Street to Indiana Avenue and south from 103rd Street to 111th Street. By 1890, all of Roseland had been annexed into Chicago. This postcard from that period shows Michigan Avenue at 112th Street. (Courtesy of the Calvin College Archives.)

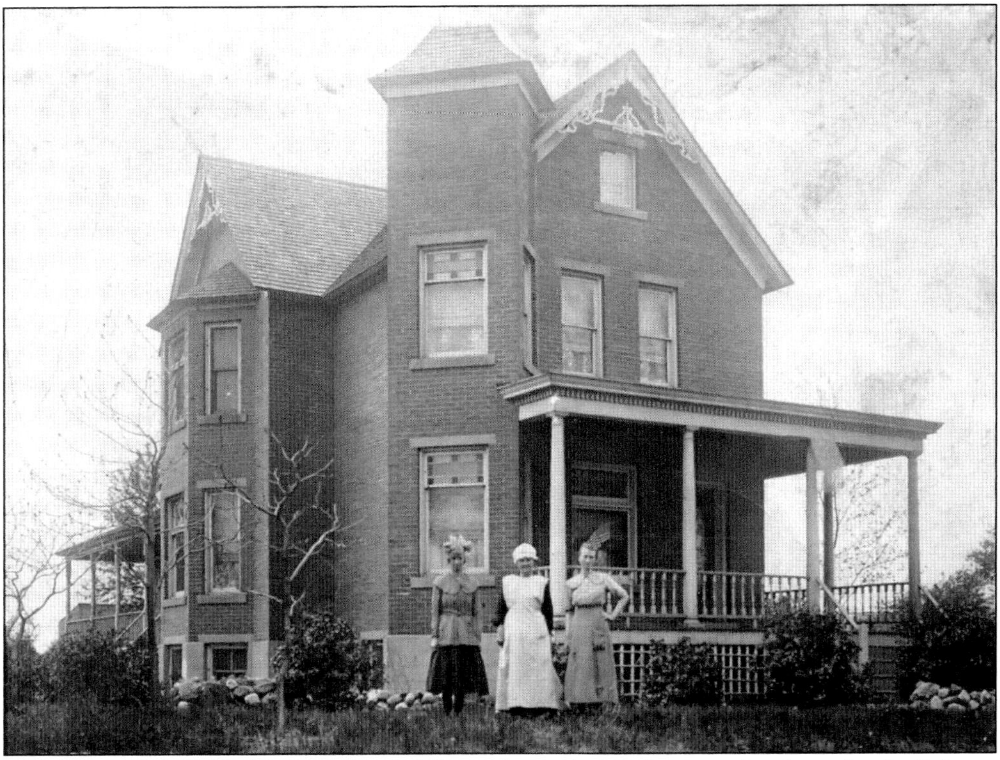

Standing in front of her home is Dora Schoon (center), with her two daughters Jacoba Schoon (left) and Mary Schoon Jaabay. Dirk and Dora Schoon's home stood at 304 Ridge Road in Munster, where an Applebee's Restaurant is now located. (Courtesy of the Munster Historical Society.)

The Gerbrand and Mary Kooy home at Ridge Road and Jackson Street in Munster is seen here in 1905. Mary was born in Reusel-de Mierden, Noord-Brabant. She was the only child of Jacob Schoon and his first wife, Elisabeth Bronder (1832–1862). (Courtesy of the Munster Historical Society.)

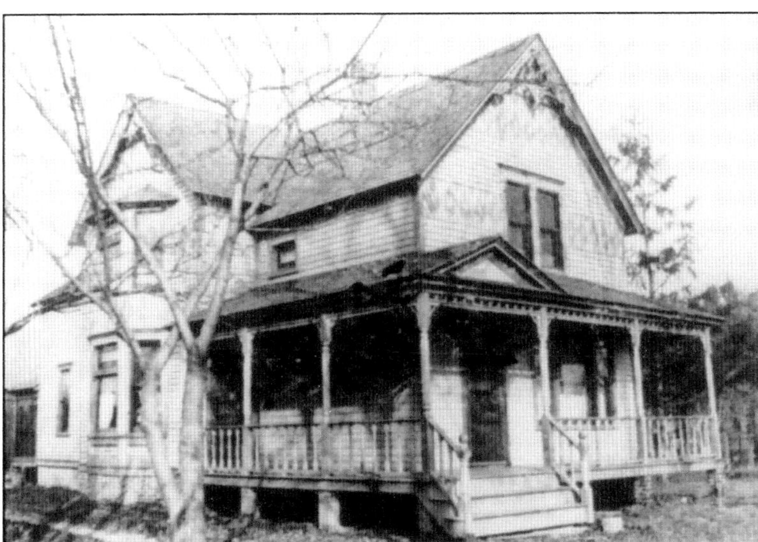

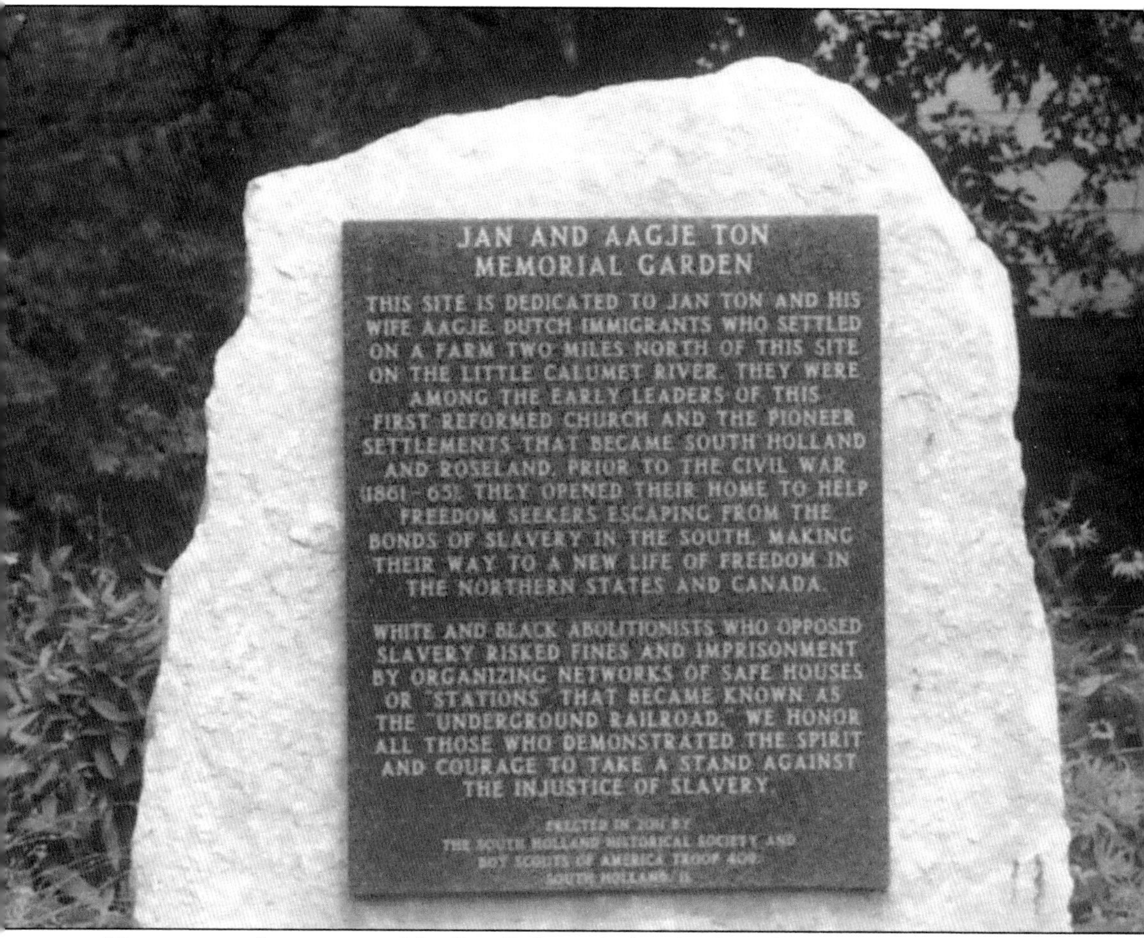

This stone on the property of the First Reformed Church of South Holland is the centerpiece of the Jan and Aagje Ton Memorial Garden. The plants selected for the garden are native to Illinois, and the boulder is a 9,000-pound hulk of limestone from the nearby Thornton quarry. Jan Ton was one of the founding fathers of High Prairie, now the Chicago neighborhood of Roseland. Jan originally settled on farmland on the north bank of the Calumet River that is now part of Riverdale. In the days before the Civil War, Jan joined with other abolitionists, including Cornelius Kuyper, and established an Underground Railroad station. Between 1849 and 1865, seven of Jan's siblings also immigrated to the Roseland area. (Photograph by the author.)

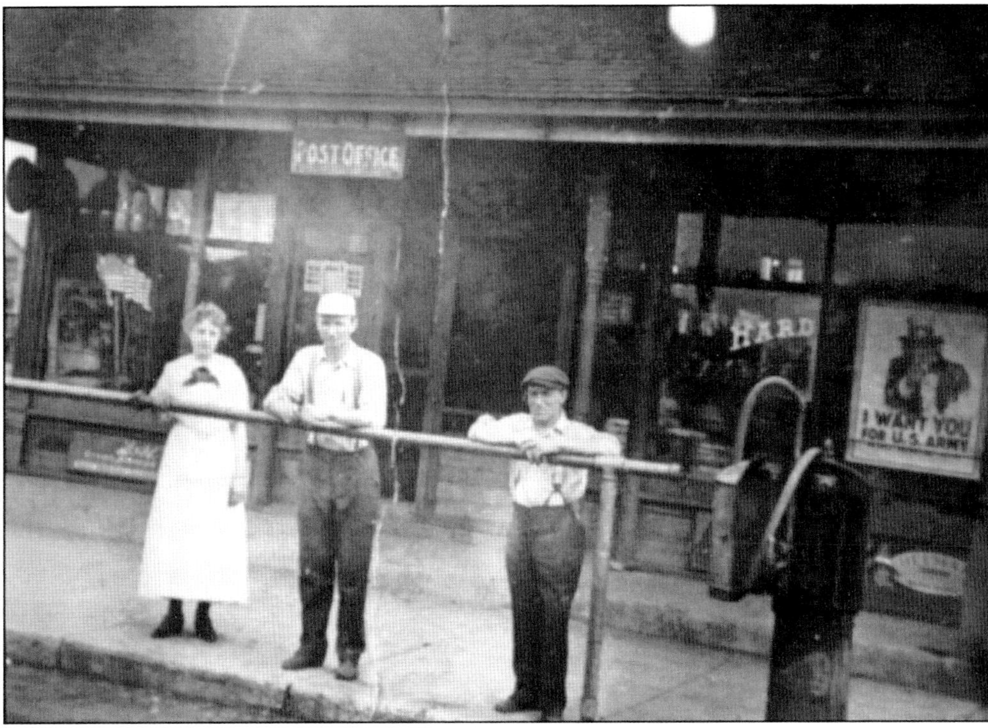

Standing in front of the Harkema Grocery Store in Highland are, from left to right, Peternell Blom, Sam Van Til, and Billy Harkema. William Lodewyk Harkema (1882–1966) and John Groot (1893–1954) ran the store as partners for a time. (Courtesy of the Highland Historical Society.)

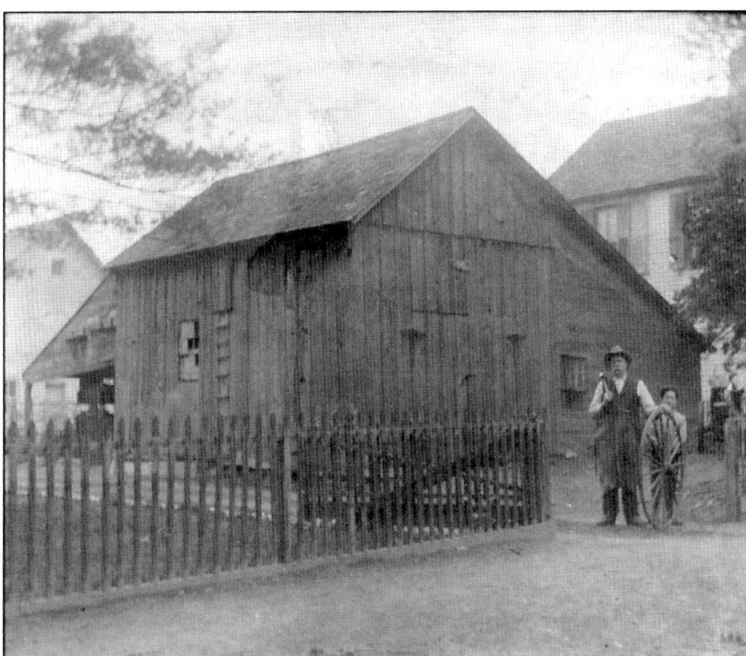

Roseland was a farming community until the late 19th century, when George M. Pullman built his failed workers' utopian town to feed labor to his railway car factory, located between Roseland and Lake Calumet. Roseland was annexed into Chicago in 1892. (Courtesy of the Lansing Historical Society.)

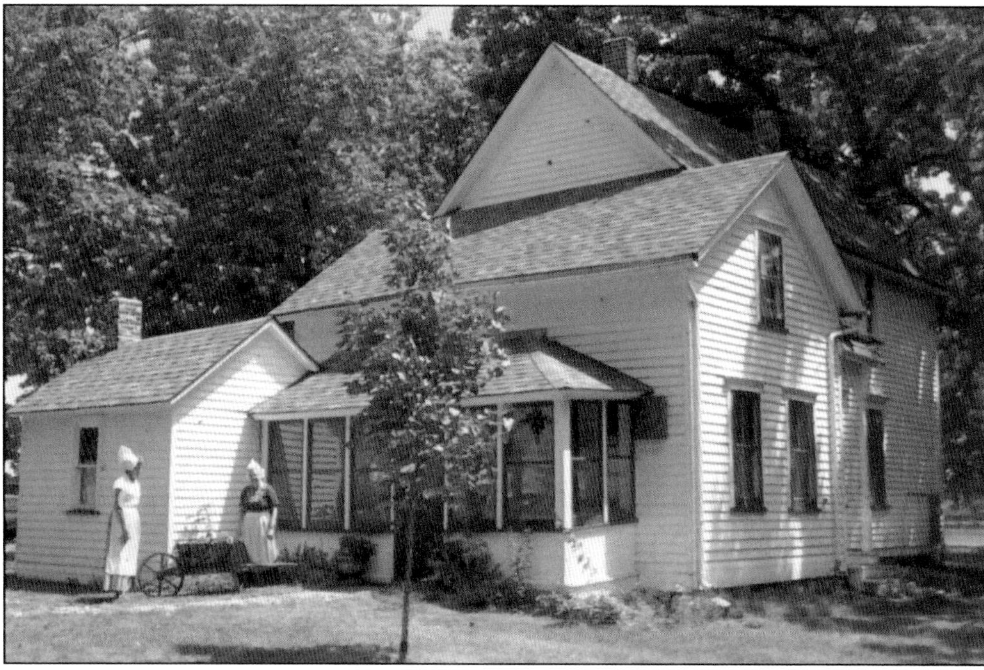

This home is on property that is a part of the land purchased by the Widow Paarlberg in 1847. The main character in Edna Ferber's fictional account of the early days in De Laage Prairie, *So Big*, was based on the Widow. The family of her son Pieter presented this home to the South Holland Historical Society in 1970. (Courtesy of the South Holland Historical Society.)

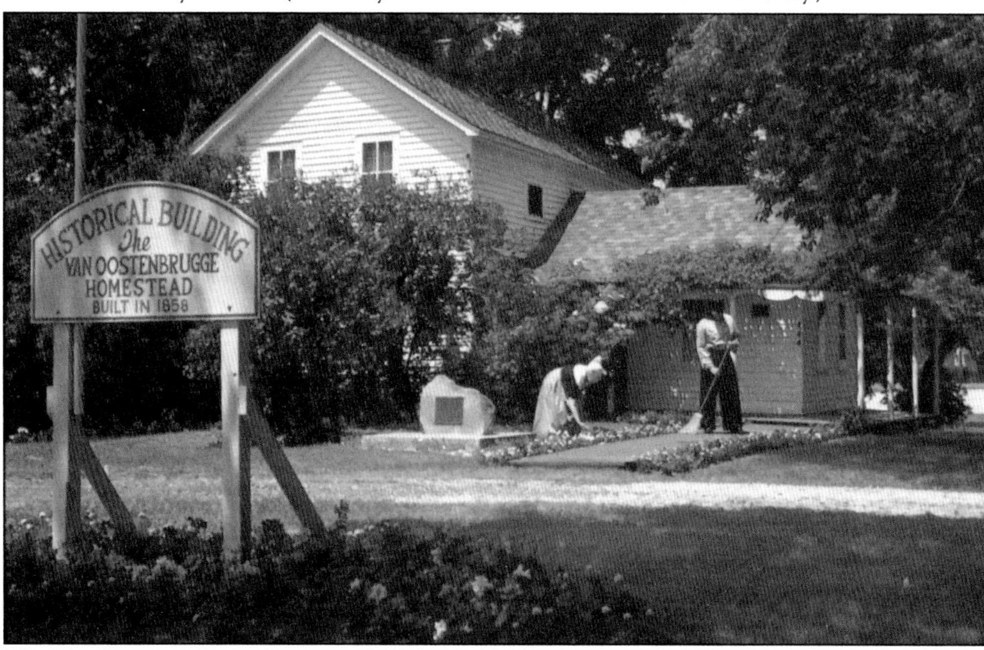

The Van Oostenbrugge Centennial Home, located at 444 East 157th Street in South Holland, was built in 1858. It was restored in 1975 by the South Holland Historical Society. Jan and Evertje Van Oostenbrugges arrived with their three children from Utrecht in the Netherlands in 1856. (Courtesy of the South Holland Historical Society.)

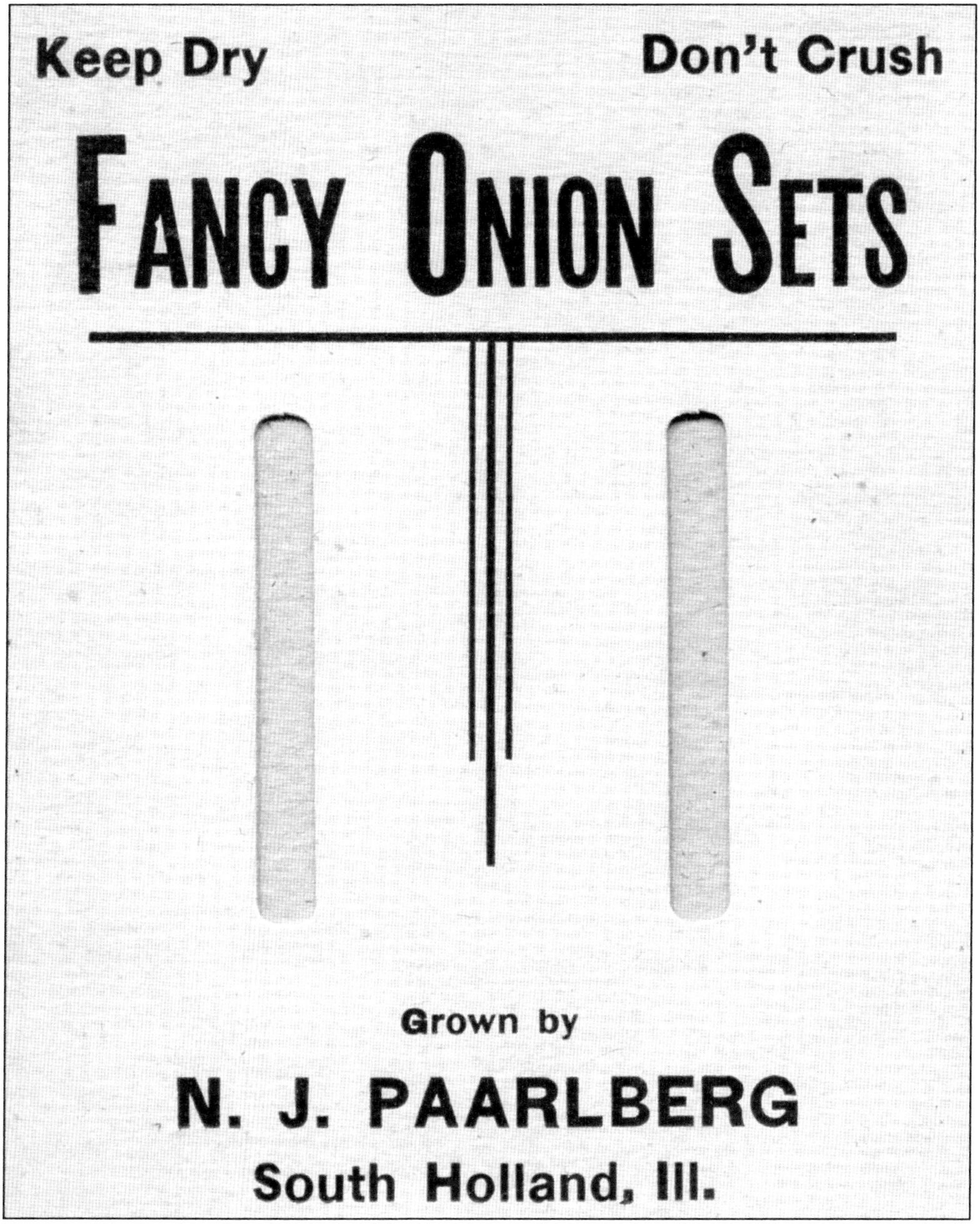

After local farmers began raising onion sets in 1892, South Holland soon became known as the "Onion Set Capital of the World." By 1940, about 2,500 acres were devoted to onion-set farming, and the area was producing more than 1.5 billion annually. (Courtesy of the South Holland Historical Society.)

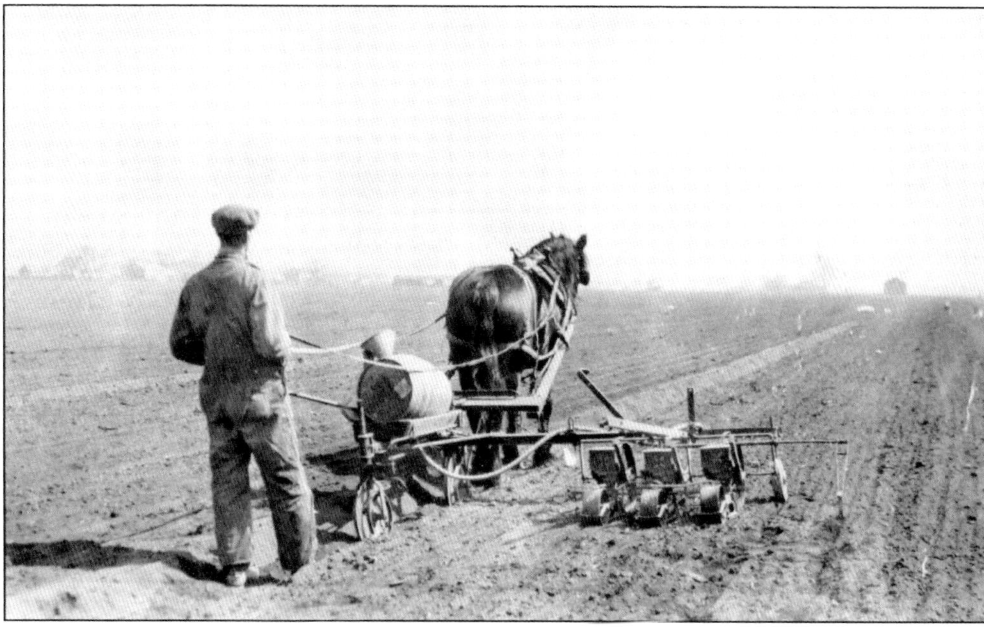

The Calumet region, with its light, sandy soils, was well suited for the production of garden crops, especially onions. In South Holland, the eventual change to onions led to the onion-set farmers and co-ops that kept agriculture a major factor in South Holland until after World War II. (Courtesy of the South Holland Historical Society.)

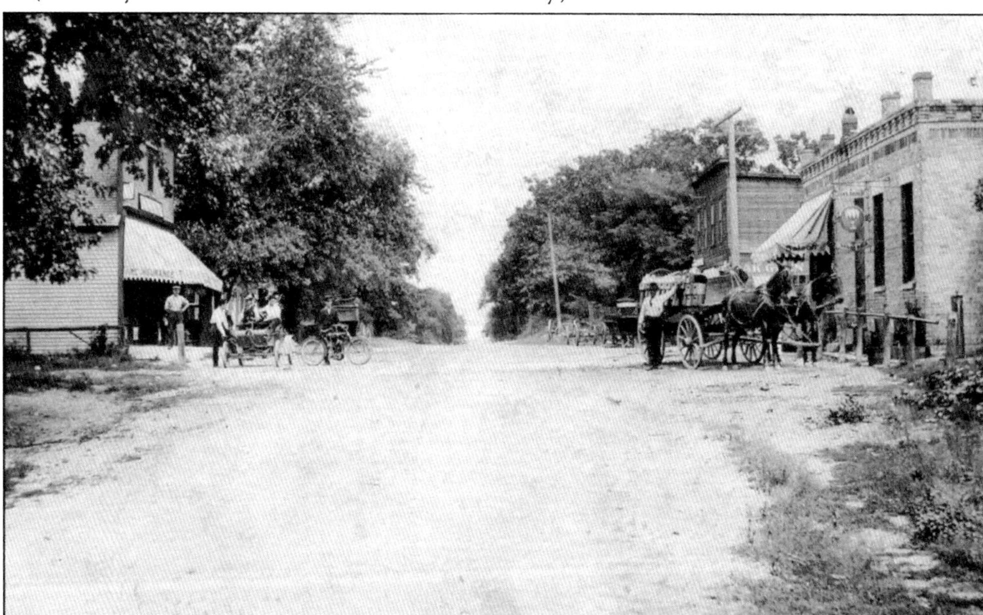

Among the early Dutch settlers of the Lansing area was the Ooms family. Adam (1825–1885) and Janna (1835–1895) Ooms arrived from the Netherlands in 1866 and rented a farm on the Little Calumet River just west of Torrence Avenue. They raised potatoes, oats, and corn. The family also had about 15 milk cows. This photograph shows an early Lansing street scene. (Courtesy of the Lansing Historical Society.)

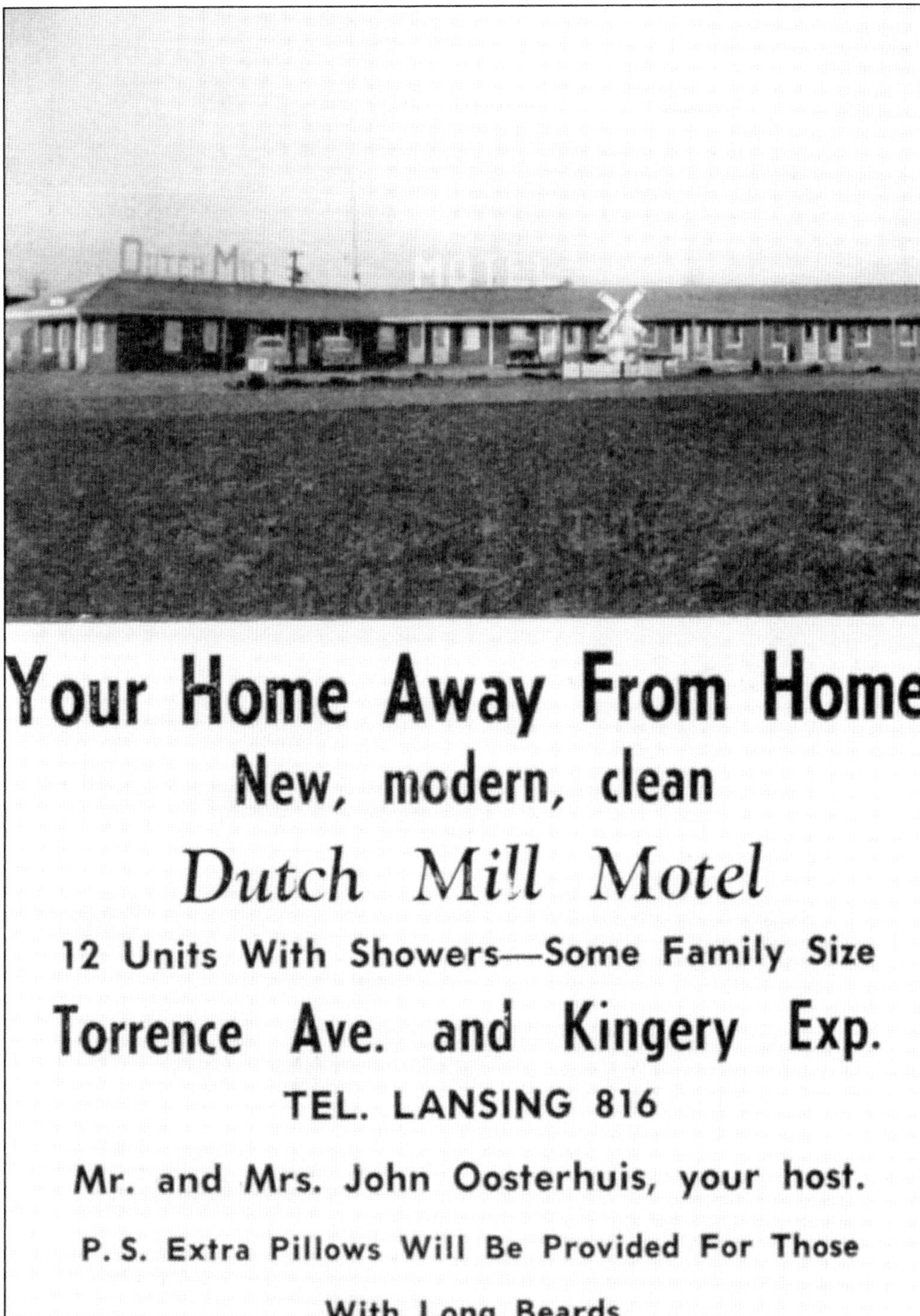

This advertisement from the centennial book (1854–1954) of Lansing, Illinois, illustrates just how much Dutch culture had permeated the region. Many of these Dutch-themed businesses still dot the landscape. Note the special accommodations for those with long beards. (Courtesy of Carol Krencik.)

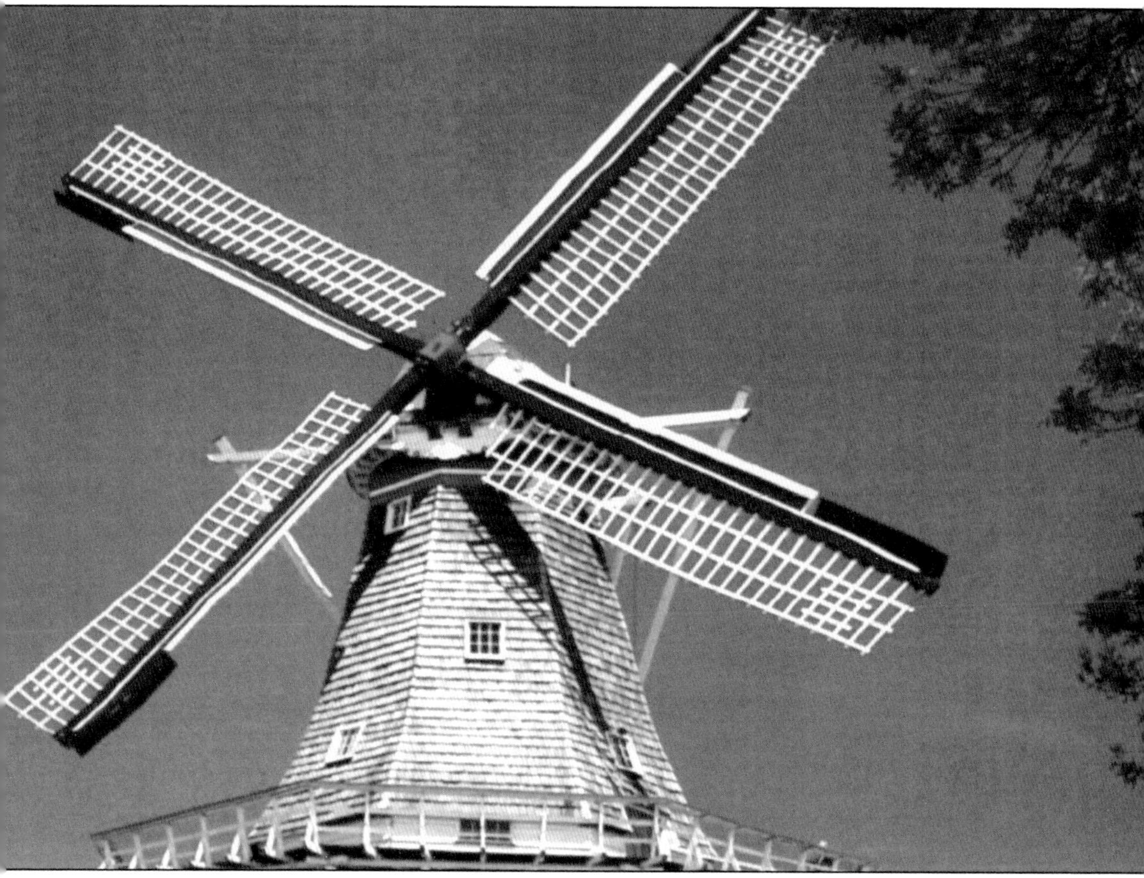

Albertus Van Raalte led the Dutch immigrants who founded the city of Holland, Michigan, in 1846. Hendrick Pieter Scholte led 800 Dutch in 1847 to Iowa, where they created the town of Pella. They were seceders from the Church of the Netherlands. If these leaders had not seceded in 1834 and eventually immigrated to the United States, the history of the Calumet region may have been very different. (Photograph by the author.)

BIBLIOGRAPHY

Cook, Richard A. A *History of South Holland, Illinois [1846–1966]*. South Holland, IL: South Holland Trust and Savings Bank, 1966.

Dodson, Linden Seymour. "The Organizing and Conserving Force of the Church in Social Change in South Holland, Illinois." Part of PhD dissertation, University of Chicago, 1932.

"Dutch." *Encyclopedia of Chicago*. Accessed May 9, 2011, encyclopedia.chicagohistory.org/pages/399.html

Hahn, Arvin William. *The South Holland Onion Set Industry*. South Holland, IL: South Holland Trust and Savings Bank, 1952.

Swierenga, Robert P. *Dutch Chicago: A History of the Hollanders in the Windy City*. Grand Rapids, MI: A.C. Van Raalte Institute, Hope College, 2002.

———. "1834 and 1857—Church Secessions and the Dutch Emigration." Robert P. and Joan Swierenga family website. Accessed May 9, 2011, www.swierenga.com/Grafscap_pap.html

Swierenga, Robert P., Donald Sinnema, and Hans Krabbendam. *The Dutch in Urban America*. Holland, MI: Joint Archives of Holland, Hope College, 2004.

Van Hinte, Jacob. *Netherlanders in America: A Study of Emigration and Settlement in the Nineteenth and Twentieth Centuries of the United States of America*. Grand Rapids, MI: Baker Book House, 1985.

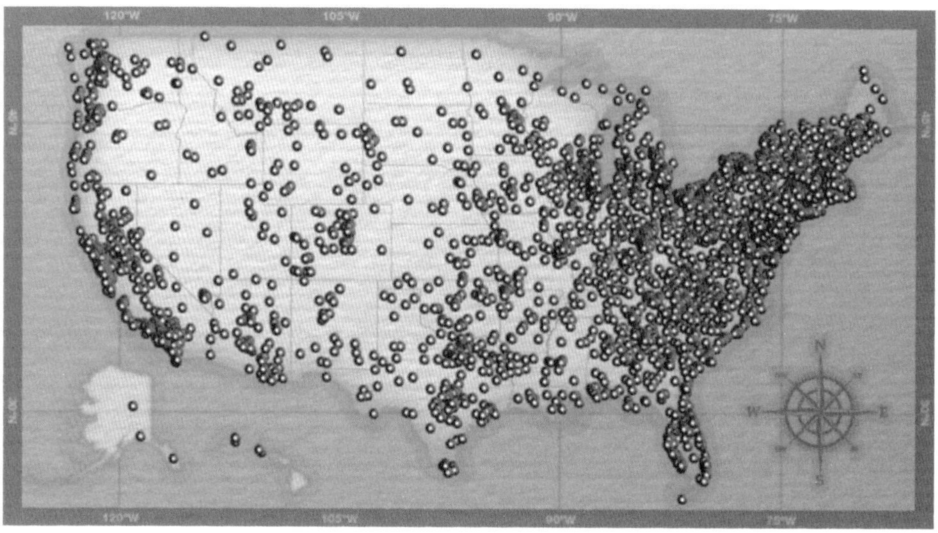